THE BIG BOOK OF BREAKFAST

THE BIG BOOK OF BREAKFAST

SERIOUS COMFORT FOOD FOR ANY TIME OF THE DAY

BY MARYANA VOLLSTEDT

CHRONICLE BOOKS
SAN FRANCISCO

Text copyright © 2003 by Maryana Vollstedt.
Cover photograph copyright © 2003 by Lisa Hubbard.
All rights reserved. No part of this book may be reproduced in any form without written permission from the publisher.

Library of Congress Cataloging-in-Publication Data:

Vollstedt, Maryana.
The big book of breakfast: serious comfort food for any time of the day / by Maryana Vollstedt; cover photograph by Lisa Hubbard.
p. cm.
ISBN 0-8118-3338-0 1. Breakfasts. I. Title.
TX733 .V57 2003
641.5'2—dc21
2002003063

Manufactured in the United States of America

Food styling by Margarette Adams
Designed and illustrated by Cyclone Design Inc.

Distributed in Canada by Raincoast Books
9050 Shaughnessy Street
Vancouver, BC V6P 6E5

10 9 8 7 6 5 4

Chronicle Books LLC
85 Second Street
San Francisco, California 94105

www.chroniclebooks.com

DEDICATION

To my husband, Reed, who is my advisor, tester, shopper, confidant, and best friend plus computer person. He has encouraged and supported me throughout my years of writing cookbooks. My books are really a team effort, and I couldn't have produced them without him. Thank you, Reed.

ACKNOWLEDGMENTS

To Bill LeBlond, editorial director, cookbooks, Chronicle Books, and the Chronicle Books staff who suggested the idea for my third Big Book, *The Big Book of Breakfast*, following *The Big Book of Casseroles* and *The Big Book of Soups & Stews*.

To Amy Treadwell at Chronicle Books for her help and advice during the writing of the book and to Rebecca Pepper for her expert copyediting and suggestions.

Special thanks to Brian Crow for his computer consulting. Also to our good neighbors who saved us from eating leftovers, my daughter Julie Glogau for developing some of the "healthy" recipes and the grandkids who tested them, and to friends and family who came to brunches and gave their critiques.

CONTENTS

CONTENTS

PREFACE

This breakfast book would not be complete without a description of the Vollstedt family's Easter celebration. For us, Easter is about as big as Christmas. It begins with a brunch, a highlight of which is our famous "egg cracking contest" and the crowning of the winner holding the champion egg. This tradition started in Germany more than 80 years ago and has been carried on by five generations of the Vollstedt clan. There are usually 40 to 50 in attendance. Everyone contributes to the meal with their favorite side dishes and pastries.

For the contest, each person holds a soft-boiled egg. They tap the eggs together, end to end, each trying to crack the other person's egg while keeping his or her own egg whole. This continues throughout the entire meal until the person holding the last uncracked egg is declared the winner. Each cracked egg must be eaten on fried potatoes and ham before another one comes into action.

The younger kids delight in the destruction, but the older kids and adults take it very seriously and try hard to hold the champion egg. No, it's not as messy as it sounds. We've had only a few accidents, and these were quickly cleaned up. In the olden days, some of the men in my husband's father's family of 12 would see who could be the first to eat a dozen eggs (this was before cholesterol became a health concern).

Another Easter tradition is making Easter nests for the bunny to fill. Commercial, frilly store-bought baskets are not allowed because no one could afford them back in the early days on the family farm. The children head for the woods, where they gather twigs, branches, cones, grass, rocks, and flowers to make their own creative baskets on the lawn. Over the years, these have become masterpieces of art. After the kids have been lured back inside, the Easter bunny finds his way to the nests and fills them with Easter goodies.

This is followed by an egg hunt for all ages. The grand prize is the golden egg, always wrapped in a five-dollar bill. (It used to be a dollar bill, but over the years it has gone up.)

This is our tradition, but many families have their own Easter traditions of attending church services followed by a brunch at home or at a restaurant or a big potluck dinner. Easter is a time for families to be together and enjoy each other.

INTRODUCTION

In *The Big Book of Breakfast,* you will find more than 300 delicious recipes that you can combine for exciting breakfasts and impressive brunches.

Learn all about eggs and how to cook them plus some of the basics, and updated tips and helpful hints.

Start the day right with a healthful breakfast that will get you going. Wake up to a bowl of hot whole-grain cereal or a satisfying stack of fluffy buttermilk pancakes with real maple syrup. You will enjoy blueberry waffles and oven-baked pepper bacon or sausage patties with a steaming cup of freshly brewed coffee. Or if you prefer, lightly scrambled eggs, or an omelet filled with cheese and mushrooms along with a heaping plate of home fries served with a fresh tropical fruit plate and a drizzle of strawberry purée.

Your brunch will be a breeze with make-ahead stratas, creative casseroles, and savory quiches enhanced by rich scones, luscious orange muffins, or melt-in-your mouth biscuits.

Just turn the pages and enjoy!

BREAKFAST

Nutritionists rate breakfast the most important meal of the day. Begin with a well-planned, well-balanced meal that will provide energy and satisfy you through the morning. A good breakfast sets the mood for the day!

If you don't have time to prepare a hearty meal of eggs, meat, pancakes, or waffles, rely on a high-fiber cereal and fresh fruit and serve breakfast another time of the day.

Breakfast fare is so good and easy to make, it shouldn't be ignored or limited to the morning meal. It can also be served for lunch, dinner, or a late-night supper.

BRUNCH

A brunch is a late-morning breakfast that drifts over into lunch. Brunches are a great way to celebrate a special event or holiday. They are easy, fairly inexpensive, casual, and a fun way to entertain. Usually held on weekends or holidays when there is leisure time for eating and conversation, brunches typically start about 11 and often last until 2.

Home brunches do not have to be as elaborate and spectacular as some of the restaurant brunches that offer an endless array of choices. Plan a menu that is comfortable for you. For a large crowd, offer a selection of complementary food arranged on a buffet table for guests to help themselves. For a smaller, informal brunch, serve waffles, omelets, or French toast, and let your guests help in the preparation.

TIPS FOR PLANNING A BRUNCH

- Make sure your menu includes a variety of dishes of contrasting colors, shapes, textures, and flavors, such as egg-based casseroles and other specialty dishes along with an assortment of breakfast meats, cheeses, a basket of fancy breads with toppings, and an exotic fruit platter or a compote of seasonal fruit.
- Plan ahead, and prepare as much food as possible in advance.
- Set the table with casual linens, tableware, and fresh flowers.
- Serve an assortment of beverages—frosty pitchers of freshly squeezed orange juice or other juices, coffee, and tea. If you like, offer champagne or other light alcoholic brunch beverages (see pages 27 to 32).

BREAKFAST BEVERAGES

Drinks for breakfast go beyond juice, coffee, and tea. Featured in this chapter are your favorite drinks with variations, plus some popular spirited brunch drinks.

Juice, coffee, and tea are the traditional breakfast drinks in the United States. Hot chocolate, more popular in Europe, can also be a warming and welcome drink on a cold winter day.

Smoothies make a quick breakfast and can also be a brunch dessert drink. They are especially appealing to children, who enjoy the process of making them.

Juices are usually served before the meal. The many choices available include a variety of citrus juices, tomato and vegetable juices, grape juice, pineapple juice, apple juice, and exotic fruit juices or a combination of juices. Freshly squeezed orange juice is the most popular breakfast juice and is superior to commercially prepared products.

COFFEE

Coffee comes from all parts of the world. The only coffee produced in the United States is the Kona variety grown in Hawaii. Commercially, coffee is the most important beverage on the market. Ground coffee is available vacuum packed in sealed containers or in packages. Fresh-roasted beans (regular and decaffeinated) are available in many blends and flavors and can be ground at the store or at home (if you have a coffee grinder). Instant coffee is available in jars in powdered form, as freeze-dried granules (crystals), and in individual packets. Espresso stands and coffee shops offer a wide choice of popular coffee drinks made with a special espresso machine, and good home espresso machines now let you prepare these drinks in you own kitchen.

TIPS FOR STORING AND MAKING COFFEE

Making a good cup of coffee depends on the coffee blend (whole beans or ground) and the coffeemaker. Adding cream and sugar is a personal choice.

- The coffeemaker must be absolutely clean; oils and residue can affect the taste. Wash it with soapy water, and dry it after each use.
- Use only fresh coffee. Buy only enough beans or ground coffee to last a week or two.
- Store coffee in an airtight container in a cool place.
- Grind coffee beans just before brewing, and grind just enough for one pot.
- Start with fresh, cold water (bottled water preferred).
- Use 2 level tablespoons coffee per cup of cold water for strong coffee, or 1½ tablespoons coffee per cup of water for medium-strength coffee. This will vary with the grind, coffeemaker, and personal preference. Experiment to see what is best for you.
- Match the coffee grind to the coffeemaker; there are several styles of coffeemakers on the market. Automatic drip makers are the most popular. Use a gold filter or paper filters.
- Do not leave brewed coffee in the coffeemaker on high heat for longer than 20 minutes. Instead, transfer coffee to a heated thermos. Reheating coffee destroys the flavor.
- Serve coffee piping hot in mugs or cups.
- When entertaining, offer both regular and decaffeinated coffee along with cream and sugar.

TEA

Tea is native to China and is the most popular drink in the world. Tea comes in many varieties and blends and is sold loose, in packages or by the pound, or in individual teabags. The three main types of tea are black tea, green tea, and oolong tea. Scientific studies have shown that tea has health benefits and increases the body's antioxidant activity.

Specialty teas are flavored with various floral or spice additions. Herbal teas are infused with herbs, flowers, and spices. Instant tea is available powdered in jars. True tea drinkers prefer the full flavor of loose tea leaves made in a teapot and steeped for a few minutes. Like coffee, tea is available in both regular and decaffeinated form.

TIPS FOR STORING AND MAKING TEA

- Store tea in a dark, dry place. Don't keep it in the refrigerator.
- Use a ceramic or glass teapot; avoid ones made of metal. Rinse the pot with boiling water.
- Start with fresh, cold water (preferably bottled water), and bring it to a boil.
- Use 1 teaspoon tea leaves or 1 teabag per cup of water. Pour boiling water over the tea, stir, and steep, covered, for 3 to 5 minutes. If using tea leaves, pour the tea through a strainer into a cup, or use a tea ball (infuser). If using a teabag, remove the bag.
- To make tea in a microwave, place 1 teabag in 1 cup cold water and microwave for 2 minutes on high. Let stand for 20 seconds, then remove the bag.
- Sun tea is made by placing 10 teabags in 1 quart of water in a glass container and allowing it to steep in the direct sun for 6 hours. Serve iced. Add more water, if needed.

HOT CHOCOLATE

Hot chocolate is made from cocoa powder or baking chocolate, water, sugar, and milk.

SMOOTHIES

Smoothies are made with fruit juice or other liquid and chopped fresh fruit and mixed in the blender. Protein powder is often added.

BRUNCH DRINKS

An introductory drink, with or without alcohol, is customarily served before a brunch. These starters get the affair going and put everyone in a party mood. Chilled drinks are generally served before the food, and hot drinks are offered during or at the end of the meal.

Offer three kinds of coffee—caffeinated, decaffeinated, and flavored. Thermos containers will allow your guests to serve themselves. In addition to sugar, milk, and cream, provide add-ins such as cocoa in shakers, orange and lemon twists, and whipped cream. Have several varieties of tea ready in teapots, kept hot on a warming tray.

In addition to the usual breakfast juices, you may want to serve a punch, champagne, or one of the many popular drinks containing a moderate amount of alcohol. If the meal is a late brunch, wine may be in order. Serve a wine that is light, crisp, and fruity.

SERVES 10 TO 12

SPICED MOCHA

If you love coffee and chocolate, here is a combination you will enjoy: a blend of coffee and cocoa spiced with cinnamon and nutmeg. The optional whipped cream topping adds extra goodness.

8 cups freshly brewed strong, hot coffee

1 cinnamon stick, broken up

2 tablespoons unsweetened cocoa powder

1 tablespoon sugar

Few gratings of nutmeg or dash of ground nutmeg

Whipped Cream (page 325) for topping (optional)

Make coffee with the cinnamon stick in the coffee grounds. When coffee has brewed, stir in cocoa, sugar, and nutmeg. Let this mixture sit for 5 minutes. Stir before serving. Top each serving with a dollop of whipped cream, if desired.

SERVES 4

HOT CHOCOLATE

Use unsweetened baking chocolate in this classic, warming drink, for a true chocolate flavor.

2 squares (2 ounces) unsweetened chocolate, cut up

1 cup water

⅓ cup sugar

Dash of salt

3 cups milk

1 teaspoon vanilla extract

In a medium saucepan over medium-high heat, melt chocolate with water, stirring constantly. Stir in sugar and salt and bring to a boil. Reduce heat to low and simmer, stirring constantly, for 3 minutes. Increase heat to medium and add milk. Stir until hot and smooth, about 2 minutes. Remove from heat and add vanilla. Pour into mugs and serve.

Note: For a foamy consistency, beat the hot chocolate with a hand beater after adding the milk.

SERVES 6

LUSCIOUS HOT CHOCOLATE

Serve this warming drink, spiked with Kahlúa, if desired, after a cold winter outing or for a buffet finale.

In a medium saucepan over medium heat, whisk together sugar, cocoa, water, and salt until smooth. Cook until it starts to bubble, then whisk in milk and half-and-half. Add Kahlúa or vanilla, if desired, and stir until hot. Serve in mugs topped with a dollop of whipped cream, if desired.

¾ cup sugar

½ cup unsweetened cocoa powder

½ cup water

Dash of salt

3 cups milk

1½ cups half-and-half

1 jigger (1½ ounces) Kahlúa liqueur, or 1 teaspoon vanilla extract (optional)

Whipped Cream (page 325) for topping (optional)

SERVES 4

HOME-BREWED CAPPUCCINO

All you need to make cappuccino at home is strong coffee and a blender for whipping the milk until it's frothy.

In a medium saucepan over medium heat, heat milk until bubbles form around edge of pan. Do not boil. Blend hot milk in a blender on high speed until frothy. Fill 4 mugs three-fourths full of coffee. Pour milk over coffee. In a small bowl, mix cocoa and sugar and sprinkle on top. Add a dash of cinnamon, if desired. Serve immediately.

1 cup milk

3 cups strong, hot coffee (use an espresso blend)

1 tablespoon unsweetened cocoa powder

1 teaspoon sugar

Ground cinnamon for topping (optional)

SERVES 1

IRISH COFFEE

Guaranteed to warm the cockles of your heart, Irish coffee is a hot drink of strong coffee, Irish whiskey, and a small amount of sugar. It is traditionally served in a glass mug with a dollop of whipped cream on top. This is fun to serve for a St. Patrick's Day brunch.

1 tablespoon brown sugar, or 1 sugar cube

1 jigger (1½ ounces) Irish whiskey

About 1 cup freshly made hot coffee

1 tablespoon heavy cream or Whipped Cream (page 325)

Place sugar in a warmed, heatproof, stemmed glass or mug. Add whiskey and stir until sugar is dissolved. Add coffee, filling the glass to within ½ inch of the top. Top with cream.

SERVES 4 TO 6

CITRUS COOLER

Serve this lively wake-up drink for a brunch or for a refreshing drink on a hot summer day. If desired, add a jigger of vodka or gin.

Ice cubes

2 cups fresh grapefruit juice

2 cups fresh orange juice

2 limes, 1 juiced and 1 sliced

2 cups club soda

Fill a large pitcher half full of ice cubes. Add juices and club soda and stir. Serve immediately in large, frosted wine glasses. Float a lime slice on top of each serving.

SERVES ABOUT 5

ORANGE-PINEAPPLE DRINK

You can mix the juices together ahead of time for this sparkling drink, keeping them chilled, and then add the ginger ale just before serving.

2 cups orange juice

2 cups pineapple juice

1 bottle (10 ounces) ginger ale

Ice cubes

Mix juices in a large pitcher. Stir in ginger ale, and pour over ice cubes in glasses.

SERVES 2 OR 3

PAPAYA COOLER

Tropical flavors star in this refreshing summer drink. It can easily be doubled.

1 papaya, peeled, seeded, and cut into chunks

2 cups water

Juice of 1 lime

¼ cup sugar

Ice cubes

Place papaya, water, lime juice, and sugar in a blender and blend until very smooth. Transfer to a pitcher filled with ice cubes. Serve immediately.

SERVES 3 TO 4

BERRY SLUSH

Strawberries and blueberries pair well in this thick, cooling drink.

1 package (16 ounces) frozen strawberries with juice

1 cup orange juice

1 tablespoon sugar

½ cup chipped ice

½ cup fresh or frozen blueberries

Combine frozen strawberries, orange juice, sugar, and ice in a blender and blend. Add blueberries and blend briefly. (Do not overblend, or the blueberries will turn the drink an unappealing color). Pour into glasses and serve.

SERVES ABOUT 3

ORANGE SLUSH

Enjoy this delicious, nonalcoholic drink, similar to an Orange Julius, while you watch the sunrise.

1 can (6 ounces) frozen orange juice concentrate

¾ cup cold water (an orange juice can full)

1 cup milk

2 tablespoons sugar

1 teaspoon vanilla extract

1 cup chipped ice

Combine all ingredients in a blender and blend until thick and frothy. Pour into glasses and serve.

SERVES 1 OR 2

ORANGE JUICE–BANANA SMOOTHIE

Kids love to make this smoothie with ingredients that are usually on hand. It's healthful and good for you, too!

- 1 cup orange juice
- 1 teaspoon vanilla extract
- 1 teaspoon sugar (optional)
- 1 ripe banana, peeled and sliced
- ½ to 1 teaspoon protein powder
- ½ cup chipped ice

Combine all ingredients in a blender and blend until smooth. Pour into glasses and serve.

SERVES 2

STRAWBERRY-BANANA PROTEIN DRINK

This fruity shake is as healthful as it is delicious.

- 1 cup plain nonfat yogurt
- 1 ripe banana, peeled and sliced
- 1 cup hulled strawberries, sliced
- ½ cup nonfat milk
- 1 tablespoon wheat germ
- 1 teaspoon vanilla extract
- 4 ice cubes

Combine all ingredients in a blender and blend until smooth. Pour into glasses and serve.

SERVES ABOUT 3

LUCY'S LEMONADE

Lemonade is the all-American cooling and refreshing summer drink. You can adjust the sugar to taste. For best results, use superfine sugar—it will dissolve faster.

3 cups cold water

1 cup strained lemon juice

½ cup granulated sugar or superfine sugar, or more to taste

Ice cubes

Mint sprigs for garnish

Mix water, juice, and sugar in a large pitcher. Stir until sugar is dissolved. Pour into glasses filled with ice cubes, and garnish each with a mint sprig.

VARIATIONS

For limeade, substitute lime juice (you'll need about 10 limes) for the lemon juice, and increase the sugar to ¾ cup.

For pink lemonade, add 1 tablespoon grenadine syrup or 1 teaspoon red food coloring.

SERVES ABOUT 3

ICED TEA

Iced tea is popular year-round, but it tastes especially good in the summer. Try serving it with Mexican food, such as Mexican Frittata (page 102).

4 teabags or 4 teaspoons loose tea leaves of your choice

4 cups boiling water

Ice cubes

Place the teabags or tea in a 4-cup glass measure. Pour in the boiling water. Let steep until strong, 10 to 15 minutes, stirring several times. Remove teabags, or pour tea through a strainer to remove the tea leaves. Cool and serve over ice cubes.

Note: If you don't have time to cool the tea before serving, add extra ice cubes, but make the tea stronger so that the ice cubes won't dilute the tea.

VARIATIONS

Add lemon or orange slices.

Add a cinnamon stick and several whole cloves to the tea while it steeps.

Garnish each glass with a sprig of mint.

Combine the brewed tea with an equal amount of orange juice just before serving.

SERVES 1 OR 2

BANANA-BLUEBERRY POWER SHAKE

Tofu, also known as soybean curd, is a good source of protein and has no cholesterol. It is considered one of today's most healthful foods. This shake is not just for health nuts, though—it is delicious.

3 ounces (¼ package) soft tofu

¾ cup milk

1 medium frozen banana (peel and freeze overnight), cut into pieces

¼ cup frozen orange juice concentrate

¼ cup frozen blueberries

Combine all ingredients in a blender and blend until smooth. Pour into glasses and serve.

VARIATION

For a strawberry shake, replace the orange juice concentrate with pineapple juice concentrate, and use ½ cup frozen strawberries instead of the blueberries.

SERVES UP TO 40

METHODIST PUNCH

This nonalcoholic punch is good when you need to serve a large group for a party or reception. It can easily be doubled.

2 cans (46 ounces each) pineapple juice

1 can (46 ounces) grapefruit juice

1 can (12 ounces) frozen lemonade concentrate, defrosted

2 cups sugar

2 cups water

2 quarts 7-Up or ginger ale

1 quart sherbet (any flavor)

In a large container, mix juices, lemonade, sugar, and water. Just before serving, add 7-Up and sherbet.

SERVES ABOUT 12

WINE PUNCH

A pretty punch bowl makes a nice centerpiece for a brunch. Provide cups and a ladle for guests to help themselves.

Place juice in a punch bowl. Add wine and ice just before serving.

- 1 can (12 ounces) frozen tropical juice concentrate, diluted as directed (to yield 48 ounces)
- 1 bottle (750 ml) dry white wine, chilled
- Ice cubes

SERVES 1

CHAMPAGNE COCKTAIL

What could be more sophisticated than this drink, served in chilled, fluted champagne glasses, for your next brunch?

Place sugar cube in a chilled champagne glass. Add bitters to moisten sugar cube. Pour in champagne. Garnish with fruit twist. Do not stir.

- 1 sugar cube
- ½ teaspoon angostura bitters
- 5 ounces chilled champagne
- Lemon or orange peel twist for garnish

SERVES 1

DELUXE BLOODY MARY

The Bloody Mary is a classic brunch drink made with tomato juice and spices and vodka or gin. It is guaranteed to wake you up!

2 or 3 ice cubes

1 jigger (1½ ounces) vodka or gin

¾ cup chilled tomato juice

1 teaspoon fresh lemon juice

2 dashes salt

Freshly ground pepper

1 teaspoon Worcestershire sauce

½ teaspoon prepared horseradish

2 to 3 drops Tabasco sauce

1 stalk celery with some leaves for garnish

1 lime wedge for garnish

Place ice cubes in a tall glass. Add vodka, tomato juice, lemon juice, salt, pepper to taste, Worcestershire sauce, horseradish, and Tabasco sauce and stir to mix. Garnish with celery and a lime wedge.

VARIATIONS

For a Virgin Mary, omit the vodka.

SERVES 1

QUICK BLOODY MARY

Here is a quick version of the Bloody Mary, which uses spicy vegetable juices as a shortcut.

Place ice cubes in a tall glass. Add vodka, Worcestershire sauce, Tabasco sauce, salt, and vegetable juice. Stir and garnish with green bean, pickle, or asparagus spear.

- 2 or 3 ice cubes
- 1 jigger (1½ ounces) vodka
- 1 teaspoon Worcestershire sauce
- 2 or 3 drops Tabasco sauce
- 2 dashes salt
- 1 can (5½ ounces) spicy vegetable juice
- Pickled green bean, dill pickle spear, or asparagus spear for garnish

SERVES 8

MIMOSA

The classic mimosa drink was created at the Ritz Hotel in Paris in 1925. It was named after the yellow blossoms on the mimosa tree. This version has Grand Marnier added. What a perfect way to start a Sunday brunch! Make just before serving.

In a large pitcher or punch bowl, mix orange juice, sugar, and liqueur, if desired. Add champagne and mix well. Serve in champagne flutes or wineglasses.

- 3 cups freshly squeezed, strained orange juice
- 1 tablespoon sugar
- 1 jigger (1½ ounces) Grand Marnier liqueur (optional)
- 1 bottle (750 ml) champagne, chilled

SERVES 8

SCREWDRIVER

Be sure to have plenty of ingredients on hand for this traditional brunch drink to serve a thirsty crowd.

8 cups freshly squeezed, strained orange juice

1 to 1½ cups vodka or gin

1 to 2 teaspoons confectioners' sugar

Ice cubes

Orange slices for garnish

In a large pitcher, mix orange juice and vodka. Add confectioners' sugar. Refrigerate briefly until serving time. Serve in tall glasses over ice cubes. Garnish with orange slices.

SERVES 1

INDIVIDUAL SCREWDRIVER

If only one person in your party wants a screwdriver, this recipe is perfect!

Ice cubes

1 jigger (1½ ounces) vodka

6 ounces orange juice

Fill a glass with ice cubes, add vodka, and top with orange juice. Stir.

SANGRÍA

SERVES 5

This traditional Spanish drink is very refreshing and makes a cooling contrast to spicy dishes.

In a large pitcher, stir juices with sugar until sugar is dissolved. Add remaining ingredients. If making ahead, add ice and club soda just before serving.

1 cup orange juice

½ cup lemon juice

¼ cup sugar

1 bottle (750 ml) dry red wine

¼ cup Cointreau or curaçao orange-flavored liqueur

1 bottle (10 ounces) club soda

1 orange, thinly sliced

2 cups ice cubes

SALTY DOG

SERVES 8

This tart-sweet cocktail is a good match for any Mexican breakfast casserole.

Place salt on a plate. Dip the rims of 8 stemmed glasses in lime juice, then into the salt. In a large pitcher, mix grapefruit juice, vodka, and confectioners' sugar. Stir to dissolve the sugar. To serve, pour grapefruit mixture over ice cubes in the prepared glasses. Garnish each with a lime slice.

Margarita salt

Lime juice for dipping the glass rim

1 can (46 ounces) unsweetened grapefruit juice

1 to 1½ cups vodka

2 tablespoons confectioners' sugar

Ice cubes

Lime slices for garnish

SERVES 10 TO 12

MINT JULEP

Host a brunch with a Kentucky Derby theme for a good excuse to serve this traditional drink.

2 cups sugar

2 cups water

16 to 20 sprigs fresh mint

Crushed ice

15 to 18 ounces Kentucky bourbon

Make a simple syrup by boiling sugar and water together for 5 minutes. Cool and place in a covered container with 6 to 8 sprigs fresh mint. Refrigerate overnight.

Make one julep at a time by filling a julep cup or short cocktail glass with crushed ice and adding 1 tablespoon mint syrup and 1 jigger (1½ ounces) bourbon to each cup. Stir rapidly with a spoon to frost the outside of the cup. Garnish each with a sprig of fresh mint.

SERVES 4

MARGARITA

This slushy tequila-lime drink is made in a blender. Margaritas are a great match with Tex-Mex or Mexican dishes, especially on a warm day.

2 cups chipped ice

½ cup fresh lime juice

6 ounces tequila

3 ounces Triple Sec

2 tablespoons sugar

1 lime, cut into wedges

Margarita salt

Place ice in a blender. Add lime juice, tequila, Triple Sec, and sugar and blend until slushy. Rub the rim of each glass with a lime wedge. Place salt on a plate and dip each glass upside down in salt to coat the rim. Fill glass with margarita slush and serve immediately.

EGG COOKERY

Eggs have always been the number one choice for breakfast. They are easy to prepare, economical, readily available, and nutritious. Eggs are so versatile, they can be prepared in many delicious ways, either alone or in combination with other ingredients for plain or fancy fare.

ALL ABOUT EGGS

Eggs are a good source of protein and are rich in vitamins A, D, and E. They also provide most of the minerals essential to nutrition. The average egg contains about 70 calories, is easy to digest, and is a popular breakfast food.

CLASSIFICATION. Eggs are classified by grade and size. Today, eggs are gathered automatically, washed and sanitized, candled (examined under light), and graded before they are marketed. Grades AA, A, and B are determined by both interior and exterior quality. Eggs are sorted according to size by weight, with sizes ranging from jumbo to small. Most recipes call for large eggs.

FERTILE EGGS. Eggs from a mated hen; if incubated they will develop into chicks. Fertile eggs are no more nutritious than nonfertile eggs and are more expensive to produce and buy.

FREE-RANGE EGGS. True free-range eggs are produced by hens that are raised outdoors or that have daily access to the outdoors. Free-range eggs are generally more expensive due to higher production costs.

ORGANIC EGGS. Eggs from hens fed on high-quality grains, free from hormones and pesticides or commercial fertilizers. (No commercial laying hens are fed hormones.)

FARM EGGS. Eggs straight from the farm. Properly stored, they are superior in taste and freshness.

TRADEMARK EGGS. Eggs marketed under different brand names from hens fed a high-quality, vegetarian diet. They contain 25 percent less fat than other eggs and are more expensive.

PASTEURIZED EGGS. Eggs of the highest quality that have been pasteurized using an all-natural process that destroys salmonella and is approved by the Food and Drug Administration. They can be purchased in liquid form, blended and separated, in a carton in the refrigerated dairy section of most supermarkets. These eggs are safe to use in all recipes that call for raw eggs. Pasteurized whole eggs are used in hospitals and commercially.

EGG SUBSTITUTES. A blend of egg whites, food starch, corn oil, skim-milk products, tofu, food coloring, and additives in liquid form that is cholesterol free. They are sold under various trade names and are available in cartons in the refrigerated section of most supermarkets. They can be used in place of eggs in egg dishes and in baking. Use ¼ cup egg substitute for each egg you are replacing.

THE PARTS OF AN EGG

SHELL. The hard, porous outer layer of the egg. The color, white or brown, is determined by the breed of the hen and has no effect on the nutritional value, quality, or flavor of the egg.

WHITE OR ALBUMEN. The thick, translucent substance surrounding the yolk. It is an excellent source of protein and riboflavin. Egg whites contain no cholesterol.

YOLK. The yellow part of the egg. How deep the color is depends on the diet of the hen. The yolk is a major source of vitamins, proteins, and minerals, and contain all of the cholesterol found in eggs. The yolk of a fresh egg should be round and high standing. As the egg ages, the yolk absorbs some of the white and flattens out.

CHALAZAE (ka-LAY-zee). The thick strands of the white that support the yolk and keep it suspended in the center. More-prominent chalazae indicate freshness. They are edible and do not need to be removed.

AIR CELL. The empty space between the white and shell at the large end of the egg. (The larger the air pocket, the older the egg.)

BLOOD SPOTS. Occasionally, tiny blood spots are missed in candling and will appear in the yolk. They are caused by a rupture of a blood vessel during formation of the egg. They are edible, but most people prefer to remove them for aesthetic reasons. They can be removed with the tip of a sharp knife.

TIPS FOR BUYING AND USING EGGS

1. PURCHASING EGGS

Buy the freshest and best-quality (AA or A) eggs available from refrigerated cases. Eggs from the supermarket are carefully dated and stored. Check the expiration date on the carton, and use the eggs before that date. Before buying, open the carton and look at the eggs. Gently jiggle each one to be sure it is not broken and sticking to the carton. Do not buy or use any unclean or cracked eggs. Cracked eggs absorb odors and bacteria. For best flavor and freshness, buy farm-fresh eggs if possible.

2. STORING EGGS

Store eggs immediately after purchase, in the carton in the coldest part of the refrigerator. The carton prevents the eggs from absorbing refrigerator odors. Store-bought eggs do not need to be washed. Store eggs point-side down to keep the yolk centered, for more appealing hard- or soft-cooked eggs. Eggs age more in 1 day at room temperature than they do in 1 week in the refrigerator. Refrigerated eggs in the carton retain their quality for 4 to 5 weeks.

Store egg dishes that you make ahead to be baked later, covered, in the refrigerator. Store leftover egg dishes, covered, in the refrigerator. To reheat, cover loosely with plastic wrap and microwave on high for 1 to 2 minutes, depending on the quantity.

3. COOKING EGGS

Allow 1 or 2 eggs per person, unless otherwise requested.

When frying eggs, use a nonstick skillet for best results. Cook eggs slowly and gently over medium-low or low heat. (The exception is omelets, which are cooked quickly at a higher temperature.) Do not cook whole eggs in the microwave; they will explode. When a recipe calls for several eggs, as in frittatas, quiches, and stratas, 2 egg whites can be substituted for 1 whole egg to cut the cholesterol content.

To separate eggs, use an egg separator, or gently crack the egg and, holding half the eggshell in each hand, pour the egg back and forth, allowing the white to flow into a bowl. If a piece of eggshell gets into the mixture, use an eggshell half to scoop it out.

4. EGG SAFETY

To destroy any harmful bacteria, such as salmonella, which is occasionally found in raw eggs, the FDA recommends cooking eggs until the yolk and white are firm. Using raw eggs in dressings, desserts, or sauces is not recommended. Pasteurized eggs are available for the home cook (see page 34).

Wash hands and utensils with soapy water before and after handling eggs to prevent cross-contamination. If eggs crack while you're boiling them, they are still safe to eat. Hard-cooked eggs used for Easter egg hunts should not be left at room temperature longer than 2 hours.

5. SERVING EGGS

Serve eggs and egg dishes immediately on warm plates with a garnish of fruit, parsley, or herb sprigs.

Author's note: While testing recipes for this cookbook, my husband Reed and I ate eggs in some form almost every day for over 10 months. We wondered how this would affect our cholesterol levels. We were relieved when our doctor reported the good news that our cholesterol had stayed the same.

SOFT-COOKED EGGS

Soft-cooked eggs have an almost firm white and a runny yolk.

Add enough water to a deep saucepan to cover the egg (or eggs) by 1 inch (see Note). Bring water to a boil. With a spoon, lower each egg slowly into the boiling water. Reduce heat to medium-low and gently simmer 4 minutes for soft, 5 minutes for medium-soft, and 6 minutes for medium-hard. Immediately run eggs under cold water to prevent further cooking and for easier handling.

To serve, cut the egg in half with a knife and scoop the egg out with a spoon into a small bowl. Season with salt and pepper and a dot of butter, if desired, and serve immediately. Soft-cooked eggs can also be eaten in the shell in an egg cup with the top cut off (English style).

Note: An egg piercer or stickpin can be used to pierce the large end of the egg before cooking to keep it from cracking while cooking. (This is optional.) Adding a dash of salt to the water can also help keep the eggs from cracking.

CODDLED EGGS

Use the same procedure as for soft-cooked eggs, except remove the pan from the heat immediately after adding the eggs, and let stand for 10 minutes. Yolk and white will be very soft and delicate. Coddled eggs are often called for in making sauces, mayonnaise, or dressing for Caesar salad.

An egg coddler is a small, decorative container with a tight-fitting lid. One egg is placed in a coddler, covered, and cooked in simmering water for about 5 minutes. The egg is served in the coddler.

HARD-COOKED EGGS

Hard-cooked eggs have a firm white and firm yolk. Fresh eggs are hard to peel; use eggs that are a few days to a week old.

Place eggs in a single layer in a deep saucepan, and add enough cold water to cover. Add 1 teaspoon salt. Bring to a boil over medium-high heat. Reduce heat to medium or medium-low, and cook at a gentle boil for 9 minutes. Immediately drain and rinse eggs under cold water to prevent further cooking and the formation of a green ring around the yolk. If a ring does appear, though unappealing, the egg is still wholesome and the flavor is not affected. If an egg cracks during cooking, it is still edible. When cool, peel and use, or store, unpeeled, in the refrigerator for up to 1 week. Mark unpeeled hard-cooked eggs with a pencil or crayon if returning them to the carton.

To peel, gently crack eggs on all sides on a countertop. Starting at the large end, peel the shell off under cold water.

To tell if an egg is raw or hard-cooked, spin it on a flat surface. A cooked egg will spin fast, a raw egg will wobble.

BAKED (SHIRRED) EGGS

This is a convenient way to cook eggs for a large number of people.

Preheat the oven to 350°F. Break eggs into buttered ramekins or muffin tins (as many as needed), and season each with salt, pepper, and 1 tablespoon cream or milk. Bake for 18 to 20 minutes. To remove eggs, run a knife around the edge of the tin and lift out with a spoon.

VARIATIONS

Top each egg with 1 tablespoon grated cheese before baking.

Add 1 tablespoon chopped ham in the bottom of each ramekin before adding the egg.

Season the eggs with herbs along with salt and pepper.

POACHED EGGS

You can poach eggs in a special egg poacher, in a steamer, or in a pan of simmering water until the white is firm and the yolk is almost set. Use the freshest eggs possible because the whites in fresh eggs will hold their shape around the yolk better.

USING AN EGG POACHER

An egg poacher consists of several individual metal containers that fit into a larger container with a lid. Water is added to the bottom of the pan. Egg poachers are the easiest and best way to make a perfectly poached egg. The eggs are cooked in the individual containers, forming a neat, uniform round shape. Follow the manufacturer's directions.

POACHING EGGS IN RAMEKINS IN A VEGETABLE STEAMER

Place eggs in lightly sprayed or oiled ramekin dishes or custard cups placed in a steamer rack in a deep pan over water. Bring the water to a boil. Reduce heat to medium-low, cover, and cook until they reach the desired doneness, 4 to 5 minutes. Run a knife around the edge of each egg and gently slide it out of the ramekin.

POACHING EGGS IN A PAN OF WATER

These eggs will look a bit more ragged than eggs poached with the other methods. Some of the white may be lost.

1 teaspoon white vinegar (optional; vinegar helps hold the shape)

1 teaspoon salt (optional)

4 large eggs

In a deep skillet or saucepan over medium-high heat, bring 1½ inches of water to a gentle boil. Reduce heat to low. Add vinegar and salt, if desired. Break 1 egg into a small bowl or cup and slip it into the water. Repeat, adding eggs clockwise. Cover and simmer for 3 to 4 minutes, or to desired doneness. Do not allow water to boil. Remove eggs with a slotted spoon in the order they were added to the pan, and blot the bottoms with a paper towel. Trim ragged edges for a neat, even look. If you won't be using them immediately, poached eggs can be stored in cold water in the refrigerator for up to 2 days and reheated in hot water.

SERVES 1

SCRAMBLED EGGS

For this classic dish, eggs are blended together with seasonings and milk or water (the liquid makes the eggs lighter, but it is optional) over moderate heat. Serve scrambled eggs for breakfast, brunch, lunch, supper, or a late-night snack. Multiply the basic recipe as necessary, being sure to use a large enough pan.

2 large eggs

2 teaspoons milk or water (optional)

Salt and freshly ground pepper

1 teaspoon butter, margarine, or vegetable spray, if using a nonstick skillet, or 1 tablespoon butter or margarine if using a conventional skillet.

BASIC SCRAMBLED EGGS

In a small bowl, whisk together eggs, milk, if desired, and salt and pepper to taste. In an 8-inch nonstick skillet over medium heat, melt butter and swirl to coat the bottom of the skillet. When butter foams, add egg mixture all at once. Let set for 20 seconds. Cook, stirring, until eggs are light and fluffy and almost dry, about 1 minute. Serve immediately.

VARIATIONS:

Add to each 2 beaten eggs just before finishing cooking:

- *1 tablespoon grated Parmesan or Asiago cheese*
- *2 tablespoons grated Cheddar or Monterey Jack cheese*
- *1 teaspoon chopped fresh herbs, or ¼ teaspoon dried herbs*
- *¼ cup chopped ham or cooked bacon*
- *¼ cup chopped sautéed mushrooms*
- *¼ cup chopped green onions*
- *1 tablespoon salsa*
- *1 tablespoon chopped tomato, drained*

SERVES 1

EXPRESS SCRAMBLED EGGS

These scrambled eggs go together fast because the ham does not have to be precooked. Serve with toast and honey for a special breakfast for one, or multiply the ingredients as needed to make more servings.

2 large eggs

2 teaspoons water

Salt and freshly ground pepper

3 tablespoons chopped cooked ham

2 tablespoons grated Cheddar cheese

1 teaspoon chopped parsley

1 teaspoon butter or margarine

In a medium bowl, whisk together eggs, water, salt and pepper to taste, ham, cheese, and parsley. In a small skillet over medium heat, melt butter and swirl to coat bottom of skillet. When butter foams, add egg mixture all at once. Let set for 20 seconds. Cook, stirring, until light and fluffy and almost dry, about 1 minute.

TIPS FOR MAKING SCRAMBLED EGGS:

- Use a whisk to blend the eggs, or a fork if you prefer streaky eggs with some white showing.
- Use a nonstick skillet for cooking.
- Use a heavy, heat-resistant plastic spoon to stir the eggs. You do not have to stir constantly.
- Stir until the eggs are light and fluffy and almost dry on top.

SERVES 1

FRIED EGGS

Use a nonstick skillet for best results and to reduce the amount of fat needed in cooking. To reduce the fat even more, use cooking spray in place of the butter or oil.

2 large eggs

1 to 2 teaspoons butter, margarine, vegetable oil, or bacon drippings

Salt and freshly ground pepper

SUNNY-SIDE UP

Break eggs into a small bowl (to be sure yolks are not broken). In an 8-inch nonstick skillet over medium heat, melt butter. Swirl to cover bottom of pan. When butter foams, gently add eggs to skillet. Cook until whites are firm and yolk is semifirm, 2 to 3 minutes, or to desired doneness. Season with salt and pepper to taste. Serve on a warm plate.

EGGS OVER EASY

Follow the directions for fried eggs, then turn the eggs over and cook for 1 minute longer, or to desired doneness.

STEAM-BASTED EGGS

Follow the directions for fried eggs, cooking them for only 1 minute. Add 2 teaspoons water to skillet. Cover and cook until whites are set and yolks are semifirm, about 2 minutes longer, or to desired doneness.

SERVES 2

SCRAMBLED EGGS WITH AVOCADO AND CHEESE

Eggs blended with avocado and cheese make a "melt in your mouth" combination. This recipe can easily be doubled.

- 4 large eggs
- 1 tablespoon water
- 1/8 teaspoon salt
- Freshly ground pepper
- 2 teaspoons butter or margarine
- 1/2 cup grated Cheddar cheese
- 1/2 avocado, diced
- Flat-leaf parsley for garnish

In a medium bowl, whisk together eggs, water, salt, and pepper to taste. In a large nonstick skillet over medium heat, melt butter and swirl to coat bottom of skillet. When butter foams, add egg mixture all at once. Let stand for 20 seconds. Cook, stirring, until light and fluffy and almost dry, 2 to 3 minutes. Add cheese and avocado and stir until blended. Serve garnished with parsley.

SERVES 4

SCRAMBLED EGGS WITH HOMINY, BACON, AND CHILES

Hominy is dried white or yellow corn kernels with the hull and germ removed. Here it is combined with eggs, bacon, and chiles for an unusual dish to serve for breakfast, lunch, or supper.

4 slices bacon, chopped

6 green onions, including some tender green tops, sliced

1 can (14½ ounces) white hominy, drained

1 can (4 ounces) diced green chiles, drained

5 large eggs

1 tablespoon milk

¼ teaspoon salt

Freshly ground pepper

Fresh Tomato Salsa (page 103) or purchased salsa for topping (optional)

In a large nonstick skillet over medium-high heat, cook bacon and green onions until bacon is crisp and onions are tender, about 5 minutes. Drain, leaving 1 tablespoon drippings in pan. Stir in hominy and chiles and mix well. In a medium bowl, whisk together eggs, milk, salt, and pepper to taste. Reduce heat to medium. Pour egg mixture over hominy mixture all at once. Let set for 20 seconds. Cook, stirring, until light and fluffy and almost dry, 2 to 3 minutes. Serve with salsa, if desired.

SERVES 4

TEX-MEX SCRAMBLE

Chorizo is a highly seasoned pork sausage flavored with garlic, chili powder, and spices. It is especially popular in the Southwest. Here chorizo is scrambled with eggs, cheese, and cilantro for a bold flavor. Serve with warm tortillas (see page 165). You may want to fill a tortilla with the egg mixture to eat in your hand.

8 ounces chorizo, casings removed

1 to 2 teaspoons vegetable oil, if needed

6 to 8 green onions, including some tender green tops, sliced

1 garlic clove, minced

8 large eggs

2 tablespoons water

¼ teaspoon salt

Freshly ground pepper

½ cup grated Monterey Jack cheese

¼ cup chopped fresh cilantro or parsley

½ cup sour cream for topping

Cilantro sprigs for garnish

In a large skillet over medium-high heat, cook chorizo, breaking it up with a wooden spoon, until browned, about 5 minutes. Add oil, if needed. Add green onions and garlic and sauté until vegetables are tender, about 2 minutes longer.

In a medium bowl, whisk together eggs, water, salt, and pepper to taste. Reduce heat to medium. Pour over meat-onion mixture. Let set for 20 seconds. Cook, stirring, until light and fluffy and almost dry, 3 to 4 minutes. Fold in cheese and cilantro and stir until blended. Add a dollop of sour cream on top of each serving. Served garnished with cilantro sprigs.

SERVES 2

SWISS SCRAMBLE

Swiss cheese and sour cream add a unique, tangy flavor to these creamy eggs.

4 large eggs

2 tablespoons sour cream

⅛ teaspoon salt

Freshly ground pepper

2 teaspoons butter or margarine

¼ cup grated Swiss cheese

In a small bowl, whisk together eggs, sour cream, salt, and pepper to taste. In a medium nonstick skillet over medium heat, melt butter and swirl to coat the bottom of the skillet. When butter foams, add eggs all at once. Let set for 20 seconds. Cook, stirring, until light and fluffy and almost dry, 2 to 3 minutes. Add cheese and cook, stirring, until blended, about 1 minute longer. Serve immediately.

SERVES 4

CONFETTI SCRAMBLE

Fresh vegetables add texture and color to this healthful egg dish. Serve with Blueberry Muffins (page 275).

- 2 tablespoons butter or margarine
- ¼ cup chopped green bell pepper
- ¼ cup chopped red bell pepper
- ¼ cup fresh or frozen corn kernels
- ½ cup chopped mushrooms
- 4 green onions, including some tender green tops, sliced
- 8 large eggs
- ¼ cup milk
- ¼ teaspoon dried thyme
- ¼ teaspoon salt
- Freshly ground pepper
- Parsley sprigs for garnish
- Sliced black olives for garnish (optional)

In a large nonstick skillet over medium heat, melt butter. Add vegetables and sauté until tender, 6 to 7 minutes.

In a medium bowl, whisk together eggs, milk, thyme, salt, and pepper to taste. Pour mixture over vegetables and let set for 20 seconds. Cook, stirring, until light and fluffy and almost dry, 3 to 4 minutes. Serve garnished with parsley and olives, if desired.

SERVES 4

SCRAMBLED EGGS WITH POBLANO CHILE

The poblano chile adds a snappy flavor to these eggs. Wrap them in a warm tortilla (see page 165) and serve with sliced oranges.

8 large eggs

2 tablespoons water

¼ teaspoon salt

Freshly ground pepper

1 tablespoon butter or margarine

1 small poblano chile, seeded and diced

6 green onions, including some tender green tops, chopped

½ cup grated Monterey Jack cheese

In a medium bowl, whisk together eggs, water, salt, and pepper to taste. In a large nonstick skillet over medium heat, melt butter and swirl to coat bottom of skillet. Add chile and green onions and sauté until tender, about 5 minutes. Pour egg mixture over vegetables and let set for 20 seconds. Cook, stirring, until light and fluffy and almost dry, 3 to 4 minutes. Add cheese and stir until blended. Serve immediately.

Note: After working with fresh chiles, wash your hands with soapy water and do not touch your eyes.

SERVES 4 TO 6

SAVORY SCRAMBLED EGGS WITH TOMATOES, GREEN ONIONS, AND SOUR CREAM

Sour cream folded into cooked eggs dotted with diced tomatoes and green onions gives these eggs a flavor boost. Serve with Date Bread (page 291).

8 large eggs

2 tablespoons water

1 tablespoon chopped fresh basil, or ½ teaspoon dried basil

⅛ teaspoon salt

Freshly ground pepper

1 medium tomato, seeded, diced, and drained

6 green onions, including some tender green tops, sliced

1 tablespoon butter or margarine

¼ cup light sour cream

In a medium bowl, whisk together eggs, water, basil, salt, and pepper to taste. Fold in tomato and green onions. In a large nonstick skillet over medium heat, melt butter and swirl to coat bottom of skillet. When butter foams, add egg mixture all at once. Let set for 20 seconds. Cook, stirring, until light and fluffy and almost dry, 3 to 4 minutes. Add sour cream and stir until blended. Serve immediately.

SERVES 4

MEXICAN SCRAMBLE

Serve this delicious combination of Mexican flavors with lots of salsa, sour cream, warm tortillas (see page 165), and a glass of Iced Tea (page 25).

8 large eggs

2 tablespoons water

½ teaspoon dried oregano

⅛ teaspoon salt

Freshly ground pepper

1 tablespoon butter or margarine

6 to 8 green onions, including some tender green tops, sliced

1 small tomato, seeded, chopped, and drained

1 can (4 ounces) diced green chiles, drained

3 tablespoons sliced ripe olives

½ cup grated Monterey Jack cheese

Sour cream for topping

Fresh Tomato Salsa (page 103) or purchased salsa for topping

In a medium bowl, whisk together eggs, water, oregano, salt, and pepper to taste. In a large skillet over medium heat, melt butter and swirl to coat bottom of skillet. When butter foams, pour in egg mixture all at once. Let set for 20 seconds. Cook, stirring, for 1 minute. Add green onions, tomato, chiles, olives, and cheese and continue cooking until light and fluffy and almost dry, 3 to 4 minutes longer. Pass the sour cream and salsa in bowls.

SERVES 4

SCRAMBLED EGGS WITH MUSHROOMS AND GARLIC

Mushrooms, garlic, and wine take these eggs beyond the ordinary. For a quick meal, serve them with Scones with Spiced Sugar-Nut Topping (page 287).

- 2 tablespoons butter or margarine
- 4 ounces medium mushrooms, chopped
- 2 garlic cloves, minced
- ¼ cup minced parsley
- 8 large eggs
- ¼ cup dry white wine
- ¼ teaspoon salt
- Freshly ground pepper
- Grated Parmesan cheese for topping

In a large nonstick skillet over medium heat, melt butter. Add mushrooms and garlic and sauté until tender, about 5 minutes. Stir in parsley. In a medium bowl, whisk together eggs, wine, salt, and pepper to taste. Pour egg mixture over vegetables all at once. Let set for 20 seconds. Cook, stirring, until light and fluffy and almost dry, 3 to 4 minutes. Serve sprinkled with Parmesan cheese.

SERVES 6

ELEGANT SCRAMBLED EGGS

Chicken and avocado go into these rich eggs, making an elegant brunch dish.

1½ tablespoons butter or margarine, divided

4 ounces medium mushrooms, sliced

1 shallot, chopped

¾ cup diced cooked chicken breast

1 avocado, diced

1 teaspoon lemon juice

8 large eggs

½ cup half-and-half or milk

1 tablespoon dry white wine (optional)

¼ teaspoon salt

⅛ teaspoon white pepper

Pimiento or roasted red pepper strips for garnish

Chopped chives for garnish

In a large nonstick skillet over medium heat, melt half the butter. Add mushrooms and shallot and sauté until tender, about 5 minutes. Stir in chicken, avocado, and lemon juice. Remove from skillet and set aside.

In a medium bowl, whisk together eggs, half-and-half, wine, salt, and pepper.

In the same skillet over medium heat, melt remaining butter and swirl to coat bottom of skillet. When butter foams, add egg mixture all at once. Let set for 20 seconds. Cook, stirring, until light and fluffy and almost dry, 3 to 4 minutes. Gently fold in chicken-avocado mixture. Garnish with pimiento strips and sprinkle chives on top.

SERVES 2

SCRAMBLED EGGS WITH SLICED TOMATO, MOZZARELLA, FRESH BASIL, AND HAZELNUTS

The combination of crunchy hazelnuts, juicy tomato, and cheesy mozzarella gives these eggs extra appeal.

- 4 large eggs
- 2 tablespoons half-and-half or milk
- ⅛ teaspoon salt
- Freshly ground pepper
- ½ cup grated mozzarella cheese
- 2 tablespoons chopped fresh basil
- 2 teaspoons butter or margarine
- 1 ripe tomato, sliced
- 1 tablespoon chopped hazelnuts

In a small bowl, whisk together eggs, half-and-half, salt, and pepper to taste. Fold in cheese and 1 tablespoon of the basil. In a large nonstick skillet over medium heat, melt butter and swirl to coat bottom of skillet. When butter foams, add egg mixture all at once. Let set for 20 seconds. Cook, stirring, until light and fluffy and almost dry, 2 to 3 minutes. Serve topped with sliced tomato, sprinkled with hazelnuts and remaining basil.

SERVES 4

GREEN EGGS AND HAM

You've read about these famous eggs; now you can eat them. Like Dr. Seuss's Sam, you'll find that you like green eggs and ham.

- 8 large eggs
- 2 tablespoons Basil Pesto (recipe follows) or purchased pesto
- ¾ cup cubed cooked ham
- ¼ teaspoon salt
- Freshly ground pepper
- 1 tablespoon butter or margarine
- Basil leaves for garnish

In a medium bowl, whisk eggs. Add pesto, ham, salt, and pepper to taste. In a large nonstick skillet over medium heat, melt butter and swirl to coat bottom of skillet. When butter foams, add egg mixture all at once. Let set for 20 seconds. Cook, stirring, until light and fluffy and almost dry, 3 to 4 minutes. Serve garnished with basil leaves.

BASIL PESTO

Makes about ½ cup

- 2 cups firmly packed fresh basil leaves, washed and dried
- 2 sprigs fresh parsley
- 2 garlic cloves, coarsely chopped
- ¼ cup pine nuts or walnuts
- ¼ cup grated Parmesan cheese
- ¼ teaspoon salt
- Freshly ground pepper
- 3 to 4 tablespoons olive oil

Place all ingredients except oil in a food processor or blender. Process until minced. With motor running, slowly pour oil through the feed tube and blend until a paste forms. Scrape down sides of bowl with a spatula. Transfer to a bowl, cover, and refrigerate until ready to use, or freeze in an airtight container for up to 3 months. Bring pesto to room temperature before using.

Note: Pesto will darken on top; this is normal. Stir before using.

SERVES 4

SCRAMBLED EGGS WITH SMOKED SALMON AND CREAM CHEESE

For a special company breakfast, serve these eggs along with Cranberry Scones (page 285).

In a medium bowl, whisk together eggs, water, salt, and pepper to taste.

In a large nonstick skillet over medium heat, melt butter. Add egg mixture and let set for 20 seconds. Cook and stir 2 minutes. Add the salmon, cheese, and onion, and cook, stirring, until light and fluffy and almost dry, about 2 minutes longer. Sprinkle with chives and serve immediately.

8 large eggs

2 tablespoons water

¼ teaspoon salt

Freshly ground pepper

1 tablespoon butter or margarine

2 ounces smoked salmon, flaked

2 ounces cream cheese, cut into small pieces

2 tablespoons diced red onion

Sliced chives or green onion tops for garnish

SERVES 3 OR 4

EGG PATTIES

These little egg pancakes are fun to make and serve. Top with salsa or ketchup and serve with Home Fries (page 255).

6 large eggs

½ cup grated Parmesan cheese

¼ cup chopped parsley

4 green onions, including some tender green tops, finely chopped

½ cup coarse dry bread crumbs

2 thick slices bacon, cooked and crumbled

¼ teaspoon salt

Freshly ground pepper

Parsley sprigs for garnish

In a medium bowl, whisk eggs. Add Parmesan, parsley, green onions, bread crumbs, bacon, salt, and pepper to taste. Mix well.

Heat a large, lightly sprayed or oiled nonstick skillet or griddle over medium heat. For each patty, drop 1 large tablespoon of egg mixture into the skillet, making 4 patties at a time. Cook patties until golden on the bottom, about 2 minutes. Turn and cook until puffed, 2 minutes longer. Serve immediately, garnished with parsley sprigs.

SERVES 4

MIGAS

When we visited friends in Austin, Texas, they took us to an old Mexican establishment that has been serving breakfast for more than 50 years. The walls were lined with faded photos of celebrities who had been customers over the years. This egg dish was one of their specialties.

In a medium bowl, whisk together eggs, water, salt, and pepper to taste. In a large nonstick skillet over medium heat, melt butter and swirl to coat bottom of skillet. When butter foams, add green onions and cook for about 1 minute. Add egg mixture all at once. Let set for 20 seconds. Cook, stirring, until almost set, 3 to 4 minutes longer. Add tomato and cheese and continue cooking and stirring until well mixed and cheese melts, about 1 minute longer. Stir in chips and serve immediately.

8 large eggs

2 tablespoons water

¼ teaspoon salt

Freshly ground pepper

2 tablespoons butter or margarine

6 green onions, including some tender green tops, sliced

1 medium tomato, seeded, chopped, and drained

1 cup grated Monterey Jack cheese

1 cup tortilla chips, broken up into large, bite-sized pieces

SERVES 4

EGGS BENEDICT

The supreme brunch dish! Crisp English muffins, slices of Canadian bacon, and delicate poached eggs are topped with a buttery, lemony Hollandaise Sauce. Forget the calories and enjoy. There are many variations of this popular dish (see the following recipes).

8 slices Canadian bacon (see Note)

4 English muffins, split and lightly toasted

8 large poached eggs (see page 40)

Hollandaise Sauce (recipe follows)

Watercress sprigs for garnish

In a medium, lightly sprayed or oiled nonstick skillet over medium heat, fry bacon for 1 to 2 minutes, turning once.

Place 2 muffin halves, cut-side up on each of 4 plates. Place a slice of bacon and a poached egg on each muffin half. Spoon Hollandaise Sauce over each egg. Serve immediately, garnished with watercress.

Note: You can replace the Canadian bacon with slices of cooked bacon or thinly sliced ham.

HOLLANDAISE SAUCE

This method of making hollandaise sauce is safe from salmonella because the egg yolks are cooked.

Makes about 1½ cups

4 egg yolks

3 tablespoons fresh lemon juice

1 tablespoon water

¼ teaspoon salt

Dash of cayenne pepper

1 cup (2 sticks) butter (no substitute), melted

In a small, heavy saucepan over medium-low heat, combine yolks, lemon juice, water, salt, and cayenne pepper. Whisk constantly until mixture bubbles and begins to thicken, 2 to 3 minutes. Scrape mixture into blender. Add butter in a slow, steady stream and blend until all the butter is used and sauce is thickened, about 30 seconds.

VARIATIONS

(to be added to the finished sauce)

Add 1 tablespoon chopped chives or parsley

Add 1 teaspoon dried mixed herbs.

Add 1 tablespoon Dijon mustard.

SERVES 4

HAM AND TOMATO BENEDICT WITH CHIVE HOLLANDAISE SAUCE

Here's a twist on the classic Benedict: Shaved ham and chopped tomato are layered on an English muffin and then topped with the traditional poached egg and Chive Hollandaise Sauce. Avocado slices and olives make flavorful garnishes.

- 4 English muffins, split, toasted, and lightly buttered
- 4 ounces shaved cooked ham
- 1 tomato, seeded, chopped, and drained
- 8 large poached eggs (see page 40)
- Chive Hollandaise Sauce (facing page)
- 1 avocado, sliced, for garnish
- 8 ripe olives for garnish

Place 2 muffin halves on each of 4 plates. Layer ham, tomato, and eggs on each muffin half, and top with Chive Hollandaise Sauce. Serve garnished with avocado slices and olives.

SERVES 4

VEGGIE EGGS BENEDICT

This meatless version of the traditional eggs Benedict has layers of tomato, avocado, onion, and poached eggs and is topped with Herbed Hollandaise Sauce.

1 bag (6 ounces) fresh spinach, stems removed and rinsed

4 English muffins, split, toasted, and lightly buttered

1 large tomato, thinly sliced

1 avocado, sliced

½ red onion, thinly sliced and separated into rings

8 large poached eggs (see page 40)

Herbed Hollandaise Sauce (page 60)

In a medium saucepan over medium heat, cook spinach in a small amount of water, tossing with a fork several times, until wilted, about 3 minutes. Drain, squeeze dry, and blot with a paper towel.

Place 2 muffin halves on each of 4 plates and top each half with about 2 tablespoons spinach. Add a tomato slice, several avocado slices, an onion ring, and a poached egg to each muffin half. Top with Herbed Hollandaise Sauce. Serve immediately.

SERVES 6

CRAB CAKES BENEDICT

Your brunch will be special when highlighted with this real delicacy: sweet, succulent crab cakes topped with Parsley Hollandaise Sauce. Serve with Cranberry Scones (page 285).

- 3 English muffins, split, toasted, and lightly buttered
- 6 Crab Cakes (recipe follows)
- 6 large poached eggs (see page 40)
- Parsley Hollandaise Sauce (page 60)
- Flat-leaf parsley for garnish
- Lemon wedges for garnish

Place 1 English muffin half on each of 6 plates. Place 1 crab cake on each muffin half. Top each with a poached egg and then with Parsley Hollandaise Sauce. Serve immediately, garnished with parsley and lemon wedges.

CRAB CAKES

Makes 6 crab cakes

- 1 pound cooked crabmeat, flaked
- 1 large egg, beaten
- 1 cup finely crushed saltines (about 25 crackers)
- 1 teaspoon fresh lemon juice
- 1 teaspoon Dijon mustard
- 2 tablespoons finely chopped green onion, including some tender green tops
- 3 tablespoons mayonnaise
- ½ teaspoon Worcestershire sauce
- ½ teaspoon salt
- ½ teaspoon Old Bay Seasoning or other seasoning salt
- ¼ teaspoon freshly ground pepper
- ¼ cup all-purpose flour
- 1 tablespoon butter or margarine
- 2 tablespoons vegetable oil

Place crabmeat in a large bowl. Add egg and crushed crackers and mix well. Then add lemon juice, mustard, green onion, mayonnaise, Worcestershire sauce, salt, Old Bay Seasoning, and pepper. Mix well and form into 6 crab cakes, each about ½ inch thick.

Place flour on a piece of waxed paper. Dust cakes lightly on both sides with flour.

In a large skillet over medium-high heat, melt butter with oil. Add cakes and cook, turning once, until golden brown, 2 to 3 minutes on each side.

SERVES 4

EGGS BENEDICT FLORENTINE

On a sunny Sunday morning, treat your guests to this popular dish with spinach added for variety and a fresh taste. Serve with a light fruit dish, such as Melon Ball Fruit Cup (page 312).

1 bag (6 ounces) fresh spinach, stems removed and rinsed

4 English muffins, split, toasted, and lightly buttered

8 thin ham slices

Dash of ground nutmeg

8 large poached eggs (see page 40)

Hollandaise Sauce (page 60)

Parsley sprigs for garnish

In a large saucepan over medium heat, cook spinach in a small amount of water, covered, until wilted, tossing once with a fork, about 3 minutes. Drain, squeeze dry, and blot with a paper towel.

Place 2 muffin halves on each of 4 plates. Top each half with a ham slice, 1 heaping tablespoon of spinach, and a sprinkling of nutmeg. Add a poached egg to each muffin half. Spoon some Hollandaise Sauce over each egg. Serve immediately, garnished with parsley sprigs.

SERVES 4

POACHED EGGS ON PORTOBELLO MUSHROOMS

Portobello mushrooms are large, mature crimini mushrooms. They have a meaty flavor and are often served as a meat substitute. Here they are used as a base for poached eggs topped with Hollandaise Sauce for a delightful dish.

- 4 portobello mushrooms, stems removed, rinsed and dried (see Note)
- Vegetable oil for brushing on mushrooms
- 4 large poached eggs (see page 40)
- Hollandaise Sauce (page 60)
- Chives for garnish

Prepare broiler. Brush both sides of mushrooms with oil. Place on a baking sheet lightly sprayed with oil, and broil for 5 minutes on each side. Place each mushroom on a plate with gill-side up. Top each with an egg. Spoon some Hollandaise Sauce over each egg. Serve immediately, garnished with chives.

Note: Portobello mushrooms readily absorb water. Rinse them quickly and dry with a paper towel immediately.

SERVES 4 TO 6

POACHED EGGS ON BLACK BEAN CAKES WITH ROASTED RED BELL PEPPER SAUCE

Wow your guests with this unforgettable combination. Have the bean cakes prepared ahead to fry at serving time. You can also make the bell pepper sauce or salsa ahead.

8 saltines, broken up

2 cans (15 ounces each) black beans, drained and rinsed

6 green onions, including some tender green tops, cut into pieces

2 garlic cloves, cut into pieces

2 sprigs cilantro or parsley, cut into pieces

1 teaspoon ground cumin

1 teaspoon chili powder

1 teaspoon salt

Freshly ground pepper

¼ cup yellow cornmeal

2 to 3 tablespoons vegetable oil

Roasted Red Bell Pepper Sauce (facing page) or Fresh Tomato Salsa (page 103)

6 large poached eggs (see page 40)

Cilantro sprigs for garnish

Place saltines in a food processor and process until crushed. Add beans, green onions, garlic, cilantro, cumin, chili powder, salt, and pepper to taste and process until chunky. Form into 6 cakes. (Mixture will be sticky). Place cornmeal in a flat dish or on waxed paper. Add cakes and turn to coat.

In a large nonstick skillet over medium heat, warm 2 tablespoons oil. Fry cakes until crisp, about 5 minutes on each side. Add more oil, if needed.

If serving with the bell pepper sauce, have the sauce warmed and ready.

To assemble, top each cake with a poached egg and a spoonful of Roasted Red Bell Pepper Sauce or Fresh Tomato Salsa. Garnish each with a sprig of cilantro and serve immediately.

Note: The black bean cakes make good vegetarian burgers.

ROASTED RED BELL PEPPER SAUCE

This sauce is also delicious on vegetables, especially asparagus.

Makes about 1 cup

2 tablespoons butter or margarine

¼ cup chopped yellow onion

1 garlic clove, minced

1 tablespoon all-purpose flour

½ cup milk

1 red bell pepper, roasted, peeled, and cut up (see Note)

¼ teaspoon paprika

¼ teaspoon salt

Freshly ground pepper

In a small saucepan over medium heat, melt butter. Add onion and garlic and sauté until tender, about 5 minutes. Add flour and stir until bubbly. Stir in milk and bring to a boil. Cook, stirring, until thickened, about 2 minutes. Sauce will be thick.

Place roasted bell pepper in food processor or blender and purée. Add onion mixture and process until smooth. Return to pan and add paprika, salt, and pepper to taste. Serve warm.

Note: To roast the pepper, preheat the broiler. Cut pepper in half lengthwise and remove seeds and ribs. Make several 1-inch slashes around the edge of each pepper half. Place skin-side up on an aluminum foil–lined baking sheet. Press peppers down with the palm of your hand to flatten them. Broil until skin is charred, about 10 minutes. Remove from broiler, fold foil tightly over peppers, and let them steam for 10 minutes. Unwrap peppers and peel off skin.

SERVES 6

POACHED EGGS ON POLENTA WITH CHUNKY TOMATO SAUCE

Baked polenta squares make a tasty base for poached eggs topped with Chunky Tomato Sauce.

POLENTA

1 cup yellow cornmeal

3½ cups cold water

½ teaspoon salt

½ cup ricotta or cottage cheese

2 tablespoons grated Parmesan cheese

1 tablespoon butter or margarine

6 large poached eggs (see page 40)

Chunky Tomato Sauce (facing page)

Grated Parmesan cheese for topping

To make the polenta: Preheat oven to 350°F. In a small bowl, mix cornmeal with 1 cup of the water. In a medium saucepan over high heat, combine remaining 2½ cups water and salt and bring to a boil. Slowly stir cornmeal mixture into boiling water. Reduce heat to low and simmer, uncovered, stirring constantly, until cornmeal mixture is thick and smooth, about 3 minutes. Remove from heat. Stir in ricotta cheese, Parmesan cheese, and butter. Turn into a lightly sprayed or oiled 8-by-8-inch baking dish. Bake until firm, about 30 minutes.

To assemble: Cut polenta into 6 squares and place each on a plate. Top each square with a poached egg. Add a few spoonfuls of Chunky Tomato Sauce and sprinkle with Parmesan cheese. Serve immediately.

CHUNKY TOMATO SAUCE

This all-purpose tomato sauce can also be used with pastas, meats, and fish.
Makes about 3 cups

- 1 tablespoon olive oil or vegetable oil
- 1 cup chopped yellow onion
- 1 or 2 garlic cloves, minced
- 1 can (14½ ounces) whole tomatoes, cut up, including juices
- 1 can (8 ounces) tomato sauce
- ½ teaspoon dried basil
- ¼ teaspoon dried oregano
- ¼ cup chopped parsley
- 1 bay leaf
- ¼ teaspoon sugar
- ¼ teaspoon salt
- Freshly ground pepper

In a medium saucepan over medium heat, warm oil. Add onion and garlic and sauté until tender, about 5 minutes. Place tomatoes and their juice in food processor or blender and process until chunky. Add to pan along with tomato sauce, herbs, sugar, salt, and pepper to taste. Simmer, uncovered, stirring occasionally, until sauce is slightly thickened and flavors are blended, 10 to 15 minutes.

Remove bay leaf and discard. Serve immediately, or cover and refrigerate for up to 1 week.

SERVES 4

POACHED EGGS ON MEDITERRANEAN RICE

These poached eggs, served on a mound of savory vegetables and rice and topped with feta cheese, have a lively, piquant flavor.

1 tablespoon vegetable oil

½ cup chopped yellow onion

½ cup chopped green bell pepper

½ cup chopped zucchini

¾ cup long-grain white rice

1½ cups chicken broth

¼ teaspoon dried oregano

¼ teaspoon salt

Freshly ground pepper

½ cup chopped tomato

1 tablespoon capers, drained

¼ cup sliced black olives

4 large poached eggs (see page 40)

¼ cup crumbled feta cheese

In a medium saucepan over medium heat, warm oil. Add onion, bell pepper, and zucchini and sauté until tender, 6 to 7 minutes. Stir in rice. Add broth, oregano, salt, and pepper to taste. Bring to a boil, then reduce heat to medium-low, cover, and cook until rice is tender, about 20 minutes. Stir in tomato, capers, and olives. Cover and keep warm over low heat.

To assemble, divide rice mixture among 4 plates. Top each with a poached egg and sprinkle with cheese.

SERVES 4

EGGS IN ORZO

Orzo is a rice-shaped pasta that lends itself well to a breakfast or brunch menu. Here, eggs are nested in cooked orzo and baked until set. Serve them with sautéed sugar snap peas, with cherry tomatoes for an accompaniment.

1 cup chicken broth

1¼ cups water

1 cup orzo

4 large eggs

¼ teaspoon salt

Freshly ground pepper

1 cup grated Monterey Jack cheese

Preheat oven to 350°F. In a medium saucepan over medium-high heat, bring broth and water to a boil. Stir in orzo. Reduce heat to low and cook, covered, until tender, about 15 minutes. Drain, if necessary. Divide orzo equally among 4 individual lightly sprayed or oiled gratin dishes. With the back of a spoon, push mixture up the sides, making an indentation (nest) in the center. Break an egg into each indentation. Season with salt and pepper to taste.

Sprinkle with cheese and bake until whites are set, yolks are almost cooked, and cheese is melted, about 15 minutes longer.

SERVES 4

SWISS BAKED EGGS

Eggs are gently baked in individual custard cups and topped with cream and cheese for a simple but elegant guest entrée. Serve with Rich Scones with Lemon Curd (page 284).

4 large eggs

¼ cup half-and-half or milk

1 teaspoon dry sherry or white wine (optional)

¼ cup grated Swiss cheese

Salt and freshly ground pepper

Paprika

Preheat oven to 350°F. Butter 4 custard cups. Break an egg into each one. In a cup, mix half-and-half with sherry, if desired. Pour evenly over the eggs. Sprinkle with cheese, salt, pepper, and paprika. Place ramekins in a baking dish or pan. Pour hot water into dish to come one third of the way up the sides of the ramekins. Bake until eggs are set, about 20 minutes. Serve immediately.

SERVES 1

EGG-IN-A-HOLE (ALSO CALLED EGG EYES)

Introduce your kids to cooking with this simple dish that is fun and easy to make. Serve with crisp bacon.

1 slice white sandwich bread

Butter

1 large egg

Spread both sides of bread with butter. With a 2½-inch round cookie cutter, cut a hole in the center of the bread. Remove the cut-out hole and set aside.

Heat an 8-inch nonstick skillet over medium heat. Add bread and fry until bottom is golden brown, 3 to 4 minutes. Flip bread over. Break the egg into the hole. Cover with a lid and cook until egg is firm, about 5 minutes. Serve immediately. Fry the cut-out hole and serve on the side.

SERVES 4

EGGS IN BAKED POTATOES

Baked potatoes make an edible container for eggs in this recipe. Start the day with this hearty combination that will keep you satisfied all morning.

4 extra-large russet potatoes (about 4 pounds), scrubbed and pierced in several places with the tip of a sharp knife

4 teaspoons butter or margarine

¼ cup sour cream

½ cup grated Cheddar or Monterey Jack cheese

Salt and freshly ground pepper

4 large eggs

Preheat oven to 375°F. Bake potatoes until tender, about 1 hour. Remove from oven. Slash potatoes lengthwise and press the edges to open. (Don't split the potatoes in half.) To each potato, add 1 teaspoon butter, 1 tablespoon sour cream, 1 tablespoon cheese, and salt and pepper to taste, and mix with a fork. Make an indentation in the center of each potato and break an egg into each one. Sprinkle with the remaining cheese. Place in a lightly sprayed or oiled baking dish, return to oven, and bake until egg is set, 15 to 18 minutes.

Note: If you don't have time to bake the potatoes in the oven, microwave them for 8 to 10 minutes on high.

SERVES 4

BAKED EGGS IN BRIOCHE

Brioche is a French creation—a light, rich yeast bread with a fluted base and a round topknot. Here eggs are baked in small individual brioches for a different and creative presentation.

- 4 small brioches (see Note)
- 2 tablespoons melted butter
- 4 large eggs
- Salt and freshly ground pepper
- ½ teaspoon dried tarragon
- 1 tablespoon chopped parsley

Preheat oven to 350°F. Cut off the topknot of each brioche and set aside. Scoop out the insides about halfway down, leaving a shell. Save bread crumbs for another purpose. Brush insides with butter. Place in a lightly sprayed or oiled baking dish and break an egg into each brioche. Sprinkle with salt and pepper to taste, tarragon, and parsley. Bake until eggs are set, about 20 minutes. Brush cut side of topknots with butter, place on a piece of foil, and bake along with eggs for the last 10 minutes of baking time. Place topknots on top of brioches and serve.

Note: Brioches can be purchased at some specialty bakeries.

SERVES 4

DEVILED EGGS

Deviled eggs are hard-cooked eggs with the yolks removed, mashed with seasonings or other ingredients, and returned to the whites. The term "devil" means to season with spicy ingredients.

4 large hard-cooked eggs (see page 39)

2 tablespoons mayonnaise

½ teaspoon prepared yellow mustard

¼ teaspoon dry mustard

¼ teaspoon salt

Freshly ground pepper

Paprika

Cut eggs in half lengthwise. Slip yolks out into a bowl. Add mayonnaise, yellow and dry mustard, salt, and pepper to taste. Mash with a fork. Fill egg whites with yolk mixture. Sprinkle with paprika. Arrange on a plate and refrigerate for several hours before serving.

VARIATIONS

Add any of the following to the yolk mixture:

- *2 tablespoons cooked crumbled bacon*
- *1 tablespoon finely chopped parsley*
- *1 tablespoon chopped, cooked shrimp*
- *1 tablespoon caviar*
- *1 tablespoon drained capers*

OMELETS

French omelets are a mixture of eggs and seasonings, quickly cooked and then folded or rolled around a filling. They are fast and easy to make and are suitable for any meal.

Although the eggs for an omelet are usually beaten together, you can make a puffy omelet by beating the yolks and whites separately (see page 36).

You can be as creative as you like with omelet fillings; typical choices include cheese, meats, vegetables, and herbs. Omelets are easier to make one at a time.

One three-egg omelet will serve one person generously. If you'll be making a number of omelets, increase the ingredient proportions.

To make omelets, you'll need an 8-inch omelet pan or an 8-inch nonstick skillet. An omelet pan is designed specifically for omelets; it has low, sloping sides so the omelet can be easily folded and rolled out onto a plate. Omelet pans must be seasoned according to the manufacturer's directions and wiped clean with a paper towel (not washed) after being used. They should be reserved for making omelets only.

TIPS FOR MAKING OMELETS

- Use fresh eggs.
- Mix the eggs with a whisk or fork until blended but not frothy.
- Adding water or milk is optional. The liquid makes the omelet fluffier.
- Prepare the filling before starting to make the omelet. The filling should be warm or at room temperature. Most vegetables need to be sautéed briefly, and meat should be cooked, before being added to the omelet.
- If you're using an omelet pan designed specifically for omelets, use another small pan or skillet for sautéing the filling ingredients. If you're making the omelet in an 8-inch nonstick skillet, you can use the same pan for both filling and omelet. Set the cooked filling aside and wipe the skillet with a paper towel before making the omelet.
- Add 1 teaspoon butter or margarine for cooking in a nonstick skillet. Increase the amount of butter if you're using an omelet pan without a nonstick coating.
- Allow about ½ cup filling for each three-egg omelet. Too much filling will make the omelet hard to fold.
- Additional filling can be served on the side or on top of the omelet.
- Suggested fillings are bacon, pancetta, ham, sausage, vegetables, beans, cottage cheese, chiles, cheeses, and herbs.
- Cook the omelet over medium heat, depending on the stove.

SERVES 1

BASIC THREE-EGG OMELET

With this basic omelet recipe, you can improvise your own filling. See the recipes that follow for ideas, and be as creative as you like.

3 large eggs

1 tablespoon water

⅛ teaspoon salt

Freshly ground pepper

1 teaspoon butter or margarine (see Note)

⅓ to ½ cup filling of your choice

In a medium bowl, whisk together eggs, water, salt, and pepper to taste. Heat an omelet pan or 8-inch nonstick skillet over medium heat. Add butter and swirl to coat the pan. When butter foams, pour in egg mixture all at once. Let set until edges start to cook, about 20 seconds. With a spatula, gently lift edges of mixture and tip skillet to allow the uncooked egg mixture to flow underneath. Continue to do this until the top is almost dry (the top may be a little lumpy, the bottom should not brown), 3 to 4 minutes. Arrange filling over one half of omelet and fold the other side over to cover. Let stand for a few seconds. Turn out onto a warmed plate and serve immediately.

Note: Butter is usually used for added flavor, but you can also use cooking spray in a nonstick pan to reduce the fat content. If you're using an omelet pan that does not have a nonstick coating, increase the amount of butter to 1 tablespoon.

FOLDING VARIATION

Arrange filling in a strip down the center of the omelet, and fold each side to the center.

SERVES 1

FAVORITE OMELET

This classic omelet with mushrooms, ham, and cheese is a favorite with everyone. The Broiled Tomato Slices complement the flavors of the filling.

FILLING

2 teaspoons butter or margarine

2 medium mushrooms, trimmed and coarsely chopped

2 green onions, including some tender green tops, chopped

½ cup chopped cooked ham or cooked crumbled bacon

2 to 3 tablespoons grated Cheddar cheese

OMELET

3 large eggs

1 tablespoon water

⅛ teaspoon salt

Freshly ground pepper

1 teaspoon butter or margarine

Broiled Tomato Slices (recipe follows)

To make the filling: In an 8-inch nonstick skillet over medium heat, melt butter. Add mushrooms, green onions, and ham and sauté until vegetables are tender, about 5 minutes. Set aside.

To make the omelet: In a medium bowl, whisk together eggs, water, salt, and pepper to taste. Heat an 8-inch omelet pan or nonstick skillet over medium heat. Add butter and swirl to coat bottom of pan. When butter foams, pour in egg mixture all at once. Let set until edges begin to cook, about 20 seconds. With a spatula, gently lift edges of mixture and tip skillet to allow the uncooked egg mixture to flow underneath. Continue to do this until the top is almost dry, 3 to 4 minutes.

Spoon mushroom and ham mixture over one half of the omelet, and sprinkle with grated cheese. Fold the other side over to cover. Let stand for a few seconds to allow cheese to melt. Turn out onto a warmed plate. Garnish with Broiled Tomato Slices and serve.

BROILED TOMATO SLICES

Makes 4 slices

1 large tomato, thickly sliced

Salt and freshly ground pepper

Grated Parmesan cheese

Preheat broiler. On a lightly sprayed or oiled baking sheet, arrange tomato slices. Sprinkle with salt, pepper, and cheese to taste. Broil until cheese melts, about 4 minutes.

SERVES 1

BRIE AND PANCETTA OMELET

If you like Brie you'll love this omelet. Serve it with Scones with Spiced Sugar-Nut Topping (page 287) and Caramelized Apples (page 319) for a classy breakfast.

2 slices pancetta or bacon, diced

3 large eggs

1 tablespoon water

⅛ teaspoon salt

Freshly ground pepper

¼ cup Brie, cut into small pieces

In an 8-inch omelet pan or nonstick skillet over medium-high heat, cook pancetta until crisp, about 5 minutes. Remove with a slotted spoon to a plate lined with a paper towel, leaving 2 teaspoons drippings in pan.

In a medium bowl, whisk together eggs, water, salt, and pepper to taste. In the same pan over medium heat, warm drippings and swirl to coat bottom of pan. Pour in egg mixture all at once and let set until edges start to cook, about 20 seconds. With a spatula, gently lift edges of mixture and tip pan to allow the uncooked egg mixture to flow underneath. Continue to do this until the top is almost dry, 3 to 4 minutes. Sprinkle Brie and pancetta over one half of omelet, and fold the other side over to cover. Let set for a few seconds. Turn out onto a warmed plate and serve immediately.

SERVES 1

RANCH OMELET

A robust filling of beans and salsa adds spark to this omelet. Serve with salsa, a basket of warm tortillas (see page 165), and a side of refried beans. You'll have enough of the refried bean mixture for about three omelets.

FILLING

1 can (16 ounces) refried beans, divided

¼ cup Fresh Tomato Salsa (page 103) or purchased salsa, slightly drained

3 tablespoons grated Monterey Jack cheese

OMELET

3 large eggs

1 tablespoon water

⅛ teaspoon salt

Freshly ground pepper

1 teaspoon butter or margarine

Sour cream for topping

Sliced ripe olives for garnish

Cilantro sprigs for garnish

To make the filling: In a small saucepan over medium heat, warm beans with salsa and set aside.

To make the omelet: In a medium bowl, whisk together eggs, water, salt, and pepper to taste. Heat an 8-inch omelet pan or nonstick skillet over medium heat. Add butter and swirl to coat bottom of pan. When butter foams, pour in egg mixture all at once. Let set until edges start to cook, about 20 seconds. With a spatula, gently lift edges of mixture and tip skillet to allow the uncooked egg mixture to flow underneath. Continue to do this until the top is almost dry, 3 to 4 minutes.

Spoon ⅓ cup of bean mixture over one half of omelet. Sprinkle with grated cheese. Fold the other side over to cover. Let stand for a few seconds to allow cheese to melt. Turn out onto a warmed plate, top with a dollop of sour cream, and garnish with olives and cilantro. Serve immediately, passing the remaining filling separately, if it's not needed for more omelets.

SERVES 1

ZUCCHINI, TOMATO, AND FRESH HERB OMELET

Make this omelet in the summer when fresh garden vegetables and herbs are in season. It goes well with Basic Baking Powder Biscuits (page 280).

FILLING

1 to 2 teaspoons olive oil

¼ cup unpeeled diced zucchini

2 green onions, including some tender green tops, sliced

1 garlic clove, minced

2 tablespoons seeded, diced, and drained tomato

1 teaspoon chopped fresh basil, or ⅛ teaspoon dried basil

1 teaspoon chopped fresh rosemary, or ⅛ teaspoon dried rosemary

Salt and freshly ground pepper

3 tablespoons grated Parmesan cheese, divided

OMELET

3 large eggs

1 tablespoon water

⅛ teaspoon salt

Freshly ground pepper

1 teaspoon butter or margarine

To make the filling: In a small nonstick skillet over medium heat, warm oil. Add zucchini, green onions, and garlic and sauté until tender, about 5 minutes. Add tomato, herbs, and salt and pepper to taste, and cook for 1 minute longer. Set aside.

To make the omelet: In a medium bowl, whisk together eggs, water, salt, and pepper to taste. Heat an 8-inch omelet pan or nonstick skillet over medium heat. Add butter and swirl to coat bottom of pan. When butter foams, pour in egg mixture all at once. Let set until edges begin to cook, about 20 seconds. With a spatula, gently lift edges of mixture and tip skillet to allow the uncooked egg mixture to flow underneath. Continue to do this until the top is almost dry, 3 to 4 minutes.

Spoon zucchini mixture over one half of omelet, and sprinkle with 2 tablespoons of the grated cheese. Fold the other side over to cover. Let stand for a few seconds. Turn out onto a warmed plate. Top with remaining cheese and serve immediately.

SERVES 1

AVOCADO AND TOMATO OMELET

Buttery avocado paired with tomato and green onion is the filling for this delicious omelet. Walnut Sour Cream Coffee Cake (page 298) makes a good accompaniment.

FILLING

¼ cup diced avocado, plus avocado slices for garnish

¼ cup seeded, drained, and diced tomato

1 green onion, including some tender green tops sliced

1 teaspoon lime or lemon juice

2 tablespoons grated Monterey Jack cheese

OMELET

3 large eggs

1 tablespoon water

⅛ teaspoon salt

Freshly ground pepper

1 teaspoon butter or margarine

To make the filling: In a small bowl, combine avocado, tomato, green onion, and lime juice. Set aside.

To make the omelet: In a medium bowl, whisk together eggs, water, salt, and pepper to taste. Heat an 8-inch omelet pan or nonstick skillet over medium heat. Add butter and swirl to coat bottom of pan. When butter foams, pour in egg mixture all at once. Let set until edges begin to cook, about 20 seconds. With a spatula, gently lift edges of mixture and tip skillet to allow the uncooked egg mixture to flow underneath. Continue to do this until the top is almost dry, 3 to 4 minutes.

Spoon avocado and tomato mixture over one half of omelet. Sprinkle with grated cheese. Fold the other side over to cover. Let stand for a few seconds. Turn out onto a warmed plate and garnish with avocado slices. Serve immediately.

SERVES 1

HAWAIIAN OMELET

The sweet and tart flavors of pineapple and coconut harmonize in this plump omelet. Make two for an intimate brunch. Serve with Banana Bread (page 292).

FILLING

⅓ cup chopped cooked ham

2 tablespoons crushed pineapple, drained

1 tablespoon flaked coconut

OMELET

3 large eggs

1 tablespoon water

⅛ teaspoon salt

Freshly ground pepper

1 teaspoon butter or margarine

Papaya slices for garnish

Mint leaf for garnish

To make the filling: In a small bowl, combine ham, pineapple, and coconut and set aside.

To make the omelet: In a medium bowl, whisk together eggs, water, salt, and pepper to taste. Heat an 8-inch omelet pan or nonstick skillet over medium heat. Add butter and swirl to coat bottom of pan. When butter foams, pour in egg mixture all at once. Let set until edges begin to cook, about 20 seconds. With a spatula, gently lift edges of mixture and tip skillet to allow the uncooked egg mixture to flow underneath. Continue to do this until the top is almost dry, 3 to 4 minutes.

Spoon ham mixture over one half of the omelet. Fold the other side over to cover. Let stand for a few seconds to allow ham mixture to warm. Turn out onto a warmed plate. Garnish with papaya slices and a mint leaf and serve immediately.

SERVES 1

LUMBERMAN'S SPECIAL OMELET

This hearty omelet makes a complete and satisfying meal. Serve any extra filling on the side, or use to make a second omelet. Bake a batch of Old-Fashioned Buttermilk Biscuits *(page 281)* *and ring the dinner bell.*

FILLING

1 tablespoon butter or margarine

½ cup cubed cooked potatoes

2 green onions, including some tender green tops, sliced

½ cup cubed cooked ham

3 tablespoons grated Cheddar cheese

OMELET

3 large eggs

1 tablespoon water

⅛ teaspoon salt

Freshly ground pepper

1 teaspoon butter or margarine

To make the filling: In a small nonstick skillet over medium-high heat, melt butter. Add potatoes, green onions, and ham and sauté until potatoes are browned, about 10 minutes. Set aside.

To make the omelet: In a medium bowl, whisk together eggs, water, salt, and pepper to taste. Heat an 8-inch omelet pan or nonstick skillet over medium heat. Add butter and swirl to coat bottom of pan. When butter foams, pour in egg mixture all at once. Let set until edges begin to cook, about 20 seconds. With a spatula, gently lift edges of mixture and tip skillet to allow the uncooked egg mixture to flow underneath. Continue to do this until the top is almost dry, 3 to 4 minutes.

Spoon ½ cup potato and ham mixture over one half of omelet and sprinkle with grated cheese. Fold the other side over to cover. Let stand for a few seconds. Turn out onto a warmed plate and serve immediately.

SERVES 1

TRIPLE CHEESE OMELET

Three complementary cheeses make a creamy filling in this omelet that will melt in your mouth. Cranberry Scones (page 285) make a good accompaniment.

FILLING

3 tablespoons cottage cheese with chives

2 tablespoons grated Cheddar cheese

1 tablespoon grated Parmesan cheese

OMELET

3 large eggs

1 tablespoon water

⅛ teaspoon salt

Freshly ground pepper

1 teaspoon butter or margarine

Parsley sprigs for garnish

To make the filling: In a small bowl, combine the cheeses and set aside.

To make the omelet: In a medium bowl, whisk together eggs, water, salt, and pepper to taste. Heat an 8-inch omelet pan or nonstick skillet over medium heat. Add butter and swirl to coat bottom of pan. When butter foams, pour in egg mixture all at once. Let set until edges start to cook, about 20 seconds. With a spatula, gently lift edges of mixture and tip skillet to allow the uncooked egg mixture to flow underneath. Continue to do this until the top is almost dry, 3 to 4 minutes.

Spoon filling over one half of the omelet. Fold the other side over to cover. Let stand for a few seconds to allow cheeses to melt. Turn out onto a warmed plate. Garnish with parsley and serve immediately.

SERVES 1

OMELET LORRAINE

Swiss cheese and bacon give this omelet a classic flavor, inspired by the famous quiche Lorraine. Serve with Fresh Fruit Compote (page 308).

FILLING

2 thick slices bacon, cooked and crumbled

3 tablespoons grated Swiss cheese

1 green onion, including some tender green tops, sliced

OMELET

3 large eggs

1 tablespoon water

⅛ teaspoon salt

Dash of ground nutmeg

Dash of cayenne pepper

1 teaspoon butter or margarine

Parsley sprigs for garnish

To make the filling: In a small bowl, combine bacon, cheese, and green onion.

To make the omelet: In a medium bowl, whisk together eggs, water, salt, nutmeg, and cayenne. Heat an 8-inch omelet pan or nonstick skillet over medium heat. Add butter and swirl to coat bottom of pan. When butter foams, pour in egg mixture all at once. Let set until edges begin to cook, about 20 seconds. With a spatula, gently lift edges of mixture and tip skillet to allow the uncooked egg mixture to flow underneath. Continue to do this until the top is almost dry, 3 to 4 minutes.

Spoon filling over one half of the omelet. Fold the other side over to cover. Let stand for a few seconds to allow cheese to melt. Turn out onto a warmed plate. Garnish with parsley and serve immediately.

SERVES 1

MUSHROOM, RED BELL PEPPER, AND CHEESE OMELET

This omelet, with its wonderful combination of tastes and textures, is meant to be savored. Serve it with toasted English muffins and a Cappuccino (page 19).

FILLING

1 tablespoon butter or margarine

2 tablespoons chopped red bell pepper

2 tablespoons chopped green bell pepper

2 tablespoons chopped yellow onion

2 medium mushrooms, chopped

2 drops Tabasco sauce

1 tablespoon chopped parsley

2 tablespoons grated Monterey Jack cheese

OMELET

3 large eggs

1 tablespoon water

⅛ teaspoon salt

Freshly ground pepper

1 teaspoon butter or margarine

Grated Parmesan cheese for topping

Parsley sprigs for garnish

Tomato wedges for garnish

To make the filling: In a small nonstick skillet over medium heat, melt butter. Add bell peppers, onion, and mushrooms and sauté until tender, about 5 minutes. Stir in Tabasco sauce and parsley and set aside.

To make the omelet: In a medium bowl, whisk together eggs, water, salt, and pepper to taste. Heat an 8-inch omelet pan or nonstick skillet over medium heat. Add butter and swirl to coat bottom of pan. When butter foams, pour in egg mixture all at once. Let set until edges begin to cook, about 20 seconds. With a spatula, gently lift edges of mixture and tip skillet to allow the uncooked egg mixture to flow underneath. Continue to do this until the top is almost dry, 3 to 4 minutes.

Spoon vegetable mixture over one half of the omelet, and sprinkle with the grated Monterey Jack cheese. Fold the other side over to cover. Let stand for a few seconds to allow cheese to melt. Turn out onto a warmed plate. Sprinkle with grated Parmesan and garnish with parsley and tomato wedges. Serve immediately.

SERVES 1

ASIAN OMELET

Looking for something different? Try this omelet inspired by Asian cuisine. A Tropical Fruit Platter with Strawberry Purée (page 307) makes a great accompaniment.

FILLING

2 teaspoons vegetable oil

¼ cup diced green bell pepper

3 green onions, including some tender green tops, sliced

2 water chestnuts, chopped

1 teaspoon soy sauce

OMELET

3 large eggs

1 tablespoon water

⅛ teaspoon salt

Freshly ground pepper

1 teaspoon butter or margarine

To make the filling: In a small nonstick skillet over medium heat, warm oil. Add bell pepper and green onions and sauté until tender, about 5 minutes. Add water chestnuts and soy sauce and set aside.

To make the omelet: In a medium bowl, whisk together eggs, water, salt, and pepper to taste. Heat an 8-inch omelet pan or nonstick skillet over medium heat. Add butter and swirl to coat bottom of pan. When butter foams, pour in egg mixture all at once. Let set until edges begin to cook, about 20 seconds. With a spatula, gently lift edges of mixture and tip skillet to allow the uncooked egg mixture to flow underneath. Continue to do this until the top is almost dry, 3 to 4 minutes.

Spoon filling mixture over one half of the omelet. Fold the other side over to cover. Let stand for a few seconds. Turn out onto a warmed plate and serve immediately.

SERVES 1

GREEK OMELET

This delicious omelet combines spinach and feta cheese for a blend of Greek flavors. Toasted Pocket Bread Wedges round out the Greek theme.

FILLING

3 tablespoons chopped, cooked spinach, squeezed dry

1½ tablespoons crumbled feta cheese

1 tablespoon sour cream

2 teaspoons toasted pine nuts (see Note)

OMELET

3 large eggs

1 tablespoon water

¼ teaspoon dried dill weed

⅛ teaspoon salt

Freshly ground pepper

1 teaspoon butter or margarine

Dill sprig for garnish

3 pitted kalamata olives for garnish

Toasted Pocket Bread Wedges (recipe follows) as an accompaniment

3 pocket or pita breads

¼ cup olive oil

To make the filling: In a small bowl, mix filling ingredients together and set aside.

To make the omelet: In a medium bowl, whisk together eggs, water, dill, salt, and pepper to taste. Heat an 8-inch omelet pan or nonstick skillet over medium heat. Add butter to coat bottom of pan. When butter foams, pour in egg mixture. Let set until edges begin to cook. Gently lift edges of mixture and tip skillet to allow the uncooked egg mixture to flow underneath. Continue to do this until the top is almost dry, 3 to 4 minutes.

Spoon filling mixture over one half of the omelet. Fold the other side over to cover. Let stand a few seconds to allow cheese to melt. Turn out onto a warmed plate. Garnish with a dill sprig and olives and serve immediately with Toasted Pocket Bread Wedges.

Note: To toast pine nuts, place nuts in a small skillet over high heat. Stir and shake until golden, about 2 minutes.

TOASTED POCKET BREAD WEDGES

These can also be served with hors d'oeuvres.

Makes 48 wedges

Preheat oven to 300°F. Halve pocket bread, and cut each half into 4 wedges. Open wedges, split them into triangles, and place smooth-side down on a baking sheet. Brush with oil and bake until slightly browned, about 10 minutes.

SERVES 1

CHICKEN OMELET

This chicken filling makes a substantial and satisfying omelet. Serve with freshly baked Rich Scones with Lemon Curd (page 284).

FILLING

2 teaspoons vegetable oil

2 tablespoons finely chopped celery

½ cup diced cooked chicken

1 tablespoon sliced pimiento-stuffed green olives

OMELET

3 large eggs

1 tablespoon water

⅛ teaspoon salt

Freshly ground pepper

1 teaspoon butter or margarine

Sour cream for topping

4 pimiento-stuffed green olives for garnish

To make the filling: In a small nonstick skillet over medium heat, warm oil. Add celery and sauté until tender, about 3 minutes. Add chicken and olives and cook until warmed, about 2 minutes longer. Set aside.

To make the omelet: In a medium bowl, whisk together eggs, water, salt, and pepper to taste. Heat an 8-inch omelet pan or nonstick skillet over medium heat. Add butter and swirl to coat bottom of pan. When butter foams, pour in egg mixture all at once. Let set until edges start to cook, about 20 seconds. With a spatula, gently lift edges of mixture and tip skillet to allow the uncooked egg mixture to flow underneath. Continue to do this until the top is almost dry, 3 to 4 minutes.

Spoon chicken and celery mixture over one half of the omelet. Fold the other side over to cover. Let stand for a few seconds. Turn out onto a warmed plate. Top with sour cream, garnish with olives, and serve immediately.

SERVES 1

TURKEY-CRANBERRY OMELET

For an easy omelet filling, use leftover turkey with a touch of cranberry sauce and cream cheese. Start the meal with Orange-Pineapple Drink (page 21).

FILLING

½ cup diced cooked turkey

2 tablespoons drained cranberry sauce

¼ teaspoon grated orange zest

1 tablespoon cream cheese, cut into small pieces

OMELET

3 large eggs

1 tablespoon water

⅛ teaspoon salt

Freshly ground pepper

1 teaspoon sugar

1 teaspoon butter or margarine

Orange slices for garnish

To make the filling: In a small bowl, combine turkey, cranberry sauce, and orange zest. Set aside.

To make the omelet: In a medium bowl, whisk together eggs, water, salt, pepper to taste, and sugar. Heat an 8-inch omelet pan or nonstick skillet over medium heat. Add butter and swirl to coat bottom of pan. When butter foams, pour in egg mixture all at once. Let set until edges begin to cook, about 20 seconds. With a spatula, gently lift edges of mixture and tip skillet to allow the uncooked egg mixture to flow underneath. Continue to do this until the top is almost dry, 3 to 4 minutes.

Spoon turkey-cranberry mixture over one half of the omelet. Scatter cream cheese pieces on top. Fold the other side over to cover. Let stand for a few seconds. Serve immediately, garnished with orange slices.

SERVES 1

SMOKED SALMON OMELET

This omelet is a real delicacy, with subtle flavors of smoked salmon and cream cheese. Serve it for brunch or lunch, along with Cranberry Scones (page 285).

FILLING

3 tablespoons (1 ounce) smoked salmon, flaked

1 tablespoon cream cheese, cut into small pieces

1 green onion, including some tender green tops, sliced

⅛ teaspoon dried dill weed

OMELET

3 large eggs

1 tablespoon water

⅛ teaspoon salt

Freshly ground pepper

1 teaspoon butter, margarine, or vegetable oil

Dill sprig for garnish

To make the filling: In a small bowl, mix filling ingredients.

To make the omelet: In a medium bowl, whisk together eggs, water, salt, and pepper to taste. Heat an 8-inch omelet pan or nonstick skillet over medium heat. Add butter and swirl to coat bottom of pan. When butter foams, pour in egg mixture all at once. Let set until edges start to cook, about 20 seconds. With a spatula, gently lift edges of mixture and tip skillet to allow the uncooked egg mixture to flow underneath. Continue to do this until the top is almost dry, 3 to 4 minutes.

Sprinkle salmon mixture over half of the omelet. Fold the other side over to cover. Let stand for a few seconds. Turn out onto a warmed plate. Garnish with a dill sprig and serve immediately.

SERVES 1

SHRIMP OMELET

Other seafood, such as cooked scallops, crab, or whitefish, or a combination, can be substituted for the shrimp in this terrific omelet. Serve it with melon slices and lime wedge.

FILLING

½ cup chopped small cooked shrimp (reserve 3 or 4 shrimp for garnish)

2 tablespoons grated Cheddar cheese

2 tablespoons chopped tomato, drained

OMELET

3 large eggs

1 tablespoon water

⅛ teaspoon salt

Freshly ground pepper

1 teaspoon butter or margarine

Chopped parsley for garnish

To make the filling: In a small bowl, mix filling ingredients.

To make the omelet: In a medium bowl, whisk together eggs, water, salt, and pepper to taste. Heat an 8-inch omelet pan or nonstick skillet over medium heat. Add butter and swirl to coat bottom of pan. When butter foams, pour in egg mixture all at once. Let set until edges begin to cook, about 20 seconds. With a spatula, gently lift edges of mixture and tip skillet to allow the uncooked egg mixture to flow underneath. Continue to do this until the top is almost dry, 3 to 4 minutes.

Spoon shrimp mixture over one half of the omelet. Fold the other side over to cover. Let stand for a few seconds. Turn out onto a warmed plate, garnish with reserved shrimp and chopped parsley, and serve immediately.

SERVES 3 TO 4

MEXICAN OMELET

This large omelet, with its fresh and lively filling, will take you straight to Mexico. Top with a dollop of sour cream for a cooling touch.

FILLING

2 teaspoons vegetable oil

¼ cup diced green bell pepper

¼ cup diced red bell pepper

6 green onions, including some tender green tops, sliced

2 tablespoons canned diced green chiles

2 tablespoons chopped black olives

¼ cup grated Monterey Jack cheese

OMELET

5 large eggs

2 tablespoons milk

¼ teaspoon salt

¼ teaspoon ground cumin

Freshly ground pepper

1 tablespoon butter or margarine

Parsley sprigs for garnish

Sour cream for topping

To make the filling: In a small nonstick skillet over medium heat, warm oil. Add bell peppers and green onions and sauté until tender, about 5 minutes. Stir in chiles and olives and set aside.

To make the omelet: In a medium bowl, whisk together eggs, milk, salt, cumin, and pepper to taste. Heat a 10-inch omelet pan or nonstick skillet over medium heat. Add butter and swirl to coat bottom of pan. When butter foams, pour in egg mixture all at once. Let set until edges begin to cook, about 20 seconds. With a spatula, gently lift edges of mixture and tip skillet to allow the uncooked egg mixture to flow underneath. Continue to do this until the top is almost dry, 3 to 4 minutes.

Spoon filling over one half of the omelet, and sprinkle with grated cheese. Fold the other side over to cover. Let stand for a few seconds to allow cheese to melt. Turn out onto a warmed plate and garnish with parsley. Cut into slices and serve immediately, passing the sour cream separately.

SERVES 4

PUFFY CHEESE OMELET SOUFFLÉ

Puffy omelets are airy and foamy and look impressive. You give this omelet its "lift" by beating the egg whites separately from the yolks. After cooking the mixture briefly on the stovetop, it is then finished in the oven. Puffy omelets lend themselves to sauces rather than fillings.

6 large eggs, separated

¼ teaspoon salt

⅛ teaspoon white pepper

¼ cup grated Cheddar cheese

1 tablespoon butter or margarine

Quick Tomato Sauce (page 170) or Mushroom Sauce (page 225) for topping

Preheat oven to 425°F. In a medium bowl, using an electric mixer, beat egg whites until peaks form. In a medium bowl, beat yolks with salt until lemon colored. Add pepper and cheese. Fold egg whites into yolk mixture.

In a large ovenproof skillet over medium heat, melt butter. When butter foams, add egg mixture all at once and cook until bottom is set, about 1 minute. Transfer skillet to oven and bake until top is puffed up and golden but still moist, 9 to 10 minutes. Serve immediately with Quick Tomato Sauce or Mushroom Sauce.

SERVES 1

PUFFY CHEESE OMELET WITH SPINACH AND FRESH HERB FILLING, TOPPED WITH TOMATO SALSA

Serve this omelet with a tasty filling to your guests at a late morning brunch. It is delicious as well as appealing and was selected for the book cover photo.

3 large eggs, separated

⅛ teaspoon salt

1 tablespoon cold water

⅛ teaspoon white pepper

1 teaspoon butter

½ cup Spinach and Fresh Herb Filling (recipe follows) or filling of your choice

¼ cup grated Cheddar cheese

Fresh Tomato Salsa (page 103) for topping

Preheat oven to 425°F. In a medium bowl, using an electric mixer, beat egg whites on high until peaks form. In another medium bowl, beat yolks with salt until lemon colored, about 30 seconds. Add cold water and pepper and blend. Fold egg whites into yolk mixture.

In an 8-inch ovenproof nonstick skillet over medium heat, melt butter. When butter foams, add egg mixture all at once and cook until bottom is set, about 1 minute. Do not stir. Transfer skillet to oven and bake until top is puffed up, about 4 minutes. Remove from oven. Arrange filling over one half of the omelet and sprinkle with cheese. Fold the other side over to cover. Return to the oven to bake until top is golden and cheese is melted, about 2 minutes longer. Turn out onto a warmed plate and serve immediately with Tomato Salsa.

SPINACH AND FRESH HERB FILLING

Makes enough for 1 serving

1 teaspoon butter or margarine

1 small shallot, finely chopped

1 cup firmly packed fresh baby spinach, chopped

½ teaspoon chopped fresh thyme leaves

½ teaspoon chopped fresh marjoram leaves

½ teaspoon chopped fresh tarragon leaves

½ teaspoon chopped fresh rosemary leaves

⅛ teaspoon salt

Freshly ground pepper

In a small skillet over medium-high heat, melt butter. Add shallot and sauté, about 3 minutes. Add spinach, herbs, salt, and pepper to taste and sauté until spinach is wilted, 2 to 3 minutes longer.

SERVES 2

ITALIAN OMELET

Wake up to some Italian flavors in this highly seasoned omelet for two. Serve with Melon Ball Fruit Cup (page 312) and a Cappuccino (page 19).

FILLING

2 thick slices pancetta or bacon, diced

2 green onions, including some tender green tops, sliced

2 tablespoons diced red bell pepper

1 can (15 ounces) white beans, rinsed and drained, divided

1 tablespoon chopped fresh basil, or ½ teaspoon dried basil

OMELET

4 large eggs

2 tablespoons milk

¼ teaspoon salt

Freshly ground pepper

¼ cup grated mozzarella cheese, divided

1 to 2 teaspoons olive oil (depending on drippings left in skillet)

1 tablespoon grated Parmesan cheese

To make the filling: In a small nonstick skillet over medium heat, sauté pancetta for 2 minutes. Add green onions and bell pepper and sauté until pancetta is crisp and vegetables are tender, about 5 minutes longer. Stir in 3 tablespoons of the drained beans and basil. With a slotted spoon, remove mixture to a plate and set aside, leaving drippings in pan.

To make the omelet: In a medium bowl, whisk together eggs, milk, salt, pepper to taste, and half the grated mozzarella. In the same skillet over medium heat, warm drippings and oil. When hot, add egg mixture all at once. Let set until edges start to cook, about 20 seconds. With a spatula, gently lift edges of mixture and tip skillet to allow the uncooked egg mixture to flow underneath. Continue to do this until the top is almost dry, 3 to 4 minutes. Spoon filling over one half of the omelet. Sprinkle with remaining grated mozzarella. Fold the other side over to cover. Let stand for a few seconds. Turn out onto a warmed plate and sprinkle with grated Parmesan. Cut in half to serve. Heat remaining beans in a pan with a small amount of water and serve as a side dish.

SERVES 1

SAUTÉED APPLE OMELET

Fill the omelet with half of the sweet apple filling, and then serve the remainder on top. Complete the breakfast with Basic Muffins (page 274).

FILLING

1 tablespoon butter or margarine

1 small apple, peeled, cored, and chopped

1 teaspoon lemon juice

¼ teaspoon ground cinnamon

Dash of ground nutmeg

1 teaspoon raisins

1 teaspoon slivered almonds

1 tablespoon brown sugar

OMELET

3 large eggs

1 tablespoon water

⅛ teaspoon salt

1 teaspoon granulated sugar

¼ teaspoon vanilla extract

1 teaspoon butter or margarine

1 tablespoon Crème Fra^che (recipe follows) for topping

To make the filling: In a small nonstick skillet over medium heat, melt butter. Add apple, lemon juice, cinnamon, and nutmeg and sauté until tender, about 4 minutes. Add remaining filling ingredients and stir until sugar melts, about 1 minute longer. Set aside.

To make the omelet: In a medium bowl, whisk together eggs, water, salt, sugar, and vanilla. Heat an 8-inch omelet pan or nonstick skillet over medium heat. Add butter to coat the bottom of pan. When butter foams, pour in egg mixture all at once. Let set until edges begin to cook. With a spatula, gently lift edges of mixture and tip skillet to allow the uncooked egg mixture to flow underneath. Continue to do this until the top is almost dry, 3 to 4 minutes.

Spoon half of the apple mixture over one half of the omelet. Fold the other side over to cover. Let stand for a few seconds. Turn out onto a warmed plate, top with remaining apple mixture and crème fra^che, and serve immediately.

CRÈME FRAÎCHE

Crème fra^che is thickened cream with a nutty flavor and a velvety, rich texture. You can also purchase crème fra^che in many stores.

Makes about 1 cup

1 cup heavy cream

2 tablespoons buttermilk

Place ingredients in a glass jar. Cover and let stand at room temperature (70°F) until thick, 8 to 24 hours. Stir and refrigerate, covered, for up to 10 days.

FRITTATAS

Frittatas are the Italian version of the French omelet. The difference is that frittatas have the ingredients mixed in with eggs, not folded in the middle. They are typically cut into wedges to serve. Frittatas are great for breakfast or brunches or for an easy weeknight meal.

TIPS FOR MAKING AND SERVING FRITTATAS

- Prepare all ingredients before starting to cook.
- Use a 9- or 10-inch ovenproof skillet for cooking the frittata (a black cast-iron skillet works very well).
- Let the frittata stand for 5 to 10 minutes before serving.
- Cut the frittata into wedges and serve it from the skillet, or invert it onto a plate and cut it into wedges.

COOK FRITTATAS IN ONE OF THE FOLLOWING WAYS:

- Slowly, in a covered skillet on top of the stove and then finished under the broiler. (If the handle on the skillet is not ovenproof, wrap it in heavy-duty foil.)
- Like an omelet, in an uncovered skillet on top of the stove (tipping the pan to allow the egg mixture to flow underneath), but not folded at the end.
- In an ovenproof skillet on top of the stove and then baked in the oven.

SERVES 4

MEXICAN FRITTATA

Serve this spicy frittata for breakfast, brunch, lunch, or supper, along with warm flour tortillas *(see page 165)* *and a plate of orange and cucumber slices and radishes.*

1 tablespoon vegetable oil

½ cup chopped yellow onion

1 garlic clove, minced

½ cup chopped green bell pepper

4 ounces medium mushrooms, sliced

1 tomato, seeded, chopped, and drained

1 can (4 ounces) diced green chiles, drained

6 large eggs

2 tablespoons milk

¼ teaspoon chili powder

¼ teaspoon ground cumin

½ teaspoon salt

Freshly ground pepper

½ cup grated Monterey Jack cheese

Fresh Tomato Salsa (facing page) or purchased salsa for topping

Sour cream for topping

In a large ovenproof skillet, warm oil over medium heat. Add onion, garlic, and bell pepper and sauté for 2 minutes. Add mushrooms and tomato and sauté until vegetables are tender, about 5 minutes longer. Stir in chiles.

Preheat broiler. In a medium bowl, mix together eggs, milk, and seasonings. Pour over vegetables in skillet. Reduce heat to medium-low, cover, and cook until eggs are set and top is almost dry, 10 to 12 minutes. Sprinkle with cheese and broil until frittata is puffy and cheese is melted, about 1 minute. Let stand for 5 minutes. Cut into wedges and serve from the skillet or slide the whole frittata onto a platter. Pass Fresh Tomato Salsa and sour cream separately.

FRESH TOMATO SALSA

Salsa appears on the Mexican table at every meal and is served with almost any dish. You can make it as hot as you like by varying the amount and variety of chiles you use. It is best when made fresh.

Makes about 2½ cups

2 cups coarsely chopped tomatoes, seeded and drained

¼ cup chopped green bell pepper

2 garlic cloves, minced

2 fresh jalapeño chiles, ribs and seeds removed and finely chopped (see Note), or 2 tablespoons diced green chiles, drained

½ cup diced white onion

1 tablespoon lime or lemon juice

¼ teaspoon ground cumin

1 tablespoon chopped fresh cilantro or parsley, or more to taste

½ teaspoon salt

Freshly ground pepper

In a medium bowl, mix together all ingredients. Serve immediately.

Note: When working with fresh chiles, keep your hands away from your eyes, and wash your hands thoroughly afterwards.

SERVES 4 TO 6

COWBOY FRITTATA

Here is a hearty brunch dish of eggs combined with sausage and potatoes. Serve with Old-Fashioned Buttermilk Biscuits with Honey Butter (page 281) to complete a perfect breakfast.

8 ounces pork sausage links

¼ cup water, plus 2 tablespoons

1½ tablespoons vegetable oil

1 cup cooked cubed potatoes

½ cup chopped green onions, including some tender green tops

6 large eggs

½ cup grated Cheddar cheese

½ teaspoon salt

Freshly ground pepper

Preheat oven to 350°F. In a large ovenproof skillet over medium heat, cook sausages, covered, in ¼ cup water for about 5 minutes. Drain, remove sausages to a plate, and cut into ½-inch slices. Set aside. In the same skillet over medium heat, warm oil. Add potatoes, green onions, and sliced sausage and sauté until onions are tender and sausages are browned, 8 to 10 minutes.

In a medium bowl, whisk together eggs, the 2 tablespoons water, cheese, salt, and pepper to taste. Pour over sausage-potato mixture in skillet. Bake until eggs are set, about 25 minutes. Let stand for 5 minutes. Cut into wedges and serve from the skillet, or slide the whole frittata onto a warm plate.

SERVES 4

WEEKEND FRITTATA

On a lazy weekend, relax and enjoy this plump frittata with sausage, bell pepper, and mushrooms. Serve with Apple-Orange Fruit Compote (page 313) and sourdough toast.

8 ounces bulk pork sausage

½ red bell pepper, seeded and chopped

½ cup chopped yellow onion

4 ounces medium mushrooms, sliced

1 teaspoon vegetable oil, if needed

6 large eggs

2 tablespoons water

2 tablespoons chopped fresh basil, or ½ teaspoon dried basil

½ teaspoon salt

Freshly ground pepper

¾ cup grated Cheddar cheese

Basil leaves for garnish

In a large ovenproof skillet over medium-high heat, cook sausage and bell pepper, breaking up sausage with a spoon, for 3 minutes. Add onion and mushrooms and cook until sausage is no longer pink and vegetables are tender, about 5 minutes longer. Add oil, if needed.

Preheat broiler. In a medium bowl, whisk together eggs, water, basil, salt, and pepper to taste. Pour over sausage mixture in skillet. Reduce heat to medium-low, cover, and cook until eggs are set and top is almost dry, 10 to 12 minutes.

Sprinkle with cheese and broil until frittata is puffy and cheese melts, about 1 minute. Let stand for 5 minutes. Cut into wedges and serve from the skillet, or slide the whole frittata onto a warm plate. Garnish with basil leaves.

SERVES 4

SWEET ONION FRITTATA

A combination of three members of the onion family and creamy Swiss cheese flavor this frittata. Try it with Famous Cinnamon Rolls (page 302) and It's the Berries in Syrup (page 310).

2 tablespoons butter or margarine

2 cups coarsely chopped yellow onion (see Note)

8 green onions, including some tender green tops, sliced

2 shallots, chopped

6 large eggs

2 tablespoons water

1 teaspoon Dijon mustard

½ teaspoon dried thyme

½ teaspoon salt

Freshly ground pepper

1 cup grated Swiss cheese, divided

¼ cup chopped parsley

In a large ovenproof skillet over medium heat, melt butter. Add onion, green onions, and shallots and sauté until tender, about 5 minutes.

Preheat broiler. In a medium bowl, whisk together eggs, water, mustard, thyme, salt, pepper to taste, half the cheese, and parsley. Pour over onions in skillet. Reduce heat to medium-low. Cover and cook until eggs are set and top is almost dry, 10 to 12 minutes. Sprinkle with remaining cheese and broil until frittata is puffy and cheese is melted, about 1 minute. Cut into wedges and serve from skillet, or slide the whole frittata onto a warm plate.

Note: Use sweet Vidalia, Maui, or Walla Walla onions when they are available.

SERVES 4 TO 6

MUSHROOM, BELL PEPPER, AND HAM FRITTATA

For a more leisurely meal, chop the vegetables ahead of time, and you're ready to go for a quick breakfast dish. Serve with Truck Stop Hash Browns (page 256).

1 tablespoon vegetable oil

6 green onions, including some tender green tops, sliced

½ red bell pepper, seeded and chopped

½ green bell pepper, seeded and chopped

4 ounces medium mushrooms, sliced

1 cup cubed cooked ham

6 large eggs

2 tablespoons water

½ teaspoon salt

¼ teaspoon dried thyme

Freshly ground pepper

1½ cups grated provolone cheese, divided

¼ cup chopped flat-leaf parsley

Sour cream for topping

In a large ovenproof skillet over medium heat, warm oil. Add green onions, bell peppers, and mushrooms and sauté until tender, 6 to 7 minutes. Stir in ham.

Preheat broiler. In a medium bowl, whisk together eggs, water, salt, thyme, pepper to taste, 1 cup of the cheese, and parsley. Pour over vegetables in skillet. Reduce heat to medium-low, cover, and cook until eggs are set and the top is almost dry, 10 to 12 minutes. Sprinkle remaining ½ cup cheese on top and broil until frittata is puffy and cheese is melted, about 1 minute. Let stand for 5 minutes. Cut into wedges and serve from the skillet, or slide the whole frittata onto a warm plate. Serve with a dollop of sour cream.

SERVES 4

BOURBON STREET FRITTATA

Bourbon Street is the heart of New Orleans, and this frittata reflects that vibrant, spicy cuisine. It includes andouille sausage, a spicy smoked sausage that is a specialty of Cajun cooking.

1 tablespoon butter or margarine

¼ cup sliced green onions, including some tender green tops

4 ounces medium mushrooms, sliced

1 andouille sausage (3 ounces), sliced in half lengthwise and cut into ⅜-inch slices

6 large eggs

2 tablespoons water or milk

1½ cups grated Cheddar cheese, divided

¼ cup chopped parsley

In a large ovenproof skillet over medium heat, melt butter. Add green onions, mushrooms, and sausage and sauté until vegetables are tender and sausage is browned, about 10 minutes.

Preheat broiler. In a medium bowl, whisk together eggs, water, 1 cup of the cheese, and parsley. Pour over vegetable-sausage mixture. Reduce heat to medium-low, cover, and cook until eggs are set and top is almost dry, 10 to 12 minutes. Sprinkle remaining ½ cup cheese on top and broil until frittata is puffy and cheese is melted, about 1 minute. Let stand for 5 minutes. Cut into wedges and serve from skillet, or slide the whole frittata onto a warm plate.

SERVES 4 TO 6

FRITTATA WITH SMOKED SALMON AND ASPARAGUS

The smoked salmon adds just a subtle tinge of smoky flavor to this delicious brunch frittata. Serve with a Melon Ball Fruit Cup (page 312) and Blueberry Drop Scones (page 289). This also makes a good hors d'oeuvre or first course.

- 8 ounces asparagus, tough ends removed, cut into ⅜-inch pieces
- 6 large eggs
- 2 tablespoons water
- ½ teaspoon salt
- Freshly ground pepper
- 4 ounces smoked salmon, flaked
- ½ cup grated Monterey Jack cheese, divided
- 1 tablespoon butter or margarine

Place asparagus in a small saucepan, add salted water to cover, and bring to a boil over medium-high heat. Cook for 5 minutes. Drain and set aside. In a medium bowl, whisk together eggs, water, salt, and pepper to taste. Add asparagus, salmon, and half the cheese and mix well.

Preheat broiler. In a large ovenproof skillet over medium heat, melt butter. When butter foams, add egg mixture all at once. Reduce heat to medium-low. Cover and cook until eggs are set and top is almost dry, 10 to 12 minutes. Sprinkle with remaining cheese and broil until frittata is puffy and cheese is melted, about 1 minute. Let stand for 5 minutes. Cut into wedges and serve from skillet, or slide the whole frittata onto a warm plate.

SERVES 4

FRITTATA SALTIMBOCCA

Prosciutto is Italian ham that has been seasoned, salt-cured, and air-dried (but not smoked). Sliced very thin, it is ready to eat and is delicious wrapped around pieces of cantaloupe or fresh figs (see Fruit Platter with Prosciutto, page 311). Here prosciutto is combined in a frittata with mushrooms and mozzarella cheese.

1 tablespoon butter or margarine

¼ cup sliced green onions, including some tender green tops

¼ cup (about 2 ounces) chopped prosciutto

2 ounces chopped mushrooms

6 large eggs

1 tablespoon dry white wine

1 tablespoon chopped fresh basil, or ½ teaspoon dried basil

3 tablespoons chopped parsley

Freshly ground pepper

¼ cup grated mozzarella cheese

In a large ovenproof skillet over medium heat, melt butter. Add green onions, prosciutto, and mushrooms and sauté until prosciutto is crisp and vegetables are tender, about 5 minutes.

Preheat broiler. In a medium bowl, whisk together eggs, wine, basil, parsley, and pepper to taste. Pour egg mixture over vegetable-prosciutto mixture. Reduce heat to medium-low, cover, and cook until eggs are set and top is almost dry, 10 to 12 minutes. Sprinkle with grated cheese. Broil until frittata is puffy and cheese is melted, about 1 minute. Cut into wedges and serve from skillet, or slide the whole frittata onto a warm plate.

SERVES 4

PIZZA FRITTATA

Pizza ingredients are featured in this frittata that will appeal to all ages. Serve it with cola or Iced Tea (page 25).

8 ounces bulk Italian sausage

½ green bell pepper, seeded and chopped

2 garlic cloves, minced

6 green onions, including some tender green tops, sliced

3 ounces medium mushrooms, sliced

1 teaspoon vegetable oil, if needed

6 large eggs

2 tablespoons water

¼ teaspoon dried oregano

¼ teaspoon dried basil

¾ teaspoon salt

1 plum tomato, thinly sliced

1 ounce sliced pepperoni

¾ cup grated mozzarella cheese

In a large ovenproof skillet over medium-high heat, cook sausage and bell pepper, breaking up sausage with a spoon, for about 5 minutes. Add garlic, green onions, and mushrooms and cook until sausage is no longer pink and vegetables are tender, about 5 minutes longer. Add oil, if needed.

Preheat broiler. In a medium bowl, whisk together eggs, water, and seasonings and pour over sausage mixture in skillet. Reduce heat to medium-low, cover, and cook until eggs are set and top is almost dry, 10 to 12 minutes.

Place tomato and pepperoni slices on top of frittata, and sprinkle with cheese. Broil until frittata is puffy and cheese is melted, about 1 minute. Let stand for 5 minutes. Cut into wedges and serve from the skillet, or slide the whole frittata onto a warm plate.

SERVES 4

FRITTATA WITH MEDITERRANEAN SAUCE

The rich, herbed tomato sauce gives this frittata a Mediterranean flavor. Make the sauce ahead to allow the flavors to blend.

4 slices pancetta or bacon, diced

Oil for frying, if needed

4 ounces medium mushrooms, sliced

½ cup chopped yellow onion

6 large eggs

2 tablespoons milk

¼ teaspoon salt

Freshly ground pepper

½ cup grated mozzarella cheese

Mediterranean Sauce (facing page)

In a large ovenproof skillet over medium heat, cook pancetta until crisp, about 5 minutes. With a slotted spoon, remove it to a plate lined with a paper towel to drain, leaving 1 tablespoon drippings in skillet. (Add oil, if needed.) Add mushrooms and onion and sauté until tender, about 5 minutes. Return pancetta to skillet.

Preheat broiler. In a medium bowl, whisk together eggs, milk, salt, and pepper to taste. Pour egg mixture over pancetta-vegetable mixture in skillet. Reduce heat to medium-low, cover, and cook until eggs are set and top is almost dry, 10 to 12 minutes. Sprinkle with cheese and broil until frittata is puffy and cheese is melted, about 1 minute. Cut into wedges and serve from skillet, or slide the whole frittata onto a warm plate. Serve with Mediterranean Sauce.

MEDITERRANEAN SAUCE

This thick, flavorful sauce with olive oil, herbs, capers, and anchovy paste is also good on chicken.
Makes about 2 cups

1 tablespoon olive oil

½ cup finely chopped yellow onion

½ cup finely chopped green bell pepper

2 garlic cloves, minced

1 tablespoon capers, drained

1 teaspoon anchovy paste

1 can (16 ounces) crushed tomatoes in thick purée

½ teaspoon dried basil

½ teaspoon dried oregano

¼ teaspoon salt

Freshly ground pepper

In a medium saucepan over medium heat, warm oil. Add onion, bell pepper, and garlic and sauté until tender, about 5 minutes. Add remaining ingredients and simmer, uncovered, for 10 to 15 minutes.

SERVES 4

GARDEN VEGETABLE AND HERB FRITTATA

Tender-crisp vegetables add variety and texture to this frittata. Serve it with Coffee Crumb Cake (page 296).

1 tablespoon vegetable oil

½ cup chopped yellow onion

4 ounces medium mushrooms, sliced

1 small zucchini, unpeeled, halved lengthwise and sliced into ½-inch pieces

½ red bell pepper, seeded and chopped

1 garlic clove, minced

6 large eggs

2 tablespoons water

½ cup grated Parmesan cheese

1 teaspoon salt

Freshly ground pepper

1 tablespoon chopped fresh basil, or 1 teaspoon dried basil

1 tablespoon snipped parsley

Preheat oven to 350°F. In a large ovenproof skillet over medium heat, warm oil. Add onion, mushrooms, zucchini, bell pepper, and garlic and sauté until tender, 6 to 7 minutes.

In a medium bowl, whisk together eggs, water, cheese, salt, pepper to taste, basil, and parsley. Pour over vegetables in skillet. Transfer to oven and bake until eggs are set, about 25 minutes. Let stand for 5 minutes. Cut into wedges and serve from skillet, or slide the whole frittata onto a warm plate.

SERVES 4

SPRING FRITTATA

This frittata is a good way to use spring asparagus and leftover Easter ham. It goes well with Real Bran Muffins (page 279).

8 ounces asparagus, tough ends removed, broken into irregular pieces

1 tablespoon vegetable oil

3 medium cooked new potatoes (about 1½ pounds), cut into 1-inch cubes

½ red bell pepper, cut into 2-inch strips

¼ cup sliced green onions, including some tender green tops

2 garlic cloves, minced

1 cup cubed cooked ham

6 large eggs

2 tablespoons milk

2 tablespoons chopped parsley

1 tablespoon chopped fresh basil, or ½ teaspoon dried basil

½ teaspoon salt

Freshly ground pepper

½ cup crumbled blue cheese

Place asparagus in a small saucepan, add salted water to cover, and bring to a boil over medium-high heat. Cook for 5 minutes. Drain and set aside.

In a large ovenproof skillet over medium heat, warm oil. Add potatoes, bell pepper, green onions, and garlic, and sauté until vegetables are tender and potatoes are browned, 6 to 7 minutes. Stir in ham and asparagus.

Preheat oven to 350°F. In a medium bowl, whisk together eggs, milk, parsley, basil, salt, and pepper to taste. Pour egg mixture over vegetables in skillet. Transfer to oven and bake until puffy and eggs are set, about 25 minutes. Sprinkle with cheese and bake 1 to 2 minutes longer. Let stand for 5 minutes. Cut into wedges and serve from the skillet, or slide the whole frittata onto a warm plate.

SERVES 4 TO 6

SPINACH, MUSHROOM, AND FETA CHEESE FRITTATA

The feta cheese adds a distinctive flavor to this frittata. Make this savory dish ahead, and then bake it just before serving. Serve with Blueberry Crumb Coffee Cake (page 299).

1 bag (6 ounces) fresh spinach, stems removed and rinsed

1 tablespoon butter or margarine

1 small red bell pepper, seeded and diced

4 ounces mushrooms, sliced

6 green onions, including some tender green tops, sliced

1 small zucchini, unpeeled, diced

6 large eggs

2 tablespoons milk

3 tablespoons chopped parsley

1½ teaspoons salt

Freshly ground pepper

½ cup crumbled feta cheese

In a large saucepan over medium heat, cook spinach in a small amount of water, covered, until wilted, tossing once with a fork, about 3 minutes. Chop and squeeze dry and set aside.

Preheat oven to 350°F. In a medium nonstick skillet over medium heat, melt butter. Add bell pepper, mushrooms and green onions and sauté for 3 minutes. Add zucchini and sauté until vegetables are tender, about 3 minutes longer. Stir in spinach.

In a large bowl, whisk together eggs, milk, parsley, salt, and pepper to taste. Pour over vegetables in skillet. Sprinkle with feta cheese. Transfer to oven and bake until eggs are set, about 25 minutes. Let stand for 5 minutes. Cut into wedges and serve from skillet, or slide the whole frittata onto a warm plate.

SERVES 4

HERBED FRITTATA WITH CHEDDAR CHEESE SAUCE

This fluffy frittata is made by beating the egg yolks and whites separately to incorporate more air. Serve it with Cheddar Cheese Sauce or any sauce of your choice, along with Famous Cinnamon Rolls (page 302).

- 6 large eggs, separated
- 2 tablespoons water
- 1 tablespoon chopped fresh tarragon, or ¼ teaspoon dried tarragon
- 1 tablespoon chopped fresh thyme, or ¼ teaspoon dried thyme
- 1 tablespoon chopped fresh rosemary, or ¼ teaspoon dried rosemary
- ½ teaspoon salt
- Freshly ground pepper
- 1 tablespoon butter or margarine
- Cheddar Cheese Sauce (recipe follows)

Preheat oven to 350°F. In a large bowl, beat egg whites with an electric mixer until stiff peaks form. In another large bowl, beat egg yolks until lemon-colored, about 2 minutes. Add water and seasonings and mix well. Fold in egg whites.

In a large ovenproof skillet over medium-high heat, melt butter. When butter sizzles, pour egg mixture into skillet. Transfer to oven and bake until eggs are set, about 25 minutes. Let stand for 5 minutes. Cut into wedges in skillet, or slide the whole frittata onto a warm plate. Serve topped with Cheddar Cheese Sauce.

CHEDDAR CHEESE SAUCE

Makes about ¾ cup

- 2 tablespoons butter or margarine
- 2 tablespoons all-purpose flour
- ¼ teaspoon dry mustard
- ½ teaspoon salt
- ⅛ teaspoon white pepper
- 1¼ cups milk
- ½ cup grated Cheddar cheese
- 2 tablespoons grated Parmesan cheese

In a small saucepan over medium heat, melt butter. Add flour, dry mustard, salt, and pepper and stir until bubbly. Add milk and stir until thickened, about 2 minutes. Add cheeses and stir until melted, 1 to 2 minutes longer. Serve immediately.

SERVES 4

BROCCOLI, MUSHROOM, AND TOMATO FRITTATA

The bright green broccoli and the vivid red tomato give a splash of contrasting colors to this appealing frittata. Pair it with Walnut Sour Cream Coffee Cake (page 298).

2 tablespoons butter or margarine

4 ounces medium mushrooms, sliced

1 cup chopped broccoli florets

2 shallots, chopped

1 garlic clove, minced

6 large eggs

2 tablespoons milk

1 teaspoon Dijon mustard

¼ teaspoon dried oregano

¼ teaspoon dried basil

¼ teaspoon salt

Freshly ground pepper

1 large tomato, sliced

1 cup grated Havarti cheese

2 tablespoons grated Parmesan cheese

Preheat oven to 350°F. In a large ovenproof skillet over medium heat, melt butter. Add mushrooms, broccoli, shallots, and garlic and sauté until tender, 5 to 6 minutes. In a medium bowl, whisk together eggs, milk, mustard, and seasonings. Pour over vegetables in skillet. Arrange tomato slices on top and sprinkle with cheeses. Transfer to oven and bake until eggs are set, about 25 minutes. Let stand for 5 minutes. Cut into wedges and serve from skillet, or slide the whole frittata onto a warm plate.

BAKED INDIVIDUAL FRITTATAS

Start the morning in a festive mood with a frittata for each guest. Famous Cinnamon Rolls (page 302) make a good accompaniment.

Preheat oven to 350°F. In a medium saucepan over medium heat, combine broth, zucchini, crookneck squash, onion, garlic, and mushrooms and cook, covered, until tender, about 6 minutes. Drain, if necessary.

In a medium bowl, whisk together eggs, milk, basil, parsley, salt, pepper to taste, and cheese. Divide vegetables evenly among 8 lightly sprayed or oiled gratin dishes. Pour in egg mixture, filling each gratin dish about three-fourths full. Transfer to oven and bake until eggs are set, 20 to 25 minutes. Let stand for 5 minutes. Serve in the gratin dishes.

½ cup chicken broth or water

1 small zucchini, quartered lengthwise and sliced

1 small crookneck squash quartered lengthwise and sliced

1 cup chopped yellow onion

1 garlic clove, minced

3 ounces medium mushrooms, coarsely chopped

8 large eggs

2 tablespoons milk

1 tablespoon chopped fresh basil, or 1 teaspoon dried basil

¼ cup chopped parsley

½ teaspoon salt

Freshly ground pepper

½ cup grated Cheddar cheese

A quiche is a pastry shell filled with a savory custard made of eggs, cream, seasonings, and other ingredients such as onions, mushrooms, ham, shellfish, herbs, and cheese. They are fun to make because you can experiment with a variety of fillings.

Once considered a "ladies dish," Quiches have made a comeback and are now a favorite for brunches, lunches, and appetizers.

The most famous quiche is Quiche Lorraine (page 124), which originated in the Alsace-Lorraine region of France. Quiches became popular in the United States after World War II.

TIPS FOR MAKING QUICHES

PIE SHELL

- All ingredients should be cold.
- Use a single-crust pie shell (homemade or purchased).
- Use a 9- or 10-inch pie plate or quiche dish.
- Prebake the pie shell for 8 minutes at 450°F (see page 123).
- To prevent the pie shell from puffing in the oven, line the unbaked pie shell with foil or parchment paper and fill it with pie weights or dried beans, or line the shell with two layers of aluminum foil and press it down firmly. Remove the weights or lining before filling.
- The pie shell should be warm when filled.
- If the edges of the pie shell become too brown during baking, cover them with a strip of aluminum foil.
- To keep the bottom of the pie shell crisp, brush it with an egg wash (an egg beaten with a little water) before baking.

CUSTARD

- Use fresh eggs.
- Use half-and-half for best results. Whole milk can also be used.
- Use a whisk for blending.
- If you make the custard ahead, refrigerate it until ready to use. Add the filling just before baking.

FILLINGS

- Add small pieces of vegetables, meats, seafood, chopped herbs, and seasonings to the basic custard. Precook filling ingredients that need to be cooked.
- Add three to four filling ingredients, about 1½ to 2 cups for each quiche. Do not overfill the pie shell.
- Cheese is a traditional quiche ingredient. You can use almost any type of cheese.

SERVING

- Serve quiche warm or at room temperature.
- Cut the quiche into wedges (like a pie). One quiche will serve 4 to 6 as a main course, or up to 8 as an hors d'oeuvre.

SERVES 6

BASIC QUICHE

This simple recipe can be the basis for your own variations. For some ideas, see the quiche recipes that follow.

1½ cups half-and-half or whole milk

3 large eggs

¼ teaspoon salt

⅛ teaspoon white pepper

⅛ teaspoon ground nutmeg

9-inch Pie Shell (facing page), partially baked

1½ cups grated Monterey Jack or Cheddar cheese

In a medium bowl, whisk together half-and-half, eggs, salt, pepper, and nutmeg. Pour into pie shell. Sprinkle cheese on top. Bake until a knife inserted in the center comes out clean and the top is golden brown, 40 to 45 minutes. Let stand for 10 minutes. Cut into wedges and serve.

PIE SHELL (FOR QUICHE)

This is a "no guess" way to make pie crust—it's fast and easy and always a success. The recipe makes a single crust for a 9- or 10-inch pie plate.

Makes 1 single-crust pie shell

1½ cups all-purpose flour

1 tablespoon cold shortening, cut into small pieces

½ cup (1 stick) frozen butter, cut into small pieces

¼ teaspoon salt

¼ cup cold water

Place all ingredients in a food processor and process until dough holds together and starts to form a ball, about 25 seconds. Do not overmix.

Remove dough and shape into a 6-inch disk. Wrap in plastic wrap and chill for at least 1 hour.

Preheat oven to 450°F. Place disk on a lightly floured surface, and with a lightly floured rolling pin roll dough from the center out to the edges, changing the direction with each stroke, until the circle is ⅛ inch thick and about 1 inch larger than the pie plate. Fold dough in half and transfer to pie plate. Press gently to remove air bubbles. Fold edge under and flute. Do not prick dough for a quiche because the filling will seep under the shell. To partially bake the shell for a quiche, bake it for 8 minutes. Cool slightly on a rack. It should be slightly warm when filling is added.

Note: For a baked pastry shell for other purposes, prick the bottom thoroughly with a fork and bake at 450°F until lightly browned, 12 to 15 minutes. Cool on a rack.

SERVES 6

CLASSIC QUICHE LORRAINE

This well-known quiche was originally made with just bacon. These days, onion and Gruyère cheese are usually added. Serve with Orchard Fruit Plate (page 314).

4 to 6 slices bacon, diced

1 cup chopped yellow onion

1 shallot, chopped

1 tablespoon finely chopped parsley

3 large eggs

1½ cups half-and-half or whole milk

¼ teaspoon dry mustard

Dash of ground nutmeg

½ teaspoon salt

Freshly ground pepper

1¼ cups grated Gruyère cheese

9-inch Pie Shell (page 123), partially baked

Preheat oven to 350°F. In a medium skillet over medium-high heat, cook bacon until crisp, about 5 minutes. With a slotted spoon, remove to a plate lined with a paper towel to drain, leaving 1 tablespoon bacon drippings in skillet. Add onion and shallot and sauté until tender, about 5 minutes. Stir in parsley.

In a medium bowl, whisk together eggs, half-and-half, mustard, nutmeg, salt, and pepper to taste. Add onion mixture and bacon. Sprinkle cheese over bottom of pie shell. Pour egg mixture over all. Bake until a knife inserted in the center comes out clean and top is golden brown, 40 to 45 minutes. Let stand for 10 minutes. Cut into wedges and serve.

SERVES 6

SPINACH-SAUSAGE QUICHE

This quiche combines spinach and sausage for a great balance of flavors. Serve for a brunch with a Fresh Fruit Compote (page 308).

- 8 ounces bulk pork sausage
- 6 green onions, including some tender green tops, sliced
- 2 garlic cloves, minced
- 1 teaspoon vegetable oil, if needed
- 1 bag (6 ounces) fresh spinach, cooked, chopped, and squeezed dry, or ½ package (5 ounces) frozen chopped spinach, thawed, drained, and squeezed dry
- 1½ cups grated Monterey Jack cheese
- 9-inch Pie Shell (page 123), partially baked
- 3 large eggs
- 1½ cups half-and-half or whole milk
- ½ teaspoon salt
- ⅛ teaspoon white pepper
- ½ teaspoon dried oregano
- ¼ cup grated Parmesan cheese

Preheat oven to 350°F. In a medium nonstick skillet over medium heat, cook sausage, green onions, and garlic, breaking up sausage with a wooden spoon, until meat is no longer pink, 6 to 7 minutes. Add oil, if needed. Stir in spinach. Sprinkle grated Monterey Jack in pie shell. Add sausage-spinach mixture to pie shell.

In a medium bowl, whisk together eggs, half-and-half, salt, pepper, and oregano. Pour egg mixture over mixture in pie shell. Sprinkle with grated Parmesan. Bake until a knife inserted in the center comes out clean and top is golden brown, 40 to 45 minutes. Let stand for 10 minutes. Cut into wedges and serve.

SERVES 6

MUSHROOM AND HAM QUICHE

This quiche, studded with ham and sautéed mushrooms, makes a perfect entrée for a Mother's Day brunch. Serve it with Fresh Pear Sorbet (page 321).

1 tablespoon butter or margarine

4 ounces mushrooms, sliced

3 green onions, including some tender green tops, sliced

1 cup cubed cooked ham

3 large eggs, beaten

1½ cups half-and-half or whole milk

½ teaspoon salt

Dash of white pepper

1½ cups grated Gruyère cheese

9-inch Pie Shell (page 123), partially baked

Preheat oven to 350°F. In a medium skillet over medium heat, melt butter. Add mushrooms, green onions, and ham and sauté until vegetables are tender, about 5 minutes. In a bowl, whisk together eggs, half-and-half, salt, and pepper. Stir in cheese.

Spread ham-mushroom mixture in pie shell. Pour egg mixture over all. Bake until a knife inserted in the center comes out clean and top is golden brown, 40 to 45 minutes. Let stand for 10 minutes. Cut into wedges and serve.

SERVES 6

GREEK QUICHE

Feta cheese adds a rich, tangy flavor to this quiche, and spinach, sun-dried tomatoes, and olives provide hints of color.

3 large eggs

1½ cups half-and-half or whole milk

½ teaspoon dried oregano

½ teaspoon salt

⅛ teaspoon freshly ground pepper

1 bag (6 ounces) fresh spinach, cooked, chopped, and squeezed dry, or ½ package (5 ounces) frozen chopped spinach, thawed, drained, and squeezed dry

1 cup grated mozzarella cheese

¼ cup sun-dried tomatoes (not oil packed), soaked in boiling water for 5 minutes, drained, dried, and chopped (use kitchen scissors)

¼ cup sliced green onions, including some tender green tops

¼ cup sliced, pitted kalamata or ripe black olives

9-inch Pie Shell (page 123), partially baked

½ cup crumbled feta cheese

Preheat oven to 350°F. In a medium bowl, whisk together eggs, half-and-half, oregano, salt, and pepper. Stir in spinach, grated mozzarella, sun-dried tomatoes, green onions, and olives and mix well. Pour into pie shell. Sprinkle with crumbled feta. Bake until a knife inserted in the center comes out clean and top is golden brown, 40 to 45 minutes. Let stand for 10 minutes. Cut into wedges and serve.

SERVES 6

ARTICHOKE AND SUN-DRIED TOMATO QUICHE

Artichoke hearts and sun-dried tomatoes are a complementary combination in this quiche. Serve it with avocado slices and cherry tomatoes.

3 large eggs

1½ cups half-and-half or whole milk

2 garlic cloves, minced

½ teaspoon salt

Freshly ground pepper

1 cup grated Monterey Jack cheese

9-inch Pie Shell (page 123), partially baked

¼ cup sun-dried tomatoes (not oil-packed), soaked in boiling water for 5 minutes, drained, dried, and chopped (use kitchen scissors)

1 can (14 ounces) quartered artichoke hearts, drained

1 tablespoon chopped fresh basil, or ½ teaspoon dried basil

¼ cup grated Parmesan cheese

Preheat oven to 350°F. In a medium bowl, whisk together eggs, half-and-half, garlic, salt, and pepper to taste. Sprinkle grated Monterey Jack over bottom of pie shell. Sprinkle sun-dried tomatoes, artichoke hearts, and basil on top of cheese. Pour egg mixture over all and sprinkle with grated Parmesan.

Bake until a knife inserted in the center comes out clean and top is golden brown, 40 to 45 minutes. Let stand for 10 minutes. Cut into wedges and serve.

SERVES 6

MUSHROOM QUICHE

Mushrooms are a popular addition to quiches. You can use a variety of domestic and wild mushrooms in this version. Wild mushrooms add a rich, earthy flavor.

2 tablespoons butter or margarine

2 shallots, finely chopped

1 pound medium mushrooms (domestic or wild or a combination), trimmed and sliced

3 tablespoons dry white wine or sherry

3 large eggs

1½ cups half-and-half or whole milk

½ teaspoon salt

Dash of white pepper

½ teaspoon dried thyme

1 tablespoon chopped parsley

9-inch Pie Shell (page 123), partially baked

½ cup grated Parmesan cheese

Preheat oven to 350°F. In a medium skillet over medium heat, melt butter. Add shallots and mushrooms and sauté until tender, about 3 minutes. Add wine and sauté until liquid evaporates, about 3 minutes longer.

In a medium bowl, whisk together eggs, half-and-half, seasonings, and parsley. Arrange mushroom mixture in bottom of pie shell. Pour egg mixture over mushrooms. Sprinkle with grated Parmesan. Bake until a knife inserted in the center comes out clean and top is golden brown, 40 to 45 minutes. Let stand for 10 minutes. Cut into wedges and serve.

SERVES 6

CHICKEN QUICHE

This unusual quiche features Asian flavors that complement the chicken. The result is surprisingly delicious.

3 large eggs

1½ cups half-and-half or whole milk

2 teaspoons soy sauce

2 garlic cloves, chopped

½ teaspoon salt

¼ teaspoon ground ginger

⅛ teaspoon cayenne

1 cup diced cooked chicken

9-inch Pie Shell (page 123), partially baked

1 cup grated Cheddar cheese

Preheat oven to 350°F. In a medium bowl, whisk together eggs, half-and-half, soy sauce, garlic, salt, ginger, and cayenne. Fold in chicken. Pour mixture into pie shell and top with cheese.

Bake until a knife inserted in the center comes out clean and top is golden brown, 40 to 45 minutes. Let stand for 10 minutes. Cut into wedges and serve.

SERVES 6

SPRINGTIME QUICHE

Ham and tender spring asparagus are a classic combination in this flavorful quiche. Serve it for an early spring brunch, with Fresh Pear and Walnut Torte (page 327).

- ¼ pound asparagus, tough ends removed, cut into ¾-inch pieces
- 2 teaspoons vegetable oil
- 1 cup chopped yellow onion
- 1 garlic clove, minced
- 1 cup cubed cooked ham
- 3 large eggs
- 1½ cups half-and-half or whole milk
- 1 teaspoon soy sauce
- ¼ teaspoon salt
- Freshly ground pepper
- 1 cup grated Swiss cheese
- 9-inch Pie Shell (page 123), partially baked

Preheat oven to 350°F. Place asparagus in a medium skillet over medium-high heat, and add water to cover. Boil for 5 minutes. Drain and set aside.

In the same skillet over medium heat, warm oil. Add onion and garlic and sauté until tender, about 5 minutes. Stir in ham.

In a medium bowl, whisk together eggs, half-and-half, soy sauce, salt, and pepper to taste. Sprinkle cheese over bottom of pie shell. Top with asparagus and onion-ham mixture. Pour egg mixture over all. Bake until a knife inserted in the center comes out clean and top is golden brown, 40 to 45 minutes. Let stand for 10 minutes. Cut into wedges and serve.

SERVES 6

ROASTED RED PEPPER AND CARAMELIZED ONION QUICHE

The bold flavors of roasted red pepper, sautéed onion, and blue cheese are a lively combination. Serve it with Apple-Orange Fruit Compote (page 313).

1 red bell pepper, roasted and peeled (see page 67)

1 tablespoon butter or margarine

1 tablespoon vegetable oil

1 small yellow onion, sliced and separated into rings

9-inch Pie Shell (page 123), partially baked

½ cup crumbled blue cheese

3 large eggs

1½ cups half-and-half or whole milk

½ teaspoon dried thyme

¼ teaspoon salt

Freshly ground pepper

Cut roasted pepper into 1-inch pieces. Set aside.

Preheat oven to 350°F. In a large skillet over medium heat, melt butter with oil. Add onion and cook, stirring occasionally, until very tender, about 15 minutes. Arrange onion on bottom of pie shell. Add red pepper and blue cheese.

In a medium bowl, whisk together eggs, half-and-half, thyme, salt, and pepper to taste. Pour mixture over vegetables in pie shell. Bake until a knife inserted in the center comes out clean and top is golden brown, 40 to 45 minutes. Let stand for 10 minutes. Cut into wedges and serve.

SERVES 4

FIESTA QUICHE

Say goodbye to ho-hum breakfasts with this zesty quiche, served with Fruit Salsa and Chunky Guacamole.

½ pound lean ground beef

¼ cup chopped yellow onion

½ cup chopped, unpeeled zucchini

½ teaspoon chili powder

½ teaspoon ground cumin

1 teaspoon vegetable oil, if needed

1 can (4 ounces) diced green chiles, drained

1 small tomato, seeded, chopped, and drained

1½ cups grated Cheddar cheese, divided

9-inch Pie Shell (page 123), partially baked

3 large eggs

1½ cups half-and-half or whole milk

½ teaspoon salt

Freshly ground pepper

Chunky Guacamole (page 177) for topping

Fruit Salsa (recipe follows)

Preheat oven to 375°F. In a medium skillet over medium-high heat, combine beef, onion, zucchini, chili powder, and cumin and cook, breaking up meat with a spoon and adding oil, if needed, until meat is no longer pink, 6 to 7 minutes. Stir in chiles and tomato. Sprinkle 1 cup of the grated Cheddar over bottom of pie shell. Top with meat mixture.

In a medium bowl, whisk together eggs, half-and-half, salt, and pepper to taste. Pour over beef mixture. Sprinkle with remaining ½ cup cheese. Bake until a knife inserted in the center comes out clean and top is golden brown, 40 to 45 minutes. Let stand for 10 minutes. Cut into wedges and top with a tablespoon of guacamole. Pass the salsa separately.

FRUIT SALSA

This is best when served freshly made.

Makes about 2 cups

1 ripe diced papaya, peeled, seeded

1 avocado, peeled and cut into ¼-inch dice

2 plum tomatoes, seeded and finely chopped

1 small jalapeño pepper, finely chopped

3 tablespoons finely chopped red onion

1 garlic clove, minced

3 to 4 tablespoons fresh lime juice

1 teaspoon grated lime zest

2 or 3 basil leaves, finely chopped

Combine all ingredients in a large bowl. Cover and chill for 1 hour.

SERVES 6

SHRIMP AND CRAB QUICHE

Here the two most popular shellfish are combined in a savory custard accented with dill. Serve with Apricot and Blueberry Flan (page 324) for a special occasion.

1 tablespoon butter or margarine

¼ cup finely chopped yellow onion

¼ cup diced celery

¼ cup diced red bell pepper

3 large eggs

1 cup half-and-half or whole milk

¼ teaspoon dried dill weed

1 tablespoon chopped parsley

¼ teaspoon salt

Freshly ground pepper

9-inch Pie Shell (page 123), partially baked

4 ounces small cooked shrimp

4 ounces crabmeat, flaked

1 cup grated Monterey Jack cheese

Preheat oven to 350°F. In a medium skillet over medium heat, melt butter. Add onion, celery, and bell pepper and sauté until tender, about 5 minutes.

In a medium bowl, whisk together eggs, half-and-half, dill, parsley, salt, and pepper to taste. Spoon vegetable mixture over bottom of pie shell. Top with shrimp and crab. Pour egg mixture over all. Sprinkle with cheese. Bake until set and top is golden brown, 45 to 50 minutes. Let stand for 10 minutes. Cut into wedges and serve.

SERVES 6

SALMON QUICHE

The special whole-wheat crust, with nuts and cheese added, makes this quiche extra good. Freshly cooked salmon is best, but you can also use canned salmon.

- 1 large egg
- 1 cup sour cream
- ½ cup whole milk
- ¼ cup mayonnaise
- ½ cup grated Cheddar cheese
- 3 green onions, including some tender green tops, finely chopped
- ¼ teaspoon dried dill weed
- 3 drops Tabasco sauce
- 1 cup cooked salmon, flaked
- 9-inch Whole-Wheat Nut Cheddar Crust (recipe follows), partially baked

Preheat oven to 375°F. In a medium bowl, whisk together egg, sour cream, milk, and mayonnaise. Fold in cheese, green onions, dill, Tabasco sauce, and salmon. Pour into crust. Sprinkle reserved crust mixture on top. Bake until a knife inserted in the center comes out clean and top is golden brown, 40 to 45 minutes. Let stand for 10 minutes. Cut into wedges and serve.

Note: If using canned salmon, drain and remove dark skin.

WHOLE-WHEAT NUT CHEDDAR CRUST

Makes 1 single-crust pie shell

- 1 cup whole-wheat flour
- ¾ cup grated Cheddar cheese
- ¼ cup chopped almonds or walnuts
- ½ teaspoon salt
- ¼ teaspoon paprika
- 6 tablespoons vegetable oil

Preheat oven to 400°F In a medium bowl, combine all ingredients and mix well. Set aside ½ cup for topping. Using fingers, press remaining mixture into bottom and up the sides of a 9-inch pie plate. To partially bake the crust, bake it for 10 minutes. Cool on a rack.

STRATAS

Stratas can be made the night before and then baked in the morning. They are a perfect dish to serve overnight guests or for a late-morning brunch. Baked in a casserole, they are conveniently served from oven to table with minimum cleanup. They are also a great way to use day-old bread.

A strata consists of layers of bread, cheese, and other ingredients with an egg-milk mixture poured over the top and baked in the oven, like a savory bread pudding. They need to be refrigerated for several hours or overnight to allow the bread to soak up the egg-milk mixture, resulting in a fluffy consistency.

TIPS FOR MAKING STRATAS

- Use day-old bread or dried bread (see Note).
- Use whole milk (or half-and-half for a richer strata).
- Make the strata several hours ahead or the night before to allow the bread to absorb the custard. Press the bread down to be sure it is fully covered with custard.
- Bring the strata to room temperature before baking, or allow an extra 10 minutes of baking time.
- If the strata becomes too brown on top, cover it with foil for the rest of the baking time.
- Let the strata stand for 10 minutes before serving.

Note: To dry bread, place bread slices in a single layer on a baking sheet and toast in a 200°F oven for about 15 minutes, or air-dry the slices on the counter for several hours, turning once.

SERVES 6

EGG-SAUSAGE STRATA

Avoid the last-minute chore of cooking eggs and frying sausage by making this overnight strata. Sensational Scones (page 288) make a good accompaniment.

8 ounces bulk Italian pork sausage

4 green onions, including some tender green tops, sliced

4 ounces medium mushrooms, sliced

2 teaspoons vegetable oil, if needed

2 cups day-old bread cubes

1 cup grated Cheddar cheese

4 large eggs

2 cups whole milk

¼ teaspoon dry mustard

¼ teaspoon dried oregano

¼ teaspoon dried basil

½ teaspoon salt

Freshly ground pepper

In a medium nonstick skillet over medium heat, cook sausage, green onions, and mushrooms, breaking up sausage with a spoon and adding oil, if needed, until pink is no longer showing in sausage, about 10 minutes. Set aside. Place bread cubes in the bottom of a lightly sprayed or oiled 8-by-11½-inch baking dish. Add sausage mixture and sprinkle with cheese. In a medium bowl, whisk together eggs, milk, mustard, oregano, basil, salt, and pepper to taste. Pour over bread-sausage mixture. Cover and refrigerate for several hours or overnight.

Preheat oven to 350°F. Bring strata to room temperature before baking. Bake, uncovered, until set, 45 to 50 minutes. Let strata stand for 10 minutes. Cut into squares and serve.

SERVES 8 TO 10

CRAB STRATA SUPREME

Rise and shine with this classy strata of crab, mushrooms, and cheese. Serve with Tropical Fruit Platter with Strawberry Purée (page 307), and entertain in style.

½ large loaf day-old French bread, cut into ½-inch cubes

2 tablespoons butter

4 ounces medium mushrooms, sliced

½ cup diced red bell pepper

6 green onions, including some tender green tops, chopped

¾ cup diced celery

2 cups grated Swiss cheese

8 ounces crabmeat, flaked

8 large eggs

1¼ cups whole milk

¼ cup dry white wine

1 teaspoon dry mustard

¼ teaspoon salt

⅛ teaspoon black pepper

1 cup sour cream

½ cup grated Parmesan cheese

Place bread cubes in a lightly sprayed or oiled 9-by-13-inch baking dish.

In a medium nonstick skillet over medium heat, melt butter. Add mushrooms, bell pepper, green onions, and celery and sauté until tender, 6 to 7 minutes. Spoon mushroom-onion mixture evenly over bread. Layer grated Swiss and crab over this mixture.

In a medium bowl, whisk together eggs, milk, wine, and seasonings. Fold in sour cream. Pour over bread mixture. Cover and refrigerate for several hours or overnight.

Preheat oven to 350°F. Bring strata to room temperature before baking. Bake, covered with foil, until set, about 35 minutes. Remove foil and sprinkle with grated Parmesan. Bake, uncovered, until bubbly, about 10 minutes longer. Let stand for 10 minutes. Cut into squares and serve.

MAKES 10 TO 12

SHRIMP AND ARTICHOKE STRATA

Make this outstanding strata the night before and you will have time to prepare a delicious Fresh Fruit Trifle (page 329) in the morning for a very special brunch.

2 tablespoons butter

⅓ cup sliced green onions, including some tender green tops

1 garlic clove, minced

6 ounces medium mushrooms, sliced

8 ounces small cooked shrimp

1 can (14 ounces) quartered artichoke hearts, drained

8 slices day-old white bread, crusts removed, if desired, and cut into ½-inch cubes, divided

2 cups grated Swiss cheese, divided

8 large eggs

1½ cups whole milk

½ teaspoon salt

Freshly ground pepper

1 tablespoon chopped fresh thyme leaves, or ¾ teaspoon dried thyme

2 tablespoons grated Parmesan cheese

Thyme sprigs for garnish

Cherry tomatoes for garnish

In a large nonstick skillet over medium heat, melt butter. Add green onions, garlic, and mushrooms and sauté until tender, about 5 minutes. Stir in shrimp and artichoke hearts and mix well.

Place half the bread cubes in a lightly sprayed or oiled 9-by-13-inch baking dish. Top with the seafood-vegetable mixture. Sprinkle with half the Swiss cheese. Top with remaining bread cubes.

In a large bowl, whisk together eggs, milk, salt, pepper to taste, and thyme. Pour over bread, covering it completely. Sprinkle with remaining grated Swiss and the grated Parmesan. Cover and refrigerate for several hours or overnight.

Preheat oven to 350°F. Bring strata to room temperature before baking. Bake, uncovered, until set, 45 to 50 minutes. Let stand for 10 minutes. Cut into squares and serve garnished with thyme sprigs and cherry tomatoes.

SERVES 8

HOLIDAY STRATA

Your open house will be a breeze when you make the main course the night before. Sourdough bread and sausage links give this strata a special tang. Serve with purchased croissants and Apple-Orange Fruit Compote (page 313) for a smashing affair.

1½ tablespoons butter or margarine

6 ounces medium mushrooms, sliced

8 slices day-old sourdough bread, crusts trimmed, buttered, and cut into cubes, divided

1¼ pounds link sausage, cooked (page 250) and cut into bite-sized pieces

2 cups grated Cheddar cheese, divided

4 large eggs

2 cups whole milk

½ teaspoon salt

⅛ teaspoon white pepper

1 teaspoon dry mustard

In a medium skillet over medium heat, melt butter. Add mushrooms and sauté until tender, about 5 minutes.

Place half of the bread in a lightly sprayed or oiled 9-by-13-inch baking dish. Add sausage, mushrooms, half of the cheese, and remaining bread.

In a large bowl, whisk together eggs, milk, salt, pepper, and mustard. Pour over bread-sausage mixture. Sprinkle with remaining cheese. Cover and refrigerate for several hours or overnight.

Preheat oven to 350°F. Bring strata to room temperature before baking. Bake, uncovered, until set and bubbly, 45 to 50 minutes. Let stand for 10 minutes. Cut into squares and serve.

SERVES 4

HAM AND CHEESE BREAKFAST STRATA

English muffins replace the bread in this strata. Slip it into the oven in the morning and serve with a pitcher of Citrus Cooler (page 20) for a hassle-free breakfast.

Butter or margarine

2 English muffins, split

1½ cups diced cooked ham

1 cup grated Cheddar cheese

4 large eggs

2 cups whole milk

½ teaspoon salt

Freshly ground pepper

A few drops of Tabasco sauce

1 teaspoon Worcestershire sauce

Lightly butter cut side of each muffin half. Place cut-side up in a lightly sprayed or buttered 8-by-8-inch baking dish. Sprinkle with ham and cheese.

In a large bowl, whisk together eggs, milk, salt, pepper to taste, Tabasco sauce, and Worcestershire sauce. Pour mixture over muffins. Cover and refrigerate for several hours or overnight.

Preheat oven to 350°F. Bring strata to room temperature before baking. Bake, uncovered, until set, 40 to 45 minutes. Let stand for 10 minutes before serving. Cut into squares and serve.

SERVES 8

CHICKEN STRATA, MEXICAN STYLE

This strata was served at a friend's late-summer poolside brunch, along with spicy Bloody Marys (page 28), cornmeal muffins, and seasonal fruit for a memorable day.

10 slices sourdough French bread, crusts removed, if desired, divided

3 cups grated Monterey Jack cheese, divided

2 cups cubed cooked chicken breast, divided

2 cups medium salsa, divided

1 cup sliced green onions, including some tender green tops, divided

1 can (15 ounces) black beans, drained and rinsed, divided

4 large eggs

2¼ cups whole milk

1 can (4 ounces) diced green chiles, drained

½ teaspoon salt

Freshly ground pepper

Chunky Guacamole (page 177) for topping

Sour cream for topping

Fit half the bread into a lightly sprayed or oiled 9-by-13-inch baking dish (the slices can overlap slightly). Top with half the cheese, half the chicken, half the salsa, half the green onions, and half the beans. Repeat the layers.

In a medium bowl, whisk together eggs, milk, chiles, salt, and pepper to taste. Pour over top of bread mixture. Cover and refrigerate for several hours or overnight.

Preheat oven to 375°F. Bring strata to room temperature. Bake, uncovered, until set and bubbly, 50 to 55 minutes. Let stand for 10 minutes. Cut into squares and serve with Chunky Guacamole and sour cream.

SERVES 6

VEGETABLE STRATA

This hearty vegetarian strata packed with a variety of vegetables has a fresh garden flavor. Serve with a pot of herbal tea.

1 tablespoon butter or margarine

½ cup chopped yellow onion

½ cup chopped green bell pepper

½ cup chopped red bell pepper

1 small crookneck squash, chopped

1 cup chopped mushrooms

2 garlic cloves, chopped

4 large eggs

2 cups whole milk

½ teaspoon salt

Freshly ground pepper

2 or 3 drops Tabasco sauce

½ loaf day-old or French bread, sliced, buttered, and then cut into cubes

1½ cups grated provolone cheese, divided

In a large nonstick skillet over medium heat, melt butter. Add onion, bell peppers, squash, mushrooms, and garlic. Sauté until tender, 6 to 7 minutes.

In a medium bowl, whisk together eggs, milk, salt, pepper to taste, and Tabasco sauce. Place bread cubes in a lightly sprayed or oiled 8-by-11½-inch baking dish. Top with all of the vegetables and half the cheese. Pour egg-milk mixture over all. (Be sure bread is completely covered with mixture.) Sprinkle remaining cheese on top. Cover and refrigerate for several hours or overnight.

Preheat oven to 350°F. Bring strata to room temperature before baking. Bake, uncovered, until set, 45 to 50 minutes. Let stand for 10 minutes. Cut into squares and serve.

SERVES 4 TO 6

BACON AND CHEESE STRATA

Start with some fresh fruit and a steaming cup of hot coffee while this easy strata bakes. It's like a quiche Lorraine, with the bread adding texture and substance.

4 slices day-old white bread, crusts removed

6 slices bacon, cooked and crumbled

6 large eggs

1½ cups whole milk

¼ teaspoon salt

Freshly ground pepper

2 drops Tabasco sauce

½ cup grated Cheddar cheese

3 tablespoons chopped parsley

½ cup grated Monterey Jack cheese

½ red bell pepper, seeded, and cut into rings

Arrange bread slices, slightly overlapping, in a lightly sprayed or oiled 8-by-11½-inch baking dish. Scatter bacon over the top.

In a large bowl, whisk together eggs, milk, salt, pepper to taste, and Tabasco sauce. Fold in grated Cheddar and parsley. Pour egg mixture over bread and bacon. Sprinkle with grated Monterey Jack. Cover and refrigerate for several hours or overnight.

Preheat oven to 350°F. Bring strata to room temperature before baking. Arrange bell pepper rings on top. Bake, uncovered, until set, 45 to 50 minutes. Let stand for 10 minutes. Cut into squares and serve.

SERVES 4 TO 6

APPLE STRATA

This spiced strata with apples and cream cheese makes a good fall entrée. A topping of confectioners' sugar or maple syrup enhances the sweetness of the apple.

6 slices day-old sourdough bread, cubed, divided

4 ounces cream cheese, cubed

1 apple, peeled and chopped

½ cup raisins (optional)

6 large eggs

1¼ cups whole milk

1 tablespoon brown sugar

1 teaspoon ground cinnamon

¼ teaspoon ground cloves

Dash of ground nutmeg

Confectioners' sugar or maple syrup for topping

Place half the bread cubes in a lightly sprayed or oiled 8-by-11½-inch baking dish. Distribute cream cheese cubes over bread cubes. Top with apples and raisins, if desired, and cover with remaining bread cubes.

In a medium bowl, whisk together eggs, milk, brown sugar, cinnamon, cloves, and nutmeg. Pour over bread mixture in dish. Be sure bread is completely covered. Cover and refrigerate for several hours or overnight.

Preheat oven to 375°F. Bring strata to room temperature before baking. Bake, uncovered, until set, 50 to 55 minutes. Let stand for 10 minutes. Sprinkle with confectioners' sugar, or pass maple syrup at the table. Cut into squares and serve.

BREAKFAST CASSEROLES

Breakfast casseroles are a combination dish baked in the oven that includes an assortment of ingredients, such as eggs, vegetables, and often meats. They deliver variety and substance to the menu and are usually the highlight of the meal.

Casseroles are convenient to serve for company because they can be made ahead and will serve a number of people.

SERVES 8

CHILE EGG PUFF

This brunch dish has always been a favorite with friends and family because it is easy to make and is rich and flavorful. Serve with fresh berries and yogurt and Broiled Ham Slice with Cheese (page 241).

10 large eggs

¼ cup all-purpose flour

1 teaspoon baking powder

½ teaspoon salt

⅛ teaspoon white pepper

3 cups grated Cheddar cheese, divided

2 cups lowfat cottage cheese

¼ cup melted butter

1 can (4 ounces) diced green chiles, drained

Fresh Tomato Salsa (page 103) or purchased salsa for topping

Sour cream for topping

Sliced green onions for topping

Chopped avocado for topping

Preheat oven to 350°F. In a large bowl, whisk eggs. Add flour, baking powder, salt, pepper, half the Cheddar cheese, all of the cottage cheese, butter, and chiles and mix well.

Place in a lightly sprayed or oiled 8-by-11½-inch baking dish. Bake, uncovered, for 30 minutes. Sprinkle remaining cheese on top and bake until eggs are set and cheese melts, about 10 minutes longer. Let stand for 10 minutes. To serve, cut into squares. Pass the toppings separately.

SERVES 8

BRUNCH BAKE

This casserole of eggs, ham, mushrooms, and green chiles was a winner at one of our tasting brunches. Be sure to try it with the salsa and guacamole. Walnut Sour Cream Coffee Cake (page 298) is a good match.

- 2 tablespoons butter or margarine
- 8 ounces medium mushrooms, sliced
- 10 green onions, including some tender green tops, sliced
- 12 large eggs
- 1 cup milk
- ¼ cup all-purpose flour
- ½ teaspoon baking powder
- 3 cups grated Monterey Jack cheese
- 1 cup diced cooked ham
- ½ teaspoon salt
- Freshly ground pepper
- 1 can (7 ounces) whole green chiles, split and seeded
- Fresh Tomato Salsa (page 103) or purchased salsa as an accompaniment
- Chunky Guacamole (page 177) or avocado slices as an accompaniment

Preheat oven to 350°F. In a medium skillet over medium heat, melt butter. Add mushrooms and green onions and sauté until tender, about 5 minutes. In a large bowl, whisk together eggs, milk, flour, and baking powder. Add cheese, ham, salt, pepper to taste, and mushroom mixture. Arrange chiles on the bottom of a lightly sprayed or oiled 9-by-13-inch baking dish.

Pour egg-milk mixture over chiles. Bake, uncovered, until set, about 40 minutes. Let stand for 10 minutes. Cut into squares and serve, passing the salsa and guacamole separately.

SERVES 8 TO 10

EGG CASSEROLE WITH SAUSAGE, MUSHROOMS, AND SALSA

This hearty concoction with lots of goodies will please Dad for a Father's Day brunch. Include Screwdrivers (page 30), Cranberry Scones (page 285), and melon wedges with lime juice on the menu.

12 ounces bulk Italian pork sausage

2 teaspoons vegetable oil, if needed

8 ounces medium mushrooms, sliced

½ cup chopped yellow onion

12 large eggs

1 cup milk

½ cup Fresh Tomato Salsa (page 103) or purchased salsa

2 tablespoons all-purpose flour

½ teaspoon baking powder

4 cups grated Cheddar or Monterey Jack cheese, divided

½ teaspoon salt

Freshly ground pepper

Sour cream for topping

Preheat oven to 350°F. In a large skillet over medium heat, cook sausage, breaking it up with a spoon, until it starts to brown, about 5 minutes. Add oil, if needed. Add mushrooms and onion, and cook until pink is no longer showing in sausage and vegetables are tender, about 10 minutes longer. Transfer to a lightly sprayed or oiled 9-by-13-inch baking dish.

In a bowl, whisk together eggs, milk, salsa, flour, and baking powder. Add half of the cheese, salt, and pepper to taste and pour over meat mixture. Sprinkle with the remaining cheese. Bake, uncovered, until set, about 40 minutes. Let stand for 10 minutes. Serve topped with sour cream.

SERVES 6 TO 8

BAKED EGGS FLORENTINE

Spinach and cottage cheese team up with eggs in this easy-to-make casserole. Serve it with Oven-Baked Bacon (page 240) and Baked Pears in Wine with Chocolate Sauce (page 328).

Preheat oven to 350°F. In a large bowl, combine all ingredients. Pour into a lightly sprayed or oiled 8-by-11½-inch baking dish. Bake, uncovered, until eggs are set, about 40 minutes. Let stand for 10 minutes. Cut into squares and serve.

1 package (10 ounces) frozen spinach, thawed and squeezed dry

1 cup cottage cheese

½ cup light sour cream

8 large eggs, beaten

¼ teaspoon dried thyme

½ teaspoon salt

Freshly ground pepper

1 cup grated Cheddar cheese

¼ cup grated Parmesan cheese

SERVES 8

ITALIAN CASSEROLE WITH MUSHROOMS, BELL PEPPER, AND PANCETTA

Enjoy a blend of Italian flavors in this casserole. Serve it with Focaccia (page 301) when you're having guests for breakfast or brunch.

1 cup diced pancetta or thick bacon (8 slices)

Vegetable oil for sautéing, if needed

1 cup chopped yellow onion

½ cup chopped green or red bell pepper

4 ounces medium mushrooms, sliced

1 garlic clove, minced

10 large eggs

1½ cups milk

¼ cup all-purpose flour

2 tablespoons chopped parsley

1 tablespoon chopped fresh basil, or 1 teaspoon dried basil

½ teaspoon dried oregano

1 teaspoon salt

Freshly ground pepper

1½ cups grated mozzarella cheese

½ cup grated Parmesan or Romano cheese

Preheat oven to 350°F. In a medium nonstick skillet over medium heat, cook pancetta until crisp, about 5 minutes. Remove to a plate, leaving 2 tablespoons drippings in skillet (add oil, if needed). Add onion, bell pepper, mushrooms, and garlic and sauté until tender, 6 to 7 minutes. Return pancetta to skillet.

In a large bowl, whisk together eggs, milk, flour, parsley, basil, oregano, salt, and pepper to taste. Add pancetta and vegetable mixture to egg mixture. Fold in grated mozzarella.

Pour mixture into a lightly sprayed or oiled 9-by-13-inch baking dish. Sprinkle with grated Parmesan. Bake until set, about 40 minutes. Let stand for 10 minutes. Cut into squares and serve.

SERVES 6 TO 8

BACON AND POTATO CASSEROLE

This hearty casserole is one of the best and easiest brunch dishes in the book. It goes well with Apple-Orange Fruit Compote (page 313) and Chocolate Zucchini Bread (page 295).

8 large eggs

1 cup mayonnaise

1 medium yellow onion, chopped

2 medium russet potatoes (about 1 pound), peeled and grated

1 pound bacon, diced and cooked

2 cups grated Cheddar cheese

Preheat oven to 350°F. In a large bowl, whisk eggs. Whisk in mayonnaise until blended. Stir in onion, potatoes, bacon, and cheese. Pour into a lightly sprayed or oiled 9-by-13-inch baking dish. Bake, uncovered, until set, about 45 minutes. Let stand for 10 minutes. Cut into squares and serve.

SERVES 6

MUMBO JUMBO

Once you have everything ready, all you do to make this dish is layer potatoes, eggs, sausage, and bacon in a casserole dish and spread sour cream on top. It makes an outstanding brunch entrée.

8 ounces bulk pork sausage

½ pound bacon, diced

3 large russet potatoes (about 1½ pounds), peeled, cooked, quartered lengthwise, and sliced

4 large hard-cooked eggs (see page 39), sliced

1 cup sour cream

In a large nonstick skillet over medium-high heat, cook sausage and bacon, breaking sausage up with a spoon, until bacon is crisp and sausage is no longer pink, about 10 minutes. Drain.

Preheat oven to 350°F. In a lightly sprayed or oiled 8-by-11½-inch baking dish, layer potatoes, egg slices, and meat. Spread sour cream on top. Cover and bake until bubbly, about 45 minutes. Remove cover and bake 10 minutes longer.

Note: This recipe can easily be doubled.

SERVES 4

FARMER'S BREAKFAST CASSEROLE

Hash browns, cheese, and ham are layered in a baking dish, with an egg custard to meld them together. This "no fuss" brunch dish can be made the night before and refrigerated. Bring it to room temperature before baking.

- 3 cups frozen cubed hash brown potatoes, slightly thawed
- ½ cup grated pepper Jack cheese
- ⅓ cup grated Cheddar or Monterey Jack cheese
- 1 cup cubed cooked ham
- 6 to 8 green onions, including some tender green tops, sliced
- 4 large eggs
- 1½ cups milk
- ¼ teaspoon salt
- Freshly ground pepper
- Fresh strawberries for garnish

Preheat oven to 350°F. In an 8-by-8-inch lightly sprayed or oiled baking dish, arrange a layer of hash browns, grated pepper Jack and Cheddar, ham, and green onions.

In a medium bowl, whisk together eggs, milk, salt, and pepper to taste. Pour egg mixture over potato mixture. Bake, uncovered, until center is set, about 50 minutes. Let stand for 10 minutes. Cut into squares and serve garnished with strawberries.

SERVES 6

SHRIMP AND CROISSANT BRUNCH CASSEROLE

Serve this elegant combination of croissants and shrimp with a custard base as the highlight of the brunch. This casserole is best when made several hours ahead to allow the flavors to blend before baking. Serve it with Glazed Lemon Cake *(page 304)*.

6 croissants, cut or torn into ½-inch pieces

1½ cups grated Monterey Jack cheese, divided

8 ounces cooked small shrimp

6 green onions, including some tender green tops, sliced

4 large eggs

1¾ cups milk

¼ teaspoon dried thyme

½ teaspoon salt

¼ teaspoon white pepper

Place half the croissant cubes in the bottom of a lightly sprayed or oiled 8-by-11½-inch baking dish. Sprinkle with half the cheese, all the shrimp, and green onions. Top with remaining croissant cubes.

In a medium bowl, whisk together eggs, milk, thyme, salt, and pepper. Pour over mixture in baking dish. Sprinkle with remaining cheese. Cover and refrigerate for several hours. Bring to room temperature before baking.

Preheat oven to 350°F. Bake, uncovered, until set, about 40 minutes. Let stand for 10 minutes. Cut into squares and serve.

SERVES 6 TO 8

CRAB BRUNCH CASSEROLE

Succulent crab and earthy mushrooms are the principal ingredients in this rich casserole. Serve with Fresh Fruit Compote (page 308).

2 tablespoons butter or margarine

8 ounces medium mushrooms, sliced

4 green onions, including some tender green tops, sliced

4 large eggs

1 cup small-curd cottage cheese

1 cup sour cream

½ cup grated Parmesan cheese

¼ cup all-purpose flour

¼ teaspoon salt

⅛ teaspoon white pepper

2 cups grated Monterey Jack cheese

8 ounces crabmeat, flaked

Preheat oven to 350°F. In a medium skillet over medium heat, melt butter. Add mushrooms and green onions and sauté until tender, about 5 minutes. Set aside.

In a food processor or blender, blend eggs, cottage cheese, sour cream, grated Parmesan, flour, salt, and pepper. Transfer to a large bowl. Fold in grated Monterey Jack, crabmeat, and sautéed vegetables. Pour into a lightly sprayed or oiled 8-by-8-inch baking dish. Bake until casserole is puffed up and golden, about 45 minutes. Let stand for 10 minutes. Cut into squares and serve.

VARIATION

Substitute 1 cup cubed cooked ham or cubed cooked chicken for the crab.

SERVES 6

LAYERED SHRIMP AND VEGETABLE BRUNCH CASSEROLE

Entertain with confidence with this distinctive casserole featuring layers of shrimp, sautéed vegetables, and fresh spinach. Complete the menu with Apple-Orange Fruit Compote (page 313) and hot rolls.

2 tablespoons olive oil

1 cup chopped yellow onion

½ cup chopped red bell pepper

1 garlic clove, minced

4 ounces medium mushrooms, sliced

1 cup seeded, chopped, and drained tomato

1 bag (6 ounces) fresh spinach, divided

12 ounces cooked small shrimp

10 large eggs

3 tablespoons milk

½ teaspoon Tabasco sauce

½ teaspoon salt

Freshly ground pepper

2 cups grated Cheddar cheese

½ cup grated Parmesan cheese

Preheat oven to 350°F. In a medium skillet over medium heat, warm oil. Add onion, bell pepper, garlic, and mushrooms, and sauté until tender, about 5 minutes. Stir in tomato. Place sautéed vegetables in a lightly sprayed or oiled 9-by-13-inch baking dish. Add half of the spinach leaves in a layer on top of vegetables, and scatter shrimp over spinach. Layer the remaining spinach on top.

In a large bowl, whisk together eggs, milk, Tabasco sauce, salt, and pepper to taste and pour over vegetable-shrimp mixture. Sprinkle with grated Cheddar and bake until eggs are set, about 25 minutes. Sprinkle with grated Parmesan and bake for 10 minutes longer. Let stand for 10 minutes. Cut into squares and serve.

SERVES 1

BAKED HAM AND EGGS GRATIN

This single-serving recipe makes a complete breakfast entrée; you can multiply it as needed. Serve it with Walnut Sour Cream Coffee Cake (page 298) and It's the Berries in Syrup (page 310).

- 1 or 2 small, thin slices cooked ham
- 2 medium mushrooms, sliced
- 2 green onions, including some tender green tops, sliced
- 2 thin tomato slices
- 1 or 2 large eggs
- Salt and freshly ground pepper
- Grated Cheddar cheese for topping

Preheat oven to 400°F. Butter an individual gratin dish. Layer ham, mushrooms, green onions, and tomato slices in dish. Break eggs on top. Season with salt and pepper to taste. Bake until eggs are set, about 15 minutes. Sprinkle with cheese. Bake until cheese melts, about 1 minute longer.

SERVES 6

BREAKFAST GRATIN

Individual gratin dishes are piled high with a tasty combination of potatoes, sausage, tomato, and onion, and then each is topped with an egg. Include Basic Muffins (page 274) for a terrific brunch.

4 medium new potatoes (about 1½ pounds), unpeeled and halved

1 pound bulk Italian sausage

½ red onion, sliced and separated into rings

½ red bell pepper, seeded and chopped

1 to 2 teaspoons vegetable oil, if needed

1 tomato, seeded and chopped

¼ cup chopped parsley

6 large eggs

1 cup grated sharp Cheddar cheese

Sour cream as an accompaniment (optional)

In a medium saucepan over medium heat, cook potatoes, in water to cover, until tender, about 20 minutes. Drain and cool slightly. Cut into ½-inch chunks and set aside.

Preheat oven to 400°F. In a medium skillet over medium heat, combine sausage, onion, and bell pepper. Sauté, breaking up sausage with a spoon, until pink is no longer showing in meat and vegetables are tender, about 10 minutes (add oil, if needed). Stir in potatoes, tomato, and parsley. Divide mixture evenly among 6 lightly sprayed or oiled individual gratin dishes. Make a small indentation in the center of the mixture in each dish, and break in an egg. Bake until eggs are set, about 15 minutes. Sprinkle with cheese and bake until cheese melts, about 2 minutes longer. Serve with sour cream, if desired.

SERVES 1

EGGS GRATIN

Make this baked egg dish to order with a choice of tasty toppings. This recipe serves one, but you can make as many as you need. Serve with Cranberry Scones (page 285).

2 large eggs

2 teaspoons water

Salt and freshly ground pepper

1 tablespoon topping: diced mushrooms, diced green bell pepper, sliced green onion, diced cooked pancetta or bacon, diced ham

1 tablespoon grated Swiss or Cheddar cheese

Preheat oven to 350°F. Carefully break eggs into a buttered 4-by-6-inch individual gratin dish. Sprinkle water over eggs. Season with salt and pepper to taste. Add 1 tablespoon toppings of your choice and sprinkle with cheese. Bake until whites are set and cheese is melted, 15 to 18 minutes. Eggs stay very hot in the gratin dish.

SERVES 4

SPICY EGGS IN SPINACH

Eggs are baked in nests of spinach in custard cups and topped with spicy salsa and cheese. This makes a nice addition to a brunch menu.

1 bag (6 ounces) fresh spinach, cooked, drained, chopped, and squeezed dry

4 large eggs

Salt and freshly ground pepper

¼ cup Fresh Tomato Salsa (page 103) or purchased salsa

¼ cup grated Monterey Jack cheese

Preheat oven to 350°F. Divide spinach equally among 4 buttered or sprayed custard cups. Press the spinach into the cups and make an indentation in the center of each. Break an egg into each indentation. Season with salt and pepper to taste. Top each egg with 1 tablespoon salsa and 1 tablespoon cheese. Place cups in a baking dish and fill dish with hot water one third of the way up the sides of the cups. Bake until whites are set and yolks begin to firm up, about 20 minutes. Serve immediately in the custard cups.

SERVES 6 TO 8

BAKED CHEESE BLINTZ CASSEROLE

This creative casserole tastes like blintzes but takes half the time to prepare and is easier to serve. Top it with Strawberry Sauce or Fresh Blueberry Sauce for added flavor.

FILLING

8 ounces light cream cheese

15 ounces ricotta cheese

1 large egg

1 tablespoon sugar

1 teaspoon vanilla extract

BATTER

½ cup butter or margarine, melted

¼ cup sugar

6 large eggs

1 cup all-purpose flour

1 teaspoon baking powder

1 teaspoon baking soda

½ cup orange juice

Strawberry Sauce (recipe follows) or Fresh Blueberry Sauce (page 233)

To make the filling: In a medium bowl with an electric mixer, beat together all filling ingredients. Set aside.

To make the batter: Preheat oven to 350°F. In another medium bowl, with an electric mixer and with clean beaters, beat butter, sugar, and eggs. Add flour, baking powder, baking soda, and orange juice and beat well.

Pour half the batter into a lightly sprayed or oiled 9-by-13-inch baking dish. Spoon filling on top, spreading it around as much as possible. Pour remaining batter on top. Bake until firm and golden on top, about 50 minutes. Cut into squares and serve with Strawberry Sauce or Fresh Blueberry Sauce.

STRAWBERRY SAUCE

This recipe is also good on ice cream, plain cake, pancakes, and waffles.

Makes about 2 cups

1 package (16 ounces) frozen strawberries with juice, thawed

2 tablespoons sugar

1 tablespoon cornstarch

¼ cup orange juice

1 cup sliced fresh strawberries

1 tablespoon Grand Marnier liqueur (optional)

In a food processor, slightly purée thawed berries, including their juice. Transfer to a medium saucepan. Add sugar, cornstarch, and orange juice and bring to a boil over medium-high heat, whisking, until thickened, about 4 minutes. Remove from heat and add fresh berries and liqueur, if desired. Let cool, then cover and refrigerate. Serve at room temperature.

People of all ages love sandwiches, so why not serve them for breakfast? They add variety and interest to the menu and can be carried for a quick breakfast on the go. Wraps are sandwiches made with tortillas with a variety of fillings. They may appeal to children who resist eating breakfast.

BREAKFAST SANDWICHES

SERVES 4

EGG AND BLACK BEAN BURRITO

Wrap up some of your favorite ingredients in a tortilla for a Mexican-style breakfast that is filling and satisfying. Serve with Citrus Salsa (page 317).

1 can (15 ounces) black beans, drained and rinsed

6 large eggs

2 tablespoons water

¼ teaspoon salt

Freshly ground pepper

1 tablespoon butter or margarine

4 large flour tortillas, warmed (see Note)

1 cup grated Cheddar cheese

½ cup sliced green onions, including some tender green tops

Fresh Tomato Salsa (page 103) or purchased salsa

½ cup sour cream

Place beans in a small saucepan over medium heat to warm, stirring occasionally.

In a medium bowl, whisk together eggs, water, salt, and pepper to taste. In a medium nonstick skillet, melt butter. When butter foams, add egg mixture all at once. Let set for 20 seconds. Cook, stirring until eggs are light and fluffy, about 2 minutes.

To assemble, lay a tortilla on a plate and spoon some beans, eggs, cheese, a few green onions, 2 tablespoons of salsa, and a dollop of sour cream in the center of each tortilla. Roll, folding in the ends. Repeat with remaining tortillas. Serve with remaining beans on the side.

Note: Here are some ways to warm tortillas:

- *Wrap in foil and warm in a 350°F oven for 10 minutes.*
- *Wrap in paper towels and place in a microwave oven on high for 10 seconds.*
- *Fry quickly in a hot, lightly sprayed skillet.*
- *Hold over a gas flame with tongs, turning constantly.*
- *Place on a grill, and grill on each side until lightly charred, turning with tongs.*

SERVES 2

EGG AND VEGETABLE WRAP

Sautéed vegetables and scrambled eggs topped with avocado and spicy cheese in a tortilla make a complete breakfast. To accompany it, try black beans and sour cream.

- 2 teaspoons vegetable oil
- ¼ cup diced red or green bell pepper
- ¼ cup chopped yellow onion
- 1 cup chopped mushrooms
- 4 large eggs
- 1 tablespoon water
- ¼ teaspoon salt
- 2 tablespoons chopped fresh cilantro or parsley
- 2 large tomato-flavored flour tortillas, warmed (see page 165)
- ½ avocado, diced
- ½ cup grated pepper Jack cheese
- Orange or grapefruit slices for garnish

In a medium skillet over medium heat, warm oil. Add bell pepper, onion, and mushrooms and sauté until tender, 6 to 7 minutes.

In a medium bowl, whisk together eggs, water, and salt. Add egg mixture and chopped cilantro to vegetables and cook, stirring, until light and fluffy, 2 to 3 minutes.

To assemble, lay a tortilla on a plate. Add half the egg mixture, half the avocado, and half the cheese. Roll up, folding in the ends. Repeat with remaining tortilla. Garnish plate with orange or grapefruit slices.

SERVES 4

BREAKFAST PIZZA

Love pizza? Here is a simple, fast open-face sandwich for breakfast, lunch, or supper.

8 ounces bulk pork sausage

2 ounces medium mushrooms, coarsely chopped

¼ teaspoon dried oregano

Freshly ground pepper

4 English muffins, split

1 can (6 ounces) tomato paste (see Note)

1 cup grated mozzarella cheese

Preheat oven to 400°F. In a medium skillet over medium heat, combine sausage, mushrooms, oregano, and pepper to taste, and cook, breaking up sausage with a spoon, until pink is no longer showing, 6 to 7 minutes. Place muffin halves on a baking sheet. Spread tomato paste lightly on each half. Spoon sausage mixture on top and sprinkle with cheese. Bake until muffin edges are crisp and cheese is melted, about 10 minutes.

Note: Freeze any leftover tomato paste for another use.

SERVES 3 TO 4

BAGELS WITH EGG SALAD

For a different way to present eggs in your breakfast menu, mound egg salad on fresh bagels or croissants. You can make the egg salad ahead and keep it chilled until ready to use.

Egg Salad (recipe follows)

3 bagels, split

1 red bell pepper, seeded and cut into rings

Spread egg salad mixture on cut side of bagels and top each with a bell pepper ring.

EGG SALAD

Makes about 2 cups

6 large hard-cooked eggs (see page 39), peeled and cut into large pieces

¼ to ⅓ cup mayonnaise

1 teaspoon Dijon mustard

¼ teaspoon dried dill weed (optional)

¼ teaspoon salt, or more to taste

Freshly ground pepper

Place eggs, mayonnaise, Dijon mustard, dill (if desired), salt, and pepper to taste in a food processor, and pulse off and on until mixture is chunky.

VARIATIONS

Add 1 celery stalk, diced.

Add 1 or 2 small sweet pickles, chopped.

Substitute prepared yellow mustard for the Dijon mustard.

SERVES 6

SAUSAGE AND EGG BISCUIT SANDWICH

There's no need to stop at the local drive-through for this famous breakfast to go. This version is even better! Make the biscuits first and keep them warm while preparing the sausage and eggs.

1 pound bulk pork sausage

1 to 2 teaspoons vegetable oil

1 tablespoon butter or margarine

6 large eggs

Salt and freshly ground pepper

6 Old-Fashioned Buttermilk Biscuits (page 281), made using a large biscuit cutter (3 to 3½ inches in diameter)

6 slices Cheddar cheese, cut to fit biscuits

Form sausage into 6 patties. In a large nonstick skillet over medium-high heat, warm oil. Fry patties until meat is no longer pink in the center, 6 to 7 minutes on each side. Remove to a plate and cover with foil to keep warm.

In the same skillet over medium heat, melt butter. Add eggs and fry until completely set (break the yolks). Season with salt and pepper to taste.

Split biscuits and layer a slice of cheese, a sausage patty, and an egg on the bottom half of each biscuit. Replace biscuit tops. Wrap in a paper napkin. Microwave on high until cheese is melted, about 20 seconds. Serve immediately.

SERVES 4

EGGS ON TOAST WITH TOMATO SAUCE (ITALIAN STYLE)

For a hot brunch sandwich, serve this robust combination of ham, egg, and cheese topped with an herbed tomato sauce. A good sourdough bread is essential.

Quick Tomato Sauce (recipe follows)

2 tablespoons olive oil

1 garlic clove, split

4 thick slices sourdough bread

4 small ham slices

4 large poached eggs (see page 40)

4 tablespoons chopped fresh basil

1 cup grated mozzarella cheese

Basil leaves for garnish

Have Quick Tomato Sauce ready and warm. In a small bowl or jar, mix oil and garlic. Let stand for 10 minutes. Preheat broiler. Place bread on a baking sheet and broil for 2 minutes on one side. Turn and brush with garlic oil. Add a ham slice to each slice of bread and broil for about 1 minute. Keep warm. Poach the eggs.

To assemble, place toast topped with ham on 4 plates. Sprinkle each with 1 tablespoon chopped basil. Spoon warm tomato sauce over each ham slice. Top with an egg and sprinkle with cheese. Place under broiler to melt cheese, about 1 minute. Serve garnished with basil leaves.

1 can (8 ounces) tomato sauce

1 garlic clove, minced

¼ teaspoon dried oregano

¼ teaspoon dried basil

¼ teaspoon salt

Freshly ground pepper

¼ teaspoon sugar

1 tablespoon dry red wine (optional)

QUICK TOMATO SAUCE

Makes about 1 cup

In a small saucepan over high heat, stir together all ingredients and bring to a boil. Reduce heat to low and simmer, uncovered, until flavors are blended, about 5 minutes. Keep warm to serve.

SERVES 4

OPEN-FACE TURKEY STACK

English muffins are layered with scrambled eggs, turkey, tomato, avocado, and melted cheese for a delicious, quick breakfast.

4 English muffins, split

4 large eggs, scrambled (see page 42)

8 slices cooked turkey breast

2 avocados, peeled and sliced

8 thin slices tomato

Salt and freshly ground pepper

8 slices Monterey Jack cheese

Preheat broiler. Place muffin halves on a baking sheet, cut-side down. Broil until toasted, about 2 minutes. Turn and divide scrambled eggs, turkey slices, avocado slices, and tomato slices evenly among the muffin halves. Season with salt and pepper to taste. Top each with a cheese slice. Broil until heated through and cheese is melted, about 2 minutes.

SERVES 1

BLACKBOARD SPECIAL

This is a version of a popular sandwich featured at a local restaurant. It is an open-face take-off on a BLT, with bacon, tomato slices, and cheese topped with a poached egg. This makes one sandwich—multiply it to make as many as you need.

1 large slice sourdough bread

3 thick slices bacon, cooked and drained

2 thin slices plum tomato

Cheddar cheese slices to cover

1 large poached egg (see page 40)

Preheat broiler. Place bread on baking sheet. Broil on one side until toasted, about 2 minutes. Turn and arrange bacon, tomato slices, and cheese over bread. Broil until cheese melts, about 1 minute. Top with poached egg and serve immediately.

SERVES 4

SCRAMBLED EGGS WITH FETA AND DILL IN PITA BREAD

This sandwich is a great blend of savory Greek flavors tucked into pita bread for a take-out breakfast. Serve with plain nonfat yogurt.

- 8 large eggs
- 3 tablespoons water
- 1 plum tomato, chopped
- ¼ cup crumbled feta cheese
- ¼ cup chopped green onions, including some tender green tops
- ¼ teaspoon dried dill weed
- ½ teaspoon salt
- Freshly ground pepper
- 2 tablespoons butter or margarine
- 4 pita or pocket breads, ½ inch cut off the top and warmed (see Note)
- Flat-leaf parsley for garnish
- 8 cherry tomatoes for garnish
- Plain nonfat yogurt as an accompaniment

In a medium bowl, whisk together eggs and water. Add tomato, feta, green onions, dill, salt, and pepper to taste and mix well.

In a large nonstick skillet over medium heat, melt butter. When butter foams, add egg mixture all at once. Let set for 20 seconds. Cook, stirring, until light and fluffy, 3 to 4 minutes. Fill pitas with mixture. Garnish with parsley and cherry tomatoes and serve with a bowl of yogurt.

Note: To warm pita bread, wrap it in foil and place in a 350°F oven for 10 to 15 minutes.

SERVES 4

BREAKFAST BAGEL WITH SMOKED SALMON SPREAD

Smoked salmon blended with cream cheese, tomato, and onions and spread on a bagel is a "fix it fast" breakfast. It also makes a good hors d'oeuvre to serve with drinks (see Note).

6 ounces cream cheese, softened

½ cup chopped and drained tomato

½ cup sliced green onions, including some tender green tops

1 tablespoon capers, drained

4 ounces smoked salmon, flaked

4 bagels, split and lightly toasted

In a medium bowl, mix cream cheese, tomato, green onions, capers, and smoked salmon. Spread on bagel halves.

Note: Cut bagel halves into quarters to serve as an hors d'oeuvre.

SERVES 1

REED'S FRIED-EGG SANDWICH

This is my husband Reed's favorite sandwich for a quick, easy breakfast.

2 teaspoons butter or margarine

1 large egg

Salt and freshly ground pepper

1 mild green chile pepper (canned), split, rinsed, and dried

1 slice Havarti cheese

2 slices white bread, buttered

1 thin slice tomato

In a medium skillet over medium heat, melt butter. Add egg and fry, breaking the yolk. Season with salt and pepper to taste. Cook chile pepper beside egg until warmed, about 2 minutes, turning once. Place cheese slice on top of chile pepper to warm for 1 minute. Place egg on one slice of bread and top with chile pepper, cheese, and tomato slice. Add remaining slice of bread.

These entrées, all made on top of the stove, are easy to prepare. Most of the ingredients are fried together quickly for a one-dish meal with little cleanup. Skillets (or frying pans) come in various sizes. A nonstick skillet is preferred because less fat is needed for sautéing.

SKILLET ENTRÉES

SERVES 8

HUEVOS RANCHEROS (MEXICAN RANCH-STYLE EGGS)

This popular Mexican dish is a favorite with the men. Serve it for a casual brunch with Chunky Guacamole and additional warm tortillas, cold beer, and a side dish of refried beans.

Ranchero Sauce (recipe follows)

8 to 16 large poached eggs (see page 40) or fried eggs (see page 44), depending on whether you want 1 or 2 eggs per tortilla

8 corn tortillas

Salt and freshly ground pepper

2 cups grated Monterey Jack cheese

Sour cream for topping

Sliced ripe olives for garnish

Chunky Guacamole (facing page) as an accompaniment

Refried Beans (facing page) as an accompaniment

Have Ranchero Sauce and eggs ready and warm.

Wrap tortillas (4 at a time) in a napkin or paper towel. Microwave on high for about 10 seconds.

To assemble, place a tortilla on a warm plate. Spread a little Ranchero Sauce over it. Top with 1 or 2 eggs. Season with salt and pepper to taste. Cover with more sauce and sprinkle with some cheese. Top with a little sour cream, garnish with olives, and serve with Chunky Guacamole and Refried Beans.

RANCHERO SAUCE

Makes about 3 cups

2 teaspoons vegetable oil

1 cup chopped yellow onion

2 garlic cloves, minced

1 can (14½ ounces) crushed tomatoes in thick purée

1 small tomato, seeded, chopped, and drained

¾ cup Fresh Tomato Salsa (page 103) or purchased salsa

1 can (4 ounces) diced green chiles, drained

¼ teaspoon dried oregano

¼ teaspoon ground cumin

½ teaspoon salt

Freshly ground pepper

In a medium saucepan over medium heat, warm oil. Add onion and garlic and sauté until tender, about 5 minutes. Reduce heat to medium-low. Add remaining ingredients and simmer, uncovered, until slightly thickened, about 10 minutes.

CHUNKY GUACAMOLE

Enjoy this zesty guacamole with any Mexican entrée or as a dip with tortilla chips.

Makes 2½ cups

- 3 or 4 ripe avocados, halved and pitted
- 1 small tomato, seeded, chopped, and drained
- 2 tablespoons fresh lemon juice
- 1 garlic clove, minced
- 1 teaspoon Worcestershire sauce
- ½ teaspoon salt
- ⅛ teaspoon cayenne pepper
- 1 or 2 drops Tabasco sauce
- 4 green onions, including some tender green tops, finely chopped

With a spoon, scoop the avocado into a medium bowl and mash with a fork. Stir in remaining ingredients and mix well. Cover and refrigerate for several hours.

Note: For a smooth guacamole, purée avocados, lemon juice, and seasonings in a food processor or blender. Fold in tomato and olives and top with green onions.

REFRIED BEANS

Makes about 2¼ cups

- 2 tablespoons butter or lard
- 1 can (14 ounces) pinto beans, drained, rinsed, and coarsely mashed
- ½ cup grated Cheddar cheese
- Grated Parmesan cheese for topping
- Chopped green onions, including some tender green tops, for topping

In a medium skillet over medium heat, melt butter. Add beans and cook for 2 minutes. Add grated Cheddar and stir until it melts. Serve sprinkled with grated Parmesan and green onions.

Note: Canned refried beans may also be used (vegetarian preferred).

SERVES 4 TO 6

SKILLET POTATOES AND EGGS

Who can resist this hearty dish of vegetables, ham, and eggs scrambled together and served with Home Fries (page 255)?

2 to 3 tablespoons vegetable oil

2 cups peeled, cooked, and cubed russet potatoes (about 2 large potatoes)

½ cup diced cooked ham

½ cup chopped yellow onion

½ cup chopped green bell pepper

¼ cup chopped red bell pepper

6 large eggs

2 tablespoons milk

¼ teaspoon salt

Freshly ground pepper

½ cup grated Swiss cheese

¼ cup chopped parsley

In a large skillet over medium heat, warm 2 tablespoons oil. Add potatoes and fry until slightly browned, about 5 minutes. Add ham, onion, and bell peppers and cook until vegetables are tender, about 10 minutes longer. Add more oil, if needed.

In a medium bowl, whisk together eggs, milk, salt, and pepper to taste and pour over potato mixture. Cook, stirring, until eggs are almost done. Stir in cheese and parsley and cook until cheese melts, 1 to 2 minutes longer. Serve immediately.

SERVES 4

RED FLANNEL HASH

This New England hash gets its name from the beets mixed with potatoes and bacon. A bit of sweet potato makes this version different. It is traditionally served with a poached or fried egg on top.

6 slices bacon, diced

⅓ cup chopped red onion

3 cups unpeeled, cooked cubed Yukon Gold potatoes or new potatoes

1 cup cooked, cubed sweet potato

1 cup chopped cooked beets

¼ cup chopped parsley

½ teaspoon salt

Freshly ground pepper

4 large poached eggs (see page 40) or fried eggs (see page 44)

In a large skillet over medium-high heat, cook bacon and onion until bacon is crisp and onion is tender, 6 to 7 minutes. Stir in potatoes, sweet potato, beets, parsley, salt, and pepper to taste and mix well. Flatten with a spatula. Cook until slightly crusty on the bottom, about 4 minutes. Turn and continue to cook 8 to 10 minutes longer. Divide among 4 plates and top each serving with a poached egg.

SERVES 6

VEGETARIAN MEDLEY

This dish with bell pepper, mushrooms, onions, potatoes, and beans is presented in individual gratin dishes and topped with salsa and sour cream for added flavor.

2 tablespoons vegetable oil

1 red bell pepper, seeded and cut into 1-inch pieces

8 ounces mushrooms, sliced

8 green onions, including some tender green tops, sliced

4 cups peeled, cubed, and cooked potatoes (any kind)

1 can (15 ounces) black beans, drained and rinsed

½ teaspoon salt

Freshly ground pepper

About ¾ cup Fresh Tomato Salsa (page 103) or purchased salsa, plus more for topping

¾ cup grated Cheddar cheese

Sour cream for topping

In a large skillet over medium heat, warm oil. Add bell pepper, mushrooms, and green onions and sauté until tender, 6 to 7 minutes. Add potatoes, beans, salt, and pepper to taste and mix well. Cook until flavors are blended, stirring occasionally, about 5 minutes longer.

Preheat broiler. Divide bean-potato mixture evenly among 6 lightly sprayed or oiled ovenproof plates or individual gratin dishes. Spoon about 2 tablespoons of salsa over the top of each, and sprinkle each with 2 tablespoons cheese. Broil until cheese melts, about 2 minutes. Serve topped with sour cream and more salsa.

SERVES 4

COUNTRY BRUNCH SKILLET

Eggs are nestled in a mixture of hash browns, bacon, and vegetables and then topped with cheese in this "down-home" brunch dish.

4 ounces bacon, diced

¼ cup chopped green bell pepper

4 green onions, including some tender green tops, sliced

4 ounces medium mushrooms, sliced

4 cups frozen cubed hash brown potatoes, slightly thawed

4 large eggs

Salt and freshly ground pepper

1 cup grated Cheddar cheese

In a large nonstick skillet over medium-high heat, cook bacon until crisp, about 5 minutes. Remove bacon with a slotted spoon to a plate lined with a paper towel to drain, leaving 2 tablespoons drippings in the skillet. Add bell pepper, green onions, and mushrooms and sauté for 2 minutes. Add hash browns and cook, turning occasionally, until hash browns are tender and browned, 10 to 15 minutes. Stir in bacon. Make 4 indentations (nests) in potatoes. Break an egg into each one. Sprinkle with salt and pepper to taste. Reduce heat to low. Cover and cook until eggs are set, about 10 minutes. Sprinkle with cheese, cover, and let stand until cheese is melted, about 1 minute longer.

SERVES 4

TOFU TOSS

Tofu (soybean curd) is credited with many health benefits. In this vegetarian sauté, the tofu absorbs the peanut sauce, adding a delicious flavor.

1 tablespoon olive oil

4 ounces medium mushrooms, sliced

1 bag (6 ounces) baby spinach, rinsed, drained, and stemmed, if desired

1 pound tofu, cut into ½-inch cubes

¼ cup purchased Thai peanut sauce (see Note)

¼ teaspoon salt

Freshly ground pepper

1 tomato, seeded, chopped, and drained

Chopped peanuts for topping

In a large skillet over medium heat, warm oil. Add mushrooms and sauté for 3 minutes. Add spinach and toss until wilted, about 2 minutes. Add tofu, peanut sauce, salt, pepper to taste, and tomato and toss until flavors are blended, 2 to 3 minutes. Sprinkle with peanuts and serve immediately.

Note: Thai peanut sauce can be purchased in the Asian section of most supermarkets.

SERVES 6

SALMON-LEEK HASH

Fresh salmon combined with crisp potatoes, leeks, and a touch of dill, and then topped with poached eggs makes a significant entrée. Serve with Blueberry Drop Scones (page 289).

- 2 russet potatoes (about 1¼ pounds), peeled and quartered
- 1 tablespoon butter or margarine
- 1½ tablespoons vegetable oil
- 2 leeks, white and pale green parts only, chopped
- ½ cup chopped red bell pepper
- 1½ cups cooked, flaked fresh salmon (see Note)
- ½ teaspoon dried dill weed
- ½ teaspoon salt
- Freshly ground pepper
- 2 tablespoons chopped parsley
- 6 large poached eggs (see page 40)

Place potatoes in a medium saucepan over high heat with 1 cup salted water, and bring to a boil. Reduce heat to medium-low, cover, and cook until almost tender, about 15 minutes. Cool under cold water and drain. Cut into ½-inch cubes. In a large nonstick skillet over medium heat, melt butter with oil. Add potatoes, leeks, and bell pepper and cook, uncovered, until potatoes start to brown, 5 to 6 minutes. Stir in salmon, dill, salt, pepper to taste, and parsley. Cook until potatoes are browned, about 5 minutes longer. Top each serving with a poached egg.

Note: Canned salmon may be used. Drain and remove the dark parts.

SERVES 4

OYSTER HASH

Fried oysters are mingled with potatoes and vegetables and topped with a poached egg for a traditional dish. Serve it with sliced tomato wedges sprinkled with coarse pepper.

4 large new red potatoes (about 2 pounds), unpeeled, quartered

2 to 3 tablespoons vegetable oil

8 green onions, including some tender green tops, sliced

½ cup diced red bell pepper

½ teaspoon dried thyme

1 teaspoon salt, divided

Freshly ground pepper

¼ cup all-purpose flour

1 pound shucked oysters, rinsed and drained on a paper towel

3 tablespoons butter or margarine

4 large poached eggs (see page 40)

Chopped parsley for garnish

Tomato wedges as an accompaniment

Place potatoes in a medium saucepan over high heat with ½ cup salted water and bring to a boil. Reduce heat to medium-low and cook, covered, until almost tender, about 15 minutes. Cool under cold water and drain. Cut into ½-inch cubes.

In a large nonstick skillet over medium-high heat, warm 2 tablespoons oil. Add potatoes, green onions, bell pepper, thyme, ½ teaspoon salt, and pepper to taste and cook until potatoes are browned and vegetables are tender, about 10 minutes, stirring occasionally. Add more oil, if needed. Keep warm on low heat.

Meanwhile, place flour and remaining ½ teaspoon salt on a piece of waxed paper. Dredge oysters in mixture to lightly coat. In another medium skillet over medium heat, melt butter. Add oysters and sauté until browned and edges begin to curl, 4 to 5 minutes, turning occasionally. Combine with potato mixture and mix gently. Divide hash evenly among 4 plates and top each serving with a poached egg. Sprinkle with chopped parsley and serve with tomato wedges.

SERVES 4

CORNED BEEF HASH WITH POACHED EGGS

This classic "blue-plate special" is perfect for those with a hearty appetite. Corned beef is the traditional meat used in hash, but you can also use other leftover meat. Serve with a poached egg on top.

2 large russet potatoes (about 1½ pounds), peeled and quartered

1 cup chopped yellow onion

1 garlic clove, minced

½ pound corned beef or other cooked meat, finely diced

¼ cup chopped parsley

½ teaspoon salt

Freshly ground pepper

2 to 3 tablespoons vegetable oil

1 tablespoon butter or margarine

4 large poached eggs (see page 40)

Place potatoes in a medium saucepan over high heat with 1 cup salted water and bring to a boil. Reduce heat to medium-low and cook, covered, until almost tender, about 15 minutes. Cool under cold water and drain. Cut into ½-inch cubes (you should have about 4 cups).

In a large bowl, mix potatoes, onion, garlic, meat, parsley, and salt, and sprinkle generously with pepper.

In a large nonstick skillet over medium-low heat, warm 2 tablespoons oil with butter. Add potato-meat mixture and spread over bottom of skillet. Press down with a spatula, cover, and cook until mixture is crusty on the bottom, about 10 minutes. Flip hash over and press down. Add more oil, if needed. Cook, uncovered, until the other side is browned and crusty, about 5 minutes longer.

Divide hash evenly among 4 plates and top each serving with a poached egg.

SERVES 4

HANGTOWN FRY

There are many stories about how this dish got its name. Some say it is named after a rowdy town in California (now Placerville) during the gold rush days. Another legend is that a miner who struck it rich went to a saloon and ordered a breakfast "worth its weight in gold." The cook came up with the most expensive ingredients in the kitchen. In this version, the oysters are lightly breaded and pan-fried and then folded into fluffy scrambled eggs.

6 slices bacon, diced

¼ cup all-purpose flour

¼ cup yellow cornmeal

1 teaspoon coarse salt

Freshly ground pepper

16 fresh shucked oysters, drained and dried

8 large eggs

¼ cup milk

In a large skillet over medium heat, cook bacon until crisp, about 5 minutes. Remove bacon with a slotted spoon to a plate lined with a paper towel to drain, leaving 2 tablespoons drippings in the skillet. On a piece of waxed paper, mix flour, cornmeal, salt, and pepper to taste. Dredge oysters in mixture, shaking off excess. Fry oysters in bacon drippings until firm and golden, 4 to 5 minutes, turning once.

In a medium bowl, whisk together eggs and milk. Pour over oysters and cook, stirring gently, until eggs are set, about 2 minutes. Sprinkle with bacon and serve immediately.

FRENCH TOAST

French toast is a quick breakfast treat that is simple to make and is always delicious. Enjoy the variations and different toppings, fillings, and sauces you will find in this chapter.

The French call it *pain perdu,* or lost (stale) bread, and see it as a way of reviving bread that has become dry. We call it French toast, in honor of its origin.

French toast is made by dipping bread into an egg-milk mixture and then frying the soaked bread until golden brown on both sides. It is served with various toppings, such as butter, syrup, honey, confectioners' sugar, berry preserves, sautéed fruit, or brown sugar.

TIPS FOR MAKING FRENCH TOAST

- Use day-old bread, or air-dry bread for several hours on the counter or in a warm oven. Fresh bread absorbs too much of the egg mixture and will lose its shape and become soggy. You can use any type of bread: white, sourdough, rye, whole wheat, raisin, challah, French, and so on.
- Dip both sides of the bread thoroughly in the batter.
- Transfer the bread to a piece of waxed paper or a plate until all slices have been dipped.
- Preheat a nonstick skillet or griddle to medium or medium-high heat, depending on the stove.
- Add butter and cook quickly until crisp and lightly browned on both sides.
- Serve immediately or keep warm in a warm oven.
- Pass the toppings separately.

MAKES 6 SLICES

BASIC FRENCH TOAST

Follow this simple recipe for delicious French toast every time. Serve it with syrup, jam, or honey.

3 large eggs

⅔ cup half-and-half or milk

Dash of salt

6 slices day-old bread of your choice

2 tablespoons butter, margarine, or vegetable oil, divided

In a large, shallow bowl, whisk together eggs, half-and-half, and salt. Dip each slice of bread in egg mixture, turning to coat, and place on a large piece of waxed paper.

Preheat a large nonstick skillet or griddle over medium heat. Add 1 tablespoon butter and swirl to coat the skillet. When butter foams, add 3 slices of bread and cook until lightly browned, about 3 minutes on each side, turning once. Remove from skillet and keep warm. Add remaining tablespoon of butter to skillet and repeat with remaining bread. Serve with toppings of your choice.

MAKES 6 SLICES

FRENCH TOAST WITH GRAHAM CRACKER CRUST

This delicious French toast has a sweet and crunchy coating. It is one of the best!

3 large eggs

⅔ cup milk

Dash of salt

1 cup crushed graham crackers (about 6 squares)

6 slices day-old bread of your choice

2 tablespoons butter, margarine, or vegetable oil, divided

In a large, shallow bowl, whisk together eggs, milk, and salt. Place cracker crumbs on a piece of waxed paper or on a plate. Dip each slice of bread in egg mixture, turning to coat, and then coat with cracker crumbs. Place on a piece of waxed paper.

Preheat a large nonstick skillet or griddle over medium heat. Add 1 tablespoon butter and swirl to coat the skillet. When butter foams, add 3 slices of bread and cook until lightly browned, about 3 minutes on each side, turning once. Remove from skillet and keep warm. Add remaining 1 tablespoon of butter to skillet and repeat with remaining bread. Serve with toppings of your choice.

VARIATION

Substitute 1 cup crushed cornflakes for the graham crackers.

MAKES 6 SLICES

SWEET SPICED FRENCH TOAST

For variety, add a little spice and sweetness to your French toast. It is so good, you don't need syrup. Serve with Oven-Baked Pepper Bacon (page 240).

3 large eggs

½ cup milk

⅓ cup maple syrup

½ teaspoon vanilla extract

¼ teaspoon ground cinnamon

Dash of ground nutmeg

Dash of ground cloves

½ teaspoon sugar

6 slices day-old bread of your choice

1 to 2 tablespoons butter, margarine, or vegetable oil, divided

In a large, shallow bowl, whisk together eggs, milk, syrup, vanilla, cinnamon, nutmeg, cloves, and sugar. Dip each slice of bread in egg mixture, turning to coat, and place on a piece of waxed paper.

Preheat a large nonstick skillet or griddle over medium heat. Add 1 tablespoon butter and swirl to coat the skillet. Add 3 slices of bread and cook until lightly browned, about 3 minutes on each side, turning once. Add remaining tablespoon of butter and repeat with remaining bread. Serve with toppings of your choice.

MAKES 8 SLICES

PEANUT BUTTER AND HONEY FILLED FRENCH TOAST

Cut a pocket in thickly sliced bread, and then spread the pocket with peanut butter and honey before frying.

- 3 tablespoons chunky peanut butter, at room temperature
- 2 tablespoons honey
- 8 slices day-old country-style bread, cut 1 inch thick
- 6 large eggs
- 2 cups milk
- 2 to 3 tablespoons butter, margarine, or vegetable oil, divided

In a small bowl, blend together peanut butter and honey. Lay bread slices on a flat surface. With a serrated bread knife, slice bread horizontally, leaving it connected at the end, to form a pocket. Spread peanut butter–honey mixture in the pockets on one side.

In a large, shallow bowl, whisk together eggs and milk. Dip each slice of stuffed bread in egg mixture, turning to coat, and place on a piece of waxed paper.

Preheat a large nonstick skillet or griddle over medium heat. Add 1 tablespoon butter and swirl to coat the skillet. When butter foams, add 3 slices of bread and cook until lightly browned, about 3 minutes on each side, turning once. Remove from skillet and keep warm. Add remaining butter to skillet and repeat with remaining bread. Serve immediately with toppings of your choice.

MAKES 9 OR 10 SLICES

BANANA-NUT STUFFED FRENCH TOAST

French toast is always a favorite. This version, with pockets stuffed with banana slices and walnuts, is simple to make but impressive. Serve with crisp bacon or Sausage Patties (page 247).

1 large loaf day-old French bread, unsliced

2 bananas, sliced

¼ cup coarsely chopped walnuts

¼ cup packed brown sugar

4 large eggs

¾ cup milk

1 teaspoon vanilla extract

2 tablespoons butter, margarine, or vegetable oil, divided

Slice the end off the bread and discard. Cut the next slice ½ inch thick and only three fourths of the way through the loaf, forming a pocket, and cut the next ½-inch slice all the way through. Continue to do this until all the bread is sliced (you'll have 9 or 10 slices). Lay 3 slices of banana, 1 teaspoon walnuts, and 2 teaspoons brown sugar in each pocket.

In a large, shallow bowl, whisk together eggs, milk, and vanilla. Dip each slice of stuffed bread in egg mixture, turning to coat, and place on a piece of waxed paper.

Preheat a large nonstick skillet or griddle over medium heat. Add 1 tablespoon butter and swirl to coat the skillet. When butter foams, add as many bread slices as will fit and cook until lightly browned, about 3 minutes on each side, turning once. Remove from skillet and keep warm. Add remaining butter to skillet and repeat with remaining bread. Serve with toppings of your choice.

MAKES 9 OR 10 SLICES

FRENCH TOAST WITH ORANGE CREAM FILLING

When you're entertaining, you want to serve something special and delicious. This filled French toast fits the bill perfectly.

- 4 ounces light cream cheese, at room temperature
- 1 tablespoon orange juice
- 2 tablespoons sugar, divided
- 1 teaspoon grated orange zest
- 1 large loaf day-old French bread, unsliced
- 4 large eggs
- 1 cup milk
- 1 teaspoon vanilla extract
- 2 tablespoons butter, margarine, or vegetable oil, divided
- Orange marmalade for topping

In a small bowl, mix together cream cheese, orange juice, 1 tablespoon sugar, and zest until blended.

Slice the end off the bread and discard. Cut next slice ½ inch thick and only three fourths of the way through the loaf, forming a pocket, and cut the next ½-inch slice all the way through. Continue to do this until all of the bread is sliced (you'll have 9 or 10 slices). Spread about 1 tablespoon of filling in each pocket, then press together.

In a large, shallow bowl, whisk together eggs, milk, remaining 1 tablespoon sugar, and vanilla. Dip each slice of stuffed bread in batter, turning to coat, and place on a piece of waxed paper until all slices are coated.

Preheat a large nonstick skillet or griddle over medium heat. Add 1 tablespoon butter and swirl to coat the skillet. When butter foams, add as many bread slices as will fit and cook until lightly browned, about 3 minutes on each side, turning once. Remove from skillet and keep warm. Add remaining butter to skillet and repeat with remaining bread. Serve topped with orange marmalade.

MAKES 6 PIECES

CROISSANT FRENCH TOAST WITH ORANGE SAUCE

For variety this recipe calls for croissants instead of bread. This delicate breakfast is perfect topped with Orange Sauce.

6 large eggs

¾ cup milk

1 teaspoon ground cinnamon

1 teaspoon vanilla extract

6 large croissants, split

2 to 3 tablespoons butter, margarine, or vegetable oil, divided

Orange Sauce (recipe follows) for topping

In a large, shallow bowl, whisk together eggs, milk, cinnamon, and vanilla. Dip each croissant half in egg mixture, turning to coat, and place on a piece of waxed paper.

Preheat a large nonstick skillet or griddle over medium heat. Add 1 tablespoon butter and swirl to coat the skillet. When butter foams, add as many croissants as will fit and cook until lightly browned, about 2 minutes on each side, turning once. Remove from skillet and keep warm. Add remaining butter to skillet and repeat with remaining croissant halves. Serve topped with Orange Sauce.

ORANGE SAUCE

Makes about 1 cup

1 cup orange juice

1 tablespoon cornstarch

¼ cup sugar

1 tablespoon butter or margarine

1 teaspoon grated orange zest

In a small saucepan over medium-high heat, whisk together orange juice, cornstarch, and sugar until thickened, about 3 minutes, stirring constantly. Remove from heat and stir in butter and zest. Serve warm.

MAKES 8 SLICES

SPICED OVERNIGHT FRENCH TOAST

First one up in the morning slips this baked French toast in the oven for an easy company breakfast. Your guests will love the warm flavor of the spices. Serve a Citrus Cooler (page 20) while it is baking.

8 slices day-old French bread, cut 1 inch thick

6 large eggs

2 cups milk

1 tablespoon firmly packed brown sugar

1 teaspoon ground cinnamon

⅛ teaspoon ground cloves

⅛ teaspoon ground nutmeg

1 teaspoon vanilla extract

3 tablespoons butter or margarine, cut into small pieces

Arrange bread in one layer in a buttered 9-by-13-inch baking dish. In a medium bowl, whisk eggs. Add milk, brown sugar, spices, and vanilla and whisk until blended. Pour mixture over bread. Let stand for 1 minute. Turn each bread slice over. Cover with foil and refrigerate overnight. Bring to room temperature before baking.

Preheat oven to 350°F. Dot each slice of bread with 3 to 4 small pieces of butter. Bake, uncovered, until lightly browned, 45 to 50 minutes. Let stand for 5 minutes before serving. Serve with toppings of your choice.

MAKES 8 SLICES

BAKED BLUEBERRY FRENCH TOAST WITH BLUEBERRY-MAPLE SYRUP

Cream cheese adds a creamy texture to this French toast, and the berry sauce makes it even more appealing. Beat the time crunch by assembling this the night before and baking it in the morning.

8 slices (1 inch thick) day-old egg bread or French bread

1 cup fresh or frozen blueberries, thawed if frozen, rinsed and dried

8 ounces cream cheese, cubed

12 large eggs

2 cups milk

½ teaspoon salt

¼ cup maple syrup

Blueberry-Maple Syrup (page 201) for topping

Arrange bread in a lightly sprayed or oiled 9-by-13-inch baking dish. Sprinkle with blueberries and cream cheese cubes.

In a large bowl, whisk together eggs, milk, salt, and syrup, and pour over bread. Cover and refrigerate for several hours or overnight. Bring to room temperature before baking.

Preheat oven to 350°F. Bake, covered, for 30 minutes. Remove cover and bake until lightly browned on top, about 30 minutes longer. Serve with Blueberry-Maple Syrup.

MAKES 6 SLICES

FRENCH TOAST BAKE WITH STRAWBERRY-CREAM CHEESE SPREAD

You'll enjoy every bite of these filled French bread sandwiches baked in a sweet custard sauce. Be sure to allow a few hours for the bread to soak, or assemble it the night before. Serve with Sausage Patties (page 247).

- 2 ounces light cream cheese
- 12 slices day-old white bread
- ½ cup strawberry jam
- 4 large eggs
- ¾ cup milk
- 2 tablespoons sugar
- ¼ teaspoon salt
- 3 tablespoons melted butter
- 1 cup whole strawberries for garnish

Spread cream cheese on 6 slices of bread. Spread jam on remaining 6 slices and put the strawberry and cream cheese slices together, forming 6 sandwiches. Arrange sandwiches in a single layer in a lightly sprayed or oiled 9-by-13-inch baking dish.

In a medium bowl, whisk together eggs, milk, sugar, salt, and melted butter. Pour over sandwiches, and turn to coat. Cover and refrigerate for several hours or overnight. Bring to room temperature before baking.

Preheat oven to 350°F. Bake, uncovered, until lightly browned, 35 to 40 minutes. Serve garnished with fresh strawberries.

VARIATION

Orange Marmalade French Toast

Substitute orange marmalade for the strawberry jam. Garnish with orange slices instead of strawberries.

MAKES 8 SLICES

STICKY BUN FRENCH TOAST

This upside-down toast with a caramelized nut layer is delicious and easy to make. Serve it with Oven-Baked Pepper Bacon (page 240).

½ cup butter or margarine

1 cup packed brown sugar

2 tablespoons light corn syrup

½ cup coarsely chopped pecans

8 slices (1 inch thick) day-old French bread

6 large eggs

1½ cups milk

1 teaspoon vanilla extract

1 teaspoon ground cinnamon

Dash of ground nutmeg

In a medium saucepan over medium heat, melt butter with brown sugar. Add syrup and stir constantly until thickened, about 2 minutes. Stir in nuts. Pour into a 9-by-13-inch baking dish. Arrange bread on top in one layer.

In a medium bowl, whisk together eggs, milk, vanilla, cinnamon, and nutmeg until well blended. Pour over bread. Cover and refrigerate for several hours or overnight. Bring dish to room temperature before baking.

Preheat oven to 350°F. Bake, uncovered, until golden on top and crispy around the edges, 50 to 55 minutes. Let set for 5 minutes. To serve, remove each slice with a spatula and invert onto a plate.

PANCAKES

The versatile pancake has many variations and can be served as an appetizer, entrée, or dessert. There's no need to use a mix when you can make these easy recipes that will suit every taste.

Pancakes are made from a batter poured onto a hot griddle or skillet. One of the most popular foods for breakfast, they can also be served for lunch or supper. Pancakes vary in thickness from thin and delicate (crêpes) to thick and heavy (flapjacks). They are typically served with toppings, such as butter, syrup, honey, preserves, confectioners' sugar, lemon juice, cinnamon, flavored yogurt, jam, sautéed fruit, and berry purées.

TIPS FOR MAKING PANCAKES

- Do not overmix the batter.
- Use a nonstick skillet or griddle.
- Preheat the skillet or griddle and spray with vegetable spray or brush lightly with vegetable oil.
- For each pancake, pour on the amount of batter called for in the recipe.
- Use a spatula with a nonstick coating to turn the pancakes.
- Turn the pancakes when bubbles form on the surface. Turn them only once.
- Serve pancakes immediately, or keep them warm in the oven until ready to serve.
- Wipe the griddle with a paper towel before putting it away

For variety and flavor, be creative with this basic recipe by adding fruit, nuts, seasonings, or flavorings.

- 1½ cups all-purpose flour
- 2 tablespoons sugar
- 2 teaspoons baking powder
- ½ teaspoon salt
- 2 large eggs
- 1½ cups milk
- 3 tablespoons melted butter or vegetable oil

In a large bowl, combine flour, sugar, baking powder, and salt. In a medium bowl, whisk together eggs, milk, and melted butter. Add to dry ingredients and whisk until just blended.

Preheat a nonstick griddle or skillet over medium-high heat. Lightly spray or brush with vegetable oil. Pour ¼ cup batter onto griddle for each pancake. Cook until bubbles form on top, about 2 minutes. Turn and cook until other side is golden, about 1 minute longer. Serve with the toppings of your choice.

MAKES 10 TO 12 PANCAKES

SOUR CREAM PANCAKES

These are so light and tender that the friend who gave me this recipe calls them "fly off the plate" pancakes. Blueberry-Maple Syrup makes a nice topping.

1 cup all-purpose flour

¼ teaspoon salt

1 tablespoon brown sugar

1 tablespoon baking powder

1 large egg

1 cup milk

3 tablespoons sour cream

1 tablespoon melted butter

Blueberry-Maple Syrup (recipe follows) for topping

In a medium bowl, combine flour, salt, brown sugar, and baking powder. In a large bowl, whisk together egg, milk, and sour cream. Whisk in dry ingredients. Add melted butter and whisk until just blended.

Preheat a nonstick griddle or skillet over medium-high heat. Lightly spray or brush with vegetable oil. Pour ¼ cup batter onto griddle for each pancake. Cook until bubbles form on the surface, about 2 minutes. Turn and cook until other side is golden, 1 minute longer. Serve with Blueberry-Maple Syrup.

BLUEBERRY-MAPLE SYRUP

Makes about 1½ cups

½ cup maple syrup

1 cup fresh or frozen blueberries, thawed if frozen, rinsed

In a small saucepan over medium-high heat, bring syrup to a boil. Add blueberries. Reduce heat to low and simmer until slightly thickened, about 2 minutes.

MAKES ABOUT 16 PANCAKES

BLUEBERRY BUTTERMILK PANCAKES

Blueberries add a surprise burst of sweet flavor in these pancakes. Enjoy them in the summer when blueberries are in season, or use frozen berries any time of the year.

2 cups all-purpose flour

2 tablespoons packed brown sugar

2 teaspoons baking powder

½ teaspoon baking soda

½ teaspoon salt

2 large eggs

2 cups buttermilk

3 tablespoons vegetable oil

1 cup fresh or frozen blueberries, thawed if frozen, rinsed and dried

In a medium bowl, combine flour, brown sugar, baking powder, baking soda, and salt. In a large bowl, whisk together eggs, buttermilk, and oil. Add dry ingredients and whisk until just blended.

Preheat a nonstick griddle or skillet over medium-high heat. Lightly spray or brush with oil. Pour ¼ cup batter onto griddle for each pancake. Scatter a few blueberries on top of each pancake. Cook until bubbles form on the surface, about 2 minutes. Turn and cook until other side is golden, about 1 minute longer. Serve with toppings of your choice.

SPICED WHOLE-WHEAT PANCAKES WITH NUTS

These nutritious whole-wheat pancakes have a lively flavor and crunchy texture. The warm Honey-Cinnamon Topping rounds out the wholesome taste.

2 cups whole-wheat flour

1 tablespoon baking powder

1 teaspoon ground coriander

1 teaspoon ground cinnamon

¼ teaspoon ground nutmeg

½ teaspoon salt

3 large eggs

2 cups milk

¼ cup vegetable oil

3 tablespoons honey

¼ cup chopped walnuts or pecans

Honey-Cinnamon Topping (recipe follows) for topping

In a large bowl, combine flour, baking powder, spices, and salt. In a medium bowl, whisk together eggs, milk, oil, and honey. Add to dry ingredients and mix well. Fold in nuts.

Preheat a nonstick griddle or skillet over medium-high heat. Lightly spray or brush with vegetable oil. Pour ¼ cup batter onto griddle for each pancake. Cook until bubbles form on the surface, about 2 minutes. Turn and cook until other side is golden, about 1 minute longer. Serve with Honey-Cinnamon Topping.

HONEY-CINNAMON TOPPING

Makes ½ cup

½ cup honey

¼ teaspoon ground cinnamon

1 tablespoon butter

In a small saucepan over low heat, combine honey and cinnamon. Stir for 1 minute. Add butter and stir until melted. Serve warm.

MAKES 10 TO 12 PANCAKES

CHOCOLATE CHIP PANCAKES

Kids love these pancakes that include one of their favorite ingredients.

1¼ cups all-purpose flour

1 tablespoon sugar

2 teaspoons baking powder

¼ teaspoon salt

2 large eggs

1 cup milk

3 tablespoons vegetable oil

½ teaspoon vanilla extract

½ cup mini chocolate chips

In a large bowl, combine flour, sugar, baking powder, and salt. In a medium bowl, whisk together eggs, milk, oil, and vanilla. Add to dry ingredients and mix well.

Preheat a nonstick griddle or skillet over medium-high heat. Lightly spray or brush with vegetable oil. Pour ¼ cup batter onto griddle for each pancake. Scatter about 10 chocolate chips on top of each pancake. Cook until bubbles form on the surface, about 2 minutes. Turn and cook until golden on other side, about 1 minute longer. Serve with toppings of your choice.

MAKES ABOUT 12 PANCAKES

THREE-SPOT BANANA BUTTERMILK PANCAKES

The bananas in these pancakes not only provide extra flavor but add an interesting design on top.

¾ cup all-purpose flour

⅓ cup whole-wheat flour

1 tablespoon brown sugar

1½ teaspoons baking powder

½ teaspoon baking soda

¼ teaspoon salt

1 large egg

1½ cups buttermilk

3 tablespoons melted butter or margarine or vegetable oil

2 ripe bananas, sliced

In a large bowl, combine flours, brown sugar, baking powder, baking soda, and salt. In a medium bowl, whisk together egg, buttermilk, and melted butter. Add to dry ingredients and whisk until blended.

Preheat a nonstick griddle or skillet over medium-high heat. Lightly spray or brush with vegetable oil. Pour ¼ cup batter onto griddle for each pancake. Place 3 banana slices on each pancake and press lightly into batter. Cook until bubbles form on the surface, about 2 minutes. Turn and cook until golden on other side, about 1 minute longer. Serve with toppings of your choice.

MAKES ABOUT 16 PANCAKES

PUMPKIN PANCAKES

Serve these orange, allspice-scented pancakes for a fall breakfast with Fresh Pork Sausage Links (page 250) and Apple-Orange Fruit Compote (page 313).

- 1 cup all-purpose flour
- ¼ cup yellow cornmeal
- 2 tablespoons sugar
- 1 teaspoon ground allspice
- ½ teaspoon salt
- 1⅓ cups milk
- ¾ cup canned pumpkin
- 3 large eggs, separated
- 3 tablespoons melted butter
- ½ teaspoon vanilla extract

In a large bowl, combine flour, cornmeal, sugar, allspice, and salt. In a medium bowl, whisk together milk, pumpkin, egg yolks, melted butter, and vanilla. Add pumpkin mixture to dry ingredients and whisk until smooth. In a medium bowl with an electric mixer, beat egg whites until peaks form. Fold into batter.

Preheat nonstick griddle or skillet over medium-high heat. Lightly spray or brush with vegetable oil. Pour ¼ cup batter onto griddle for each pancake. Cook until bubbles form on the surface, about 2 minutes. Turn and cook until golden on the other side, 1 minute longer. Serve with toppings of your choice.

MAKES ABOUT 10 PANCAKES

GRANOLA PANCAKES

Granola adds a chewy texture and an earthy flavor to these pancakes. Serve them with warm honey or syrup.

1¼ cups all-purpose flour

1 tablespoon sugar

1 tablespoon baking powder

½ teaspoon baking soda

¼ teaspoon salt

2 large eggs

1½ to 1¾ cups buttermilk

3 tablespoons melted butter

1 cup granola

In a large bowl, combine flour, sugar, baking powder, baking soda, and salt. In a medium bowl, whisk together eggs, 1½ cups buttermilk, and melted butter. Add to dry ingredients and whisk until just blended. Stir in granola. Add more buttermilk if batter seems too thick.

Preheat a nonstick griddle or skillet over medium-high heat. Lightly spray or brush with vegetable oil. Pour ¼ cup batter onto griddle for each pancake. Cook until bubbles form on top, about 2 minutes. Turn and cook until golden on the other side, about 1 minute longer. Serve with toppings of your choice.

MAKES ABOUT 10 PANCAKES

SPICED ORANGE PANCAKES

When it comes to flavor, these pancakes topped with orange marmalade can't be beat. The spices blend with the orange for a memorable breakfast.

1¼ cups all-purpose flour

1 tablespoon sugar

1 teaspoon baking powder

½ teaspoon ground ginger

⅛ teaspoon ground cloves

Dash of ground nutmeg

¼ teaspoon salt

1¼ cups orange juice

1 large egg

2 tablespoons melted butter or margarine

1 teaspoon grated orange zest

½ teaspoon vanilla extract

Orange marmalade for topping

In a large bowl, combine flour, sugar, baking powder, spices, and salt. In a small bowl, whisk together orange juice, egg, melted butter, orange zest, and vanilla. Add to dry ingredients and mix well.

Preheat a nonstick griddle or skillet over medium-high heat. Lightly spray or brush with vegetable oil. Pour ¼ cup batter onto griddle for each pancake. Cook until bubbles form on surface, about 2 minutes. Turn and cook until golden on other side, about 1 minute longer. Serve topped with orange marmalade.

MAKES ABOUT 16 PANCAKES

AUTUMN PANCAKES

These chewy oatmeal pancakes have apples and nuts added for flavor and crunch. Serve with real maple syrup.

Place oatmeal in a small bowl. Pour boiling water over and let stand for 5 minutes. Do not drain.

In a large bowl, combine flour, baking powder, salt, sugar, and cinnamon. Add oatmeal, egg, milk, apple, nuts, and melted butter and mix well.

Preheat a large nonstick skillet or griddle over medium-high heat. Lightly spray or brush with vegetable oil. Pour ¼ cup batter onto griddle for each pancake. Cook until bubbles form on the surface, about 2 minutes. Turn and cook until golden on the other side, about 1 minute longer. Serve with toppings of your choice.

½ cup quick oatmeal

1½ cups boiling water

1½ cups all-purpose flour

2 teaspoons baking powder

⅛ teaspoon salt

3 tablespoons sugar

½ teaspoon ground cinnamon

1 large egg, beaten

1 cup milk

1 large apple, peeled, cored, and coarsely chopped

¼ cup chopped walnuts

3 tablespoons melted butter

MAKES ABOUT 10 PANCAKES

COTTAGE CHEESE AND YOGURT PANCAKES

Calories are reduced in these light and fluffy pancakes by using low-fat ingredients. Top with sugarless jam and enjoy an almost guilt-free meal.

1 cup all-purpose flour

1 teaspoon baking powder

¼ teaspoon baking soda

2 large eggs

¾ cup low-fat cottage cheese

½ cup plain nonfat yogurt

¾ cup skim milk

2 tablespoons vegetable oil

In a large bowl, combine flour, baking powder, and baking soda. In a medium bowl, whisk together eggs, cottage cheese, yogurt, milk, and oil. Add to dry mixture and mix until blended.

Preheat a nonstick griddle or skillet over medium-high heat. Lightly spray or brush with vegetable oil. Pour ¼ cup batter onto griddle for each pancake. Cook until bubbles form on the surface, about 2 minutes. Turn and cook until golden on the other side, about 1 minute longer. Serve with toppings of your choice.

MAKES ABOUT 9 PANCAKES

SPECIAL-OCCASION PANCAKES

For birthdays and holidays, serve these light and airy pancakes. They take longer to prepare, but they make breakfast festive.

4 large eggs, separated

1 cup all-purpose flour

2 tablespoons sugar

¼ teaspoon salt

1 cup milk

3 tablespoons sour cream

¼ cup melted butter or margarine

In a large bowl, using an electric mixer, beat egg yolks until lemony in color. In a medium bowl, combine flour, sugar, and salt. Add yolks. Add milk, sour cream, and melted butter and mix well. In a medium bowl, with clean beaters in the mixer, beat egg whites until soft peaks form. Fold into batter.

Preheat a nonstick griddle or skillet over medium-high heat. Lightly spray or brush with vegetable oil. Pour ¼ cup batter onto griddle for each pancake. Cook until bubbles form on top, about 2 minutes. Turn and cook until golden on the other side, about 1 minute longer. Serve with toppings of your choice.

MAKES ABOUT 10 PANCAKES

JIFFY BUTTERMILK PANCAKES

For a quick breakfast, you can't beat these fluffy pancakes made in minutes in the food processor or blender.

1 large egg

1 cup buttermilk

1 cup all-purpose flour

1 teaspoon baking powder

½ teaspoon baking soda

2 tablespoons vegetable oil

½ teaspoon salt

Honey for topping (see Note)

Place egg and buttermilk in a food processor or blender and process for 20 seconds. Add flour, baking powder, baking soda, oil, and salt and process for 1 minute longer.

Preheat a nonstick griddle or skillet over medium-high heat. Lightly spray or brush with vegetable oil. Pour ¼ cup batter onto griddle for each pancake. Cook until bubbles form on the surface, about 2 minutes. Turn and cook until golden on the other side, 1 minute longer. Serve with warm honey or syrup.

Note: Warm the honey in the microwave for a few seconds and it will pour like syrup.

MAKES ABOUT 40 SMALL PANCAKES

SWEDISH PANCAKES

Swedish pancakes are smaller and thinner than other pancakes. They are made in a special pan called a plett, but can also be made in a skillet. For a traditional Swedish treat, serve with Fresh Lingonberry Sauce.

3 large eggs

1 cup half-and-half or milk, divided

1 cup all-purpose flour

6 tablespoons melted butter or margarine

½ teaspoon salt

Fresh Lingonberry Sauce (recipe follows) for topping

In a medium bowl, using an electric mixer, beat eggs and ½ cup half-and-half for about 2 minutes. Add flour and beat until smooth. Stir in remaining ½ cup half-and-half, melted butter, and salt.

Preheat a nonstick griddle or skillet over medium-high heat. Lightly spray or brush with vegetable oil. Pour 1 tablespoon batter onto griddle for each pancake. Cook until bubbles form on the surface, about 1 minute. Turn and cook until golden on the other side, about 1 minute longer. Reduce heat, if necessary, to keep them from getting too brown. Serve with Fresh Lingonberry Sauce.

FRESH LINGONBERRY SAUCE

Makes about 2¼ cups

Lingonberries are a small, tart red berry, a member of the *Vaccinium* genus (the same genus as blueberries and cranberries). They are traditionally served with Swedish pancakes. This sauce will jell up when cold, so plan on serving it at room temperature.

3 cups lingonberries, sorted and rinsed

1¼ cups sugar

1 cup water

In a medium saucepan over high heat, combine all ingredients. Bring to a boil. Reduce heat to medium-low and simmer, uncovered, for 10 minutes, stirring occasionally. Cool, cover, and refrigerate. Bring to room temperature to serve.

MAKES ABOUT 16 PANCAKES

THREE-GRAIN PANCAKES

These pancakes, high in fiber and sweetened with honey, are tasty as well as healthful.

1 cup all-purpose flour

½ cup whole-wheat flour

2 tablespoons cornmeal

1 tablespoon oat bran

1 teaspoon baking powder

½ teaspoon ground cinnamon

½ teaspoon salt

1 large egg

1⅔ cups milk

3 tablespoons honey

1 teaspoon vanilla extract

In a medium bowl, combine flours, cornmeal, oat bran, baking powder, cinnamon, and salt. In a large bowl, whisk egg. Add milk, honey, and vanilla and mix well. Add dry ingredients and mix well.

Preheat a nonstick griddle or skillet over medium-high heat. Lightly spray or brush with vegetable oil. Pour ¼ cup batter onto griddle for each pancake. Cook until bubbles form on the surface, about 2 minutes. Turn and cook until golden on the other side, 1 minute longer. Serve with toppings of your choice.

SERVES 4 TO 6

APPLE PIE PANCAKES

This oven pancake with a layer of caramelized apples on the bottom is baked and then cut into wedges like a pie. Serve with crème fraˆche or heavy cream.

3 tablespoons butter or margarine

3 tablespoons sugar

1 teaspoon ground cinnamon

⅛ teaspoon ground nutmeg

2 baking apples, peeled, cored, and sliced

3 large eggs

½ cup milk

½ cup all-purpose flour

1 teaspoon baking powder

¼ teaspoon salt

Crème Fraˆche (page 99) or heavy cream (optional) for topping

Preheat oven to 400°F. In a large ovenproof skillet (see Note) over medium heat, melt butter. Stir in sugar, cinnamon, and nutmeg. Add apples and sauté until slightly tender, 6 to 7 minutes.

In a medium bowl, whisk eggs. Add milk, flour, baking powder, and salt and whisk until blended. Pour egg mixture over apples. Bake until puffed and golden, about 18 minutes. Remove from oven and let stand for 5 minutes. Cut into wedges and serve topped with crème fraˆche or heavy cream, if desired.

Note: A black cast-iron skillet works well.

SERVES 4

PUFF PANCAKE

This puffed-up baked pancake is light and airy and very delicious. Serve with syrup or preserves.

2 tablespoons butter or margarine

1 cup half-and-half or milk

6 large eggs

2 tablespoons honey

½ cup low-fat cottage cheese

1 cup all-purpose flour

½ teaspoon baking powder

½ teaspoon salt

Preheat oven to 425°F. Place butter in a deep-dish pie plate and melt in the oven. Place remaining ingredients in blender and blend for 1 minute. Let set for 1 minute. Pour batter into pie plate containing melted butter. Bake until puffy and golden, about 25 minutes. Cut into wedges and serve immediately with toppings of your choice.

DUTCH BABY (GERMAN PANCAKE)

This pancake baked in the oven billows up and turns golden. It is traditionally served sprinkled with lemon juice and confectioners' sugar, but it's also good with any traditional pancake topping.

- 3 large eggs
- ½ cup all-purpose flour
- ½ cup milk
- ½ teaspoon salt
- 2 tablespoons butter or margarine

Preheat oven to 400°F. In a medium bowl, whisk eggs. Add flour slowly and whisk until blended. Whisk in milk and salt.

In a large ovenproof skillet (see Note) over medium heat, melt butter. Pour batter into skillet. Place in oven and bake until lightly browned and puffed, about 20 minutes. Remove from oven. Loosen edges with a knife and turn out onto a plate. Serve with toppings of your choice.

Note: A black cast-iron skillet works well.

CRÊPES AND BLINTZES

Crêpe is the French word for pancake. Crêpes are paper-thin, delicate pancakes made of eggs, milk, flour, butter or oil, and seasonings or flavoring. They are served folded, rolled, or stacked and can fit into any meal. A variety of fillings can be used. Blintzes are a traditional Jewish crêpe. The crêpes are cooked on one side and then filled and fried or baked.

THERE ARE THREE KINDS OF CRÊPES:

- Breakfast crêpes: Filled with eggs and breakfast meats.
- Savory crêpes: Filled with a combination of meats, poultry, seafood, and vegetables and often topped with a sauce and baked.
- Sweet crêpes: Filled with fruit and cream or just sprinkled with sugar or honey.

TIPS FOR MAKING AND STORING CRÊPES

- Mix crêpe batter in a blender (more air is incorporated into the batter when a blender is used) or with an electric mixer. If possible, let the batter rest for 1 hour or longer before cooking to allow the flour to absorb the liquid, resulting in a more tender crêpe.
- Cook crêpes in a preheated 8-inch non-stick skillet or in a traditional crêpe pan.
- Stack cooked crêpes on a plate until ready to fill, or cover and keep them warm in a warm oven.
- To store, place a piece of parchment paper between each pair of crêpes. Wrap in foil and store in the refrigerator for several days, or freeze for up to 1 month. To warm, remove paper and wrap in foil. Heat in the oven for 15 minutes at 350°F, or wrap in a paper towel and microwave on High for about 10 seconds.

SUGGESTED CRÊPE FILLINGS

SAVORY CRÊPES

- Cheese—Swiss, Cheddar, Monterey Jack, and ricotta
- Sautéed mushrooms
- Cheese, avocado, and tomatoes
- Cheese, turkey, and cranberry sauce
- Spinach, cheese, and green onions
- Sautéed chicken and mushrooms
- Roasted eggplant, zucchini, and feta cheese
- Caramelized onions
- Flaked salmon, cream cheese, and dill
- Minced ham and asparagus

SWEET CRÊPES

- Strawberries and whipped cream
- Spiced apples with dates and nuts
- Blueberries and chunks of melon and pineapple with sour cream or whipped cream
- Bananas, nuts, and whipped cream
- Ricotta cheese and applesauce
- Kiwi and mango slices
- Berries and crème fra^che

MAKES 10 CRÊPES

BASIC CRÊPES

Don't be afraid to try your hand at crêpes; they are easy and quick to make. Cooking times may vary, depending on the stove.

2 large eggs

1¼ cups whole milk

1 cup all-purpose flour

1 tablespoon melted butter

¼ teaspoon salt

Blender method: Place all ingredients in a blender and pulse several times, scrape down the sides with a spatula, then blend for 30 seconds. Transfer to a pitcher. Let stand for 1 hour or longer.

Bowl method: In a medium bowl, using an electric mixer, beat eggs with milk. Add flour, melted butter, and salt and beat until well blended. Let stand for 1 hour or longer.

Preheat an 8-inch nonstick skillet over medium heat and lightly spray or oil. Pour 3 tablespoons batter into skillet. Quickly lift pan off burner and tilt it in every direction until batter covers bottom of skillet. Cook until top is dry and underside is lightly browned, about 1 minute. Turn with a rubber spatula and cook for about 30 seconds longer. Remove from pan and repeat with remaining batter. Stack crêpes on a plate between squares of parchment paper, unless using immediately.

VARIATIONS

Herb Crêpes: Add 1 teaspoon mixed dried herbs to the batter.

Dessert Crêpes: Add 1 teaspoon vanilla extract and 1 teaspoon sugar to the batter; omit the salt.

MAKES 8 CRÊPES

MORNING CRÊPES

These crêpes filled with cheese, scrambled eggs, and bacon add class to a breakfast or brunch. Serve with Broiled Pineapple Rings (page 318).

8 large eggs

2 tablespoons water

½ teaspoon salt

Freshly ground pepper

1 tablespoon butter

½ cup grated Swiss cheese

4 slices bacon, diced and cooked

8 crêpes (facing page)

Sour cream or plain nonfat yogurt for topping (optional)

In a large bowl, whisk together eggs, water, salt, and pepper to taste. In a large, nonstick skillet over medium heat, melt butter. When butter foams, add eggs all at once. Let set for 20 seconds. Cook, stirring, until light and fluffy and almost dry, about 2 minutes. Add cheese and bacon and stir until blended, about 1 minute longer.

To assemble: Fill each crêpe with about ¼ cup of egg mixture, arranging it along the center of the crêpe. Roll up and place seam-side down on a warm plate. Serve topped with sour cream or yogurt, if desired.

VARIATION

Omit bacon and add ½ cup cooked diced ham.

MAKES 8 CRÊPES

GREEK-STYLE CRÊPES

Greek ingredients come together in a delicious filling for these crêpes.

1 bag (6 ounces) fresh spinach, cooked, chopped, and squeezed dry

½ cup ricotta or cottage cheese

¼ cup crumbled feta cheese

3 tablespoons toasted pine nuts (see page 90)

½ teaspoon dried oregano

½ teaspoon salt

Freshly ground pepper

Parmesan Cheese Sauce (recipe follows)

8 crêpes (page 220)

Preheat oven to 350°F. In a large bowl, mix together spinach, cheeses, nuts, oregano, salt, pepper to taste, and 2 tablespoons Parmesan Cheese Sauce. Fill each crêpe with about ¼ cup of filling, arranging it down the middle of the crêpe. Roll and place seam-side down in a lightly sprayed or oiled 8-by-11½-inch baking dish. Pour remaining sauce on top. Bake, uncovered, until heated through, 20 to 25 minutes.

2 tablespoons butter

2 tablespoons all-purpose flour

1 cup milk

¼ cup chicken broth

¼ cup grated Parmesan cheese

1 tablespoon dry white wine (optional)

¼ teaspoon salt

Dash of white pepper

PARMESAN CHEESE SAUCE

Makes about 1½ cups

In a medium saucepan over medium heat, melt butter. Add flour and stir until bubbly. Add milk and broth and stir until smooth and thickened, about 2 minutes. Add cheese, wine (if desired), salt, and pepper and stir until cheese melts, about 1 minute longer.

MAKES 10 CRÊPES

CHICKEN DIVAN CRÊPES

All the traditional ingredients for chicken Divan are rolled into a crêpe and topped with a flavorful sauce and then baked in the oven for an elegant brunch dish.

3 tablespoons butter or margarine

¼ cup chopped yellow onion

4 ounces mushrooms, sliced

3 tablespoons all-purpose flour

1½ cups chicken broth

½ cup half-and-half or milk

½ teaspoon salt

Freshly ground pepper

2 tablespoons dry white wine

¼ cup grated Parmesan cheese

1½ cups broccoli florets, cut into small pieces

2 cups cubed, cooked chicken breast

10 crêpes (page 220)

Preheat oven to 350°F. In a medium saucepan over medium heat, melt butter. Add onion and mushrooms and sauté until tender, about 5 minutes. Add flour and stir until bubbly. Add broth, half-and-half, salt, and pepper to taste and stir until thickened, 2 to 3 minutes. Add wine and grated Parmesan and stir until blended. Set aside.

In another medium saucepan over medium heat, cook broccoli in water to cover until tender-crisp, about 3 minutes. Rinse under cold water to stop cooking process and drain. In the same pan, mix chicken, broccoli, and ½ cup of the sauce, including some of the mushrooms.

To assemble: Fill each crêpe with about ¼ cup of filling, arranging it down the middle of the crêpe. Roll up and place seam-side down in a lightly sprayed or oiled 8-by-11½-inch baking dish. Pour remaining sauce over rolled crêpes. Bake, uncovered, until heated through and bubbly, about 25 minutes.

MAKES 10 CRÊPES

TURKEY AND MUSHROOMS IN HERB CRÊPES

Leftover turkey was the inspiration for this filling with mushrooms and a creamy sauce. You can also use cooked chicken. Serve with Cranberry Sorbet (page 323).

2 tablespoons butter or margarine

4 ounces mushrooms, sliced

2 tablespoons finely chopped yellow onion

2 cups cubed, cooked turkey

½ cup mayonnaise

½ cup sour cream

½ cup grated Swiss cheese

¼ teaspoon salt

Dash of white pepper

2 tablespoons sherry or dry white wine

10 Herb Crêpes (page 220)

¼ cup toasted sliced almonds

In a medium skillet over medium heat, melt butter. Add mushrooms and onion and sauté until tender, about 5 minutes. Stir in turkey. Remove from heat.

Preheat oven to 350°F. In a medium bowl, mix together mayonnaise, sour cream, cheese, salt, pepper, and sherry. Mix half of this mixture with chicken and mushrooms. Fill each crêpe with ¼ cup of filling, arranging it down the middle of the crêpe. Roll up and place crêpes seam-side down in a lightly sprayed or oiled 9-by-13-inch baking dish. Spread remaining cream mixture on top and sprinkle with almonds. Bake until heated through, about 25 minutes.

SERVES 4

CHICKEN AND SPINACH CRÊPES WITH MUSHROOM SAUCE

A filling of chicken, fresh spinach, cottage cheese, and Parmesan cheese rolled in crêpes and topped with a mushroom sauce makes this a special dish.

- 1 bag (6 ounces) fresh spinach, stems removed and rinsed
- ¾ cup diced, cooked chicken breast
- ½ cup cottage cheese
- Dash of ground nutmeg
- ½ teaspoon salt
- Freshly ground pepper
- ¼ teaspoon dried thyme
- 2 tablespoons grated Parmesan cheese
- 8 crêpes (page 220)
- Mushroom Sauce (recipe follows)

Preheat oven to 350°F. In a medium saucepan over medium heat, cook spinach with a small amount of water, covered, until wilted, tossing once with a fork, about 3 minutes. Drain, squeeze dry, and blot with a paper towel. In a medium bowl, mix together spinach, chicken, cottage cheese, nutmeg, salt, pepper to taste, thyme, and grated Parmesan. Fill each crêpe with about ¼ cup of filling, arranging it down the middle of the crêpe. Roll up and place crêpes seam-side down in a lightly sprayed or oiled 8-by-11½-inch baking dish. Spoon Mushroom Sauce on top. Bake until heated through and bubbly, about 25 minutes.

MUSHROOM SAUCE

Makes about 1½ cups

- 2 tablespoons butter or margarine
- ¼ cup chopped yellow onion
- 4 ounces mushrooms, chopped
- 2 tablespoons all-purpose flour
- 1¼ cups half-and-half or milk
- ¼ teaspoon salt
- Freshly ground pepper
- 1 teaspoon lemon juice

In a small saucepan over medium heat, melt butter. Add onion and mushrooms and sauté until tender, about 5 minutes. Add flour and stir until bubbly. Add half-and-half and stir until thickened, about 2 minutes. Stir in salt, pepper to taste, and lemon juice.

MAKES 10 CRÊPES

CRAB AND SHRIMP CRÊPES

Crab, shrimp, and mushrooms are folded into a cheese sauce, enclosed in tender crêpes, and baked in the oven.

1 tablespoon butter or margarine

3 ounces mushrooms, sliced

4 ounces crabmeat, flaked

4 ounces small shrimp

Swiss Cheese Sauce (recipe follows)

10 crêpes (page 220)

In a medium skillet over medium heat, melt butter. Add mushrooms and sauté until tender, about 5 minutes. Stir in crab, shrimp, and ¼ cup of the cheese sauce. Set aside.

Preheat oven to 350°F. Fill each crêpe with about ¼ cup of crab-shrimp mixture, arranging it down the middle of the crêpe. Roll up and place crêpes seam-side down in a lightly sprayed or oiled 8-by-11½-inch baking dish. Spoon remaining cheese sauce on top. Bake, uncovered, until heated through and bubbly, about 25 minutes.

2 tablespoons butter or margarine

2 tablespoons all-purpose flour

1¼ cups milk

1 tablespoon dry white wine

¼ teaspoon salt

⅛ teaspoon white pepper

½ cup grated Swiss cheese

SWISS CHEESE SAUCE

Makes about 1½ cups

In a medium saucepan over medium heat, melt butter. Add flour and stir until it bubbles. Add milk, wine, salt, and pepper and whisk until smooth and thickened, 1 to 2 minutes. Add cheese and stir until it melts.

MAKES 6 CRÊPES

BLUEBERRY-PEACH DESSERT CRÊPES

Blueberries and chopped peaches make a delicious dessert crêpe filling. If you have frozen fruit, you can make these crêpes all year round.

Vanilla Custard Sauce (page 329)

1 cup fresh or frozen blueberries, thawed if frozen, rinsed and dried

1 cup peeled, chopped fresh or frozen peaches, thawed if frozen

6 Dessert Crêpes (page 220)

Place pudding in a medium bowl. Fold in blueberries and peaches.

Fill each crêpe with about ¼ cup of fruit mixture, arranging it on one side of the crêpe. Fold the other side over. Top with a spoonful of the remaining pudding mixture.

MAKES 12 BLINTZES

CHEESE BLINTZES

Top these creamy cheese-filled blintzes with Fresh Blueberry Sauce or strawberry preserves for a delicious dessert.

BATTER

1 cup all-purpose flour

¼ teaspoon salt

1¼ cups milk

2 large eggs

FILLING

1½ cups ricotta or small-curd cottage cheese, drained

2 ounces cream cheese

1 tablespoon sour cream

1 tablespoon sugar

1 teaspoon vanilla extract

1 teaspoon grated orange or lemon zest

2 to 3 tablespoons butter

Fresh Blueberry Sauce (page 233) or strawberry preserves for topping

To make the batter: In a blender, combine all batter ingredients and pulse several times, then blend until smooth, about 30 seconds. Let stand for 1 hour or longer.

To make the filling: In a medium bowl, mix ricotta, cream cheese, sour cream, sugar, vanilla, and orange zest.

To cook and assemble the blintzes: Preheat an 8-inch nonstick skillet over medium heat. Spray with nonstick spray. Pour 2½ to 3 tablespoons batter into skillet. Tip skillet in every direction until batter covers bottom of skillet. Cook until top is dry and bottom is golden, about 3 minutes. Do not turn. Remove from pan and repeat with remaining batter. Stack blintzes on a plate.

Place about 2 tablespoons filling in the center of the cooked side of a crêpe. Fold bottom up, then fold sides over to meet, and finally fold top down to make a rectangular packet. In a large skillet over medium-high heat, melt 2 tablespoons butter. Place blintzes in skillet seam-side down and cook, turning once, until golden brown, 1 to 2 minutes on each side. Add more butter, if needed. Serve with Blueberry Sauce or preserves.

Waffles are a delicious homemade treat. If you're looking for a fast, satisfying meal, waffles are the answer. To make them, you need a special waffle iron. You pour a batter similar to pancake batter onto one side of the hot iron and close the hinged lid, letting the waffle bake until lightly browned and crisp. The honeycombed surface of the waffle holds the butter and syrup, making every bite a delectable sensation.

Waffles are a timeless breakfast food that can be served any time of the day. Breakfast waffles are usually served with syrup or jam. Savory waffles, topped with creamed meats or poultry, are served for a main course, and waffles heaped with berries and a dollop of whipped cream or ice cream make a great dessert.

Conventional electric waffle irons are available in several shapes, including round, square, oblong, and heart shaped. Belgian waffle irons have larger and deeper grooves, which some people prefer. The recipes in this chapter will work with all types of waffle irons. Most waffle irons made today have nonstick grids that need to be lightly sprayed once with vegetable spray before each use.

TIPS FOR MAKING WAFFLES

- If using a new waffle iron, read and follow the manufacturer's directions carefully.
- Set the temperature control to produce the desired doneness. You may have to experiment the first time and make adjustments to fit your waffle iron and personal taste.
- Spray the waffle iron with vegetable spray, or rub it lightly with oil.
- Pour ¾ cup batter (depending on the size of the waffle iron) onto the center of a lightly sprayed waffle iron. Close the lid and bake until the steam stops and the waffle is lightly browned and crisp, 3 to 4 minutes. Some waffle irons give a beep when done.
- If the batter seems too thick, add more liquid.
- The first waffle may be a test waffle. The second one is always better.
- When you are through making waffles, unplug the iron and leave the lid open to cool.
- Wipe off any excess spray or crumbs with a paper towel. Wipe the outside of the waffle iron with a soft towel before putting it away.

MAKES 4 WAFFLES

BASIC WAFFLES

Waffles are convenient to make because the ingredients are usually on hand. Here is a basic waffle recipe that can be varied in many ways. See the suggestions that follow the recipe for some new ideas. You can use any type of waffle iron for this recipe.

2 large eggs

½ cup melted butter or margarine or vegetable oil

1¾ cups milk

2 cups all-purpose flour

1 tablespoon sugar

4 teaspoons baking powder

¼ teaspoon salt

Preheat waffle iron and spray lightly with oil. In a medium bowl, whisk eggs until foamy. Whisk in melted butter and milk. Add remaining ingredients and whisk until just smooth. Pour ¾ cup batter onto hot waffle iron. Close lid and bake until steam stops and waffle is lightly browned and crisp, 3 to 4 minutes. Remove waffle and repeat with remaining batter. Serve immediately with toppings of your choice.

VARIATIONS

Waffles with Ham: Stir ½ cup diced cooked ham into batter.

Cheese Waffles: Fold ½ cup grated Cheddar or Monterey Jack cheese into batter.

Nutty Waffles: Fold ½ cup chopped, toasted nuts into batter.

Chocolate Waffles: Fold ¼ cup unsweetened cocoa powder and ¼ cup sugar into batter.

Poppy Seed Waffles: Fold 2 tablespoons poppy seeds into batter.

MAKES 6 WAFFLES

BLUEBERRY BUTTERMILK WAFFLES

Plain waffles are good, but blueberries and buttermilk make them even better.

2 cups all-purpose flour

1 tablespoon baking powder

1 teaspoon baking soda

1 tablespoon sugar

2 large eggs

1¾ cups buttermilk or milk

½ cup melted butter or margarine

1 cup blueberries, rinsed, drained, and dried

Preheat waffle iron and spray lightly with oil. In a large bowl, combine flour, baking powder, baking soda, and sugar. In a medium bowl, whisk together eggs, buttermilk, and melted butter. Add to dry ingredients and stir until blended. Pour ¾ cup batter onto hot waffle iron. Scatter a few blueberries on top and press into the batter. Close lid and bake until steam stops and waffle is lightly browned and crisp, 3 to 4 minutes. Remove waffle and repeat with remaining batter. Serve immediately with toppings of your choice.

MAKES 4 WAFFLES

OATMEAL BUTTERMILK WAFFLES

Enjoy these hearty waffles made with whole-wheat flour and oatmeal for a healthy, filling breakfast. They are great served with Fresh Blueberry Sauce.

1 cup whole-wheat flour

1 cup quick rolled oats

1 tablespoon baking powder

½ teaspoon baking soda

1 tablespoon brown sugar

Dash of salt

2 large eggs

1½ cups buttermilk

¼ cup melted butter or vegetable oil

Fresh Blueberry Sauce (recipe follows) for topping

Preheat waffle iron and spray lightly with oil. In a large bowl, using an electric mixer, beat together flour, oats, baking powder, baking soda, brown sugar, salt, eggs, buttermilk, and melted butter until blended. Pour ¾ cup batter onto hot waffle iron. Close lid and bake until steam stops and waffle is lightly browned and crisp, 3 to 4 minutes. Remove waffle and repeat with remaining batter. Serve immediately with Fresh Blueberry Sauce.

FRESH BLUEBERRY SAUCE

This sauce is also good on ice cream.

Makes about 2 cups

3 tablespoons sugar

½ cup water

1 tablespoon cornstarch

1 tablespoon lemon juice

1 pint (2 cups) fresh or frozen blueberries

In a medium saucepan over high heat, combine sugar, water, cornstarch, and lemon juice. Whisk until blended, then add blueberries. Bring to a boil. Reduce heat to medium and cook, stirring constantly, until juice is clear and sauce is slightly thickened, about 2 minutes. Cool, then transfer to a bowl, cover, and store in refrigerator. Serve at room temperature.

MAKES 4 WAFFLES

BANANA-NUT SOUR CREAM WAFFLES

If you like bananas, you will love these pancakes with mashed bananas. Nuts are also added for crunch.

1 cup all-purpose flour

2 teaspoons baking powder

¼ teaspoon baking soda

¼ teaspoon salt

1 large egg

1 cup sour cream

¾ cup milk

¼ cup melted butter or margarine

1 ripe banana, mashed

¼ cup chopped walnuts

Preheat waffle iron and spray lightly with oil. In a large bowl, combine flour, baking powder, baking soda, and salt. In a medium bowl, whisk together egg, sour cream, milk, and melted butter. Add to dry ingredients and mix well. Stir in banana and nuts. Pour ¾ cup batter onto hot waffle iron. Close lid and bake until steam stops and waffle is lightly browned and crisp, 3 to 4 minutes. Remove waffle and repeat with remaining batter. Serve immediately with toppings of your choice.

MAKES 6 WAFFLES

BUTTERMILK WAFFLES

These crisp, flavorful waffles can be served for a quick meal any time of the day. Serve them with Sweetened Cream Cheese, nuts, and berries for an alternative to butter and syrup.

2 cups all-purpose flour
1 tablespoon baking powder
1 teaspoon baking soda
½ teaspoon salt
1 tablespoon sugar
3 large eggs
1¾ cups buttermilk
½ cup melted butter or margarine
Nuts and fresh berries for topping
Sweetened Cream Cheese (recipe follows) for topping

Preheat waffle iron and spray lightly with oil. In a large bowl, combine flour, baking powder, baking soda, salt, and sugar. In a medium bowl, whisk together eggs, buttermilk, and melted butter. Add to dry ingredients and stir until well blended. Pour ¾ cup batter onto hot waffle iron. Close lid and bake until steam stops and waffle is lightly browned and crisp, 3 to 4 minutes. Remove waffle and repeat with remaining batter. Spoon a little Sweetened Cream Cheese on top of each waffle. Sprinkle with nuts and berries.

SWEETENED CREAM CHEESE

Makes about 1 cup

8 ounces cream cheese, at room temperature, cut up
¼ cup confectioners' sugar

Blend cream cheese and sugar in a food processor.

MAKES 6 WAFFLES

HAWAIIAN WAFFLES

The addition of flaky coconut and chopped macadamias adds a fabulous flavor and texture to these waffles. Tropical Fruit Salsa enhances the flavor.

2 large eggs

½ cup melted butter or margarine or vegetable oil

1¾ cups milk

2 cups all-purpose flour

1 tablespoon sugar

4 teaspoons baking powder

¼ teaspoon salt

½ cup flaked coconut

½ cup coarsely chopped macadamia nuts

Tropical Fruit Salsa (recipe follows) for topping

Preheat waffle iron and spray lightly with oil. In a medium bowl, whisk eggs until foamy. Whisk in melted butter and milk. Add flour, sugar, baking powder, and salt and whisk until just smooth. Fold in coconut and macadamia nuts. Pour ¾ cup batter onto hot waffle iron. Close lid and bake until steam stops and waffle is lightly browned and crisp, 3 to 4 minutes. Remove waffle and repeat with remaining batter. Serve immediately with Tropical Fruit Salsa.

TROPICAL FRUIT SALSA

Make this sweet and spicy salsa about 2 hours ahead to allow the flavors to blend.

Makes about 2 cups

1 ripe mango, peeled

1 cup chopped fresh pineapple

1 fresh jalapeño chile, seeded and finely chopped

2 green onions, including some tender green tops, finely chopped

½ cup finely chopped red bell pepper

⅓ cup finely chopped parsley

2 teaspoons red wine vinegar

¼ teaspoon salt

Juice of 1 lime

Carefully cut flesh away from mango pit in horizontal spears, then cut into ¼-inch cubes. Combine in a medium bowl with remaining ingredients. Cover and refrigerate. Drain excess liquid if needed. Serve at room temperature.

Note: If you have sensitive skin, wear latex gloves when working with chiles.

MAKES 4 WAFFLES

GINGERBREAD WAFFLES

These spiced waffles are just as good as gingerbread—maybe even better. Serve with maple syrup and Filled Baked Apples (page 320).

- 1½ cups all-purpose flour
- ½ cup whole-wheat flour
- 1 tablespoon packed brown sugar
- 4 teaspoons baking powder
- 1 teaspoon ground cinnamon
- 1 teaspoon ground ginger
- ¼ teaspoon ground cloves
- 3 large eggs
- 1½ cups milk
- ¼ cup molasses
- ¼ cup melted butter or margarine or vegetable oil

Preheat waffle iron and spray lightly with oil. In a large bowl, combine flours, brown sugar, baking powder, and spices. In a medium bowl, whisk together eggs, milk, molasses, and melted butter. Add egg mixture to dry ingredients and mix until blended. Pour ¾ cup batter onto hot waffle iron. Close lid and bake until steam stops and waffle is lightly browned and crisp, 3 to 4 minutes. Remove waffle and repeat with remaining batter. Serve immediately with topping of your choice.

MAKES 5 WAFFLES

YOGURT WAFFLES

In these light, fluffy waffles made with yogurt, the eggs are beaten separately and the frothy whites are folded into the creamy batter.

1½ cups all-purpose flour

2 teaspoons baking powder

½ teaspoon baking soda

¼ teaspoon salt

2 large eggs, separated

1 cup plain nonfat yogurt

1 cup milk

3 tablespoons melted butter

Preheat waffle iron and spray lightly with oil. In a large bowl, combine flour, baking powder, baking soda, and salt. In a medium bowl, using an electric mixer, beat egg whites until peaks form. In another medium bowl, using an electric mixer, beat egg yolks until lemon colored. Add yogurt and mix. Add to dry ingredients along with milk and melted butter. Fold egg whites into batter. Pour ¾ cup batter onto hot waffle iron. Close lid and bake until steam stops and waffle is lightly browned and crisp, 3 to 4 minutes. Remove waffle and repeat with remaining batter. Serve immediately with toppings of your choice.

MEATS

Meat is often the highlight of the meal, providing substance and variety that will satisfy the hearty appetite. Meat at breakfast will prevent those 11 o'clock hunger pangs. In this chapter you will find some new and creative ways to prepare meats for breakfast or brunch, as well as some old favorites.

BACON

Bacon is side pork that has been cured and smoked. It can be purchased already sliced or cut from a slab at the deli counter.

When serving bacon, allow two to three slices per person.

To pan-fry bacon: Start bacon in a cold skillet over medium to medium-low heat, turning once. Drain on a paper towel. Discard drippings.

To broil bacon: Preheat broiler. Place bacon on top part of broiling pan, with a little water in the bottom. Broil about 5 inches from the heat for 2 minutes on each side, turning once. Drain on a paper towel.

PANCETTA

Pancetta is a flavorful Italian bacon that is cured with salt and spices but not smoked. It is used in pasta sauces and other sauces and is often interchangeable with bacon.

ALLOW 2 TO 3 SLICES PER PERSON

OVEN-BAKED BACON

This is a good way to cook bacon for a large crowd. When bacon is baked, it stays flat and crisp.

Thickly sliced bacon (as many slices as needed)

Preheat oven to 400°F. Place bacon slices on a baking sheet with a rim, arranging slices to overlap the lean edge of each slice with the fat edge of the next slice. Bake until crisp, 18 to 20 minutes. Drain on a paper towel.

VARIATION

Oven-Baked Pepper Bacon: Sprinkle coarsely ground pepper evenly over bacon slices before baking.

SERVES 4 TO 6

BREADED BREAKFAST BACON

Try this for a new twist on bacon. It is crisp and crunchy and worth the extra effort.

12 thick slices bacon

1 large egg

1 tablespoon water

1 teaspoon Dijon mustard

1 teaspoon Worcestershire sauce

1 cup fine dry bread crumbs

Preheat oven to 400°F. Place bacon slices in a single layer on a baking sheet with a rim. Bake for 10 minutes. Drain off fat.

In a large, shallow bowl, whisk egg with water. Add mustard and Worcestershire sauce and mix well. Place crumbs on a piece of waxed paper. Remove bacon from baking sheet and coat each piece on both sides with egg mixture, then in crumbs. Return to baking sheet and bake until crisp, about 15 minutes longer. Drain on a paper towel. Serve immediately.

SERVES 4

BROILED HAM SLICE WITH CHEESE

The mustard-cheese topping adds a new flavor to ham. Team it up with Potato Pancakes (page 258) and eggs cooked as you like them.

1 ham slice, ¼ inch thick (about 1 pound)

Dijon mustard for spreading on ham

½ cup grated Cheddar cheese

¼ cup grated Parmesan cheese

Preheat broiler. Place ham slice on a baking sheet. Broil for 2 minutes and turn. Spread with Dijon mustard. Sprinkle grated cheeses over mustard. Broil until cheese melts, about 1 minute longer. Cut into serving pieces and serve immediately.

SERVES 10 TO 15

HONEY-BAKED HAM WITH PINEAPPLE

The easy-to-make Honey-Mustard Glaze will have your guests coming back for more. Arrange ham slices on a platter garnished with pineapple slices and kiwi fruit and serve with one or both of the tasty sauces.

1 fully cooked ham (4 to 5 pounds)

Whole cloves

Honey-Mustard Glaze (recipe follows)

Pineapple slices for garnish

Kiwi slices for garnish

Creamy Horseradish Sauce (facing page) as an accompaniment

Spicy Mustard Sauce (facing page) as an accompaniment

Preheat oven to 350°F. Place ham on a rack in a roasting pan. Bake, uncovered, for 1½ hours. Remove ham from oven. Cut off rind, leaving a thin layer of fat. Score the fat with a long knife in a 1-inch diamond pattern. Press 1 clove in center of each diamond. Brush with Honey-Mustard Glaze. Reduce temperature to 325°F. Bake for 1 hour longer, brushing several times with glaze. Let stand for 10 to 15 minutes before carving. Garnish platter with pineapple and kiwi slices, and serve Creamy Horseradish and Spicy Mustard Sauces in bowls.

HONEY-MUSTARD GLAZE

Makes about 1 cup

¾ cup honey

¼ cup pineapple juice

2 teaspoons dry mustard

¼ teaspoon ground cloves

1 teaspoon ground cinnamon

In a medium bowl, mix together all ingredients.

CREAMY HORSERADISH SAUCE

Makes about 1 cup

- ¾ cup sour cream
- 2 teaspoons prepared horseradish sauce, or more to taste
- 1 teaspoon Dijon mustard

In a small bowl, mix together all ingredients. Cover and refrigerate until ready to use.

SPICY MUSTARD SAUCE

Makes about ½ cup

- 1 tablespoon brown sugar
- 1 teaspoon cider vinegar
- ½ teaspoon dried dill weed
- ¼ cup Dijon mustard
- 2 teaspoons vegetable oil

In a small bowl, stir together sugar with vinegar until sugar is dissolved. Add remaining ingredients and mix well. Cover and chill. Serve at room temperature.

SERVES 6 TO 8

HAM LOAF

Slices of this wonderful ham loaf will complement any breakfast menu. Serve with Mashed-Potato Cakes (page 259) and Broiled Pineapple Rings (page 318). It also makes great sandwiches the next day.

1 large egg

½ cup milk

¼ teaspoon salt

Freshly ground pepper

1 teaspoon Dijon mustard

1¼ pounds ground cooked ham

4 ounces bulk pork sausage

½ cup diced yellow onion

1 cup crushed saltines (about 20)

1 tablespoon chopped parsley

Sweet and Sour Glaze (facing page; optional)

Pineapple slices for garnish

Parsley sprigs for garnish

Creamy Cold Sauce (facing page; optional)

Preheat oven to 350°F. In a large bowl, whisk together egg, milk, salt, pepper to taste, and Dijon mustard. Add ham, sausage, onion, saltines, and parsley and mix well. Turn into a lightly sprayed or oiled 4½-by-8-by-2½-inch loaf pan. Spread glaze over loaf, if desired. Bake, uncovered, until lightly browned and bubbly, about 1 hour and 15 minutes. Let stand in pan for 10 minutes. Remove from pan and slice. Arrange on a platter and garnish with pineapple slices and parsley sprigs. Serve with Creamy Cold Sauce, if desired

SWEET AND SOUR GLAZE

Makes about ½ cup

In a small bowl, combine all ingredients.

½ cup packed brown sugar

2 tablespoons cider vinegar

1 teaspoon dry mustard

CREAMY COLD SAUCE

Makes about 1 cup

In a small bowl, combine all ingredients and mix well.

½ cup mayonnaise

½ cup sour cream

¼ teaspoon salt

¼ cup prepared mustard

1 tablespoon lemon juice

1 tablespoon sliced chives

1 tablespoon prepared horseradish sauce, or more to taste

SERVES 4

SAUSAGE AND GRAVY ON BISCUITS

Flaky biscuits covered with a fabulous sausage-milk gravy are just as good as at the truck stop. Today, sausage is so lean that you may have to add bacon drippings to make the gravy. Serve with Steam-Basted Eggs (page 44).

1 pound bulk pork sausage

3 tablespoons bacon or sausage drippings, if needed

3 tablespoons all-purpose flour

2 cups milk

½ teaspoon salt

¼ teaspoon coarse pepper

8 Old-Fashioned Buttermilk Biscuits (page 281), split

Place sausage in a large skillet over medium heat and cook, breaking up sausage with a wooden spoon, until meat is no longer pink, 5 to 6 minutes. Add 1 teaspoon bacon drippings, if needed. Remove with a slotted spoon to a plate, leaving drippings in skillet. Add bacon drippings, if needed, to total 3 tablespoons. Increase heat to medium-high. Add flour and stir until flour begins to turn brown, about 1 minute. Add milk, salt, and pepper and whisk until thickened, about 2 minutes. Return sausage to skillet and stir until flavors are blended, 1 minute longer. Serve over biscuits.

MAKES 4 TO 6 PATTIES

SAUSAGE PATTIES

Sausage patties make a good accompaniment for most egg dishes. You can make the patties a day ahead, leaving only a quick frying job for the morning. Today's sausage is so lean, that you may need oil for frying. Serve with eggs cooked as you like them and Caramelized Apples (page 319).

1 pound bulk pork sausage

½ teaspoon ground sage

2 teaspoons maple syrup

2 teaspoons vegetable oil, if needed

Combine sausage, sage, and syrup and mix well with your hands. Form mixture into 4 to 6 patties.

Place patties in a medium nonstick skillet over medium heat. Cook until meat is browned and pink is no longer showing, about 5 minutes on each side. Add oil, if needed.

MAKES ABOUT 30 MEAT BALLS

SAUSAGE BALLS

Prepare these spicy meatballs ahead to serve as a brunch side dish. Pass a bowl of Dijon Mayonnaise and provide toothpicks for spearing.

1¼ pounds bulk Italian sausage

3 tablespoons finely chopped yellow onion

1 cup coarse dry bread crumbs

3 tablespoons grated Parmesan cheese

1 tablespoon Dijon mustard

¼ cup milk

½ teaspoon salt

Freshly ground pepper

Dijon Mayonnaise (recipe follows) for dipping

In a large bowl, mix together sausage, onion, bread crumbs, grated Parmesan, mustard, milk, salt, and pepper to taste. Cover, and refrigerate for 30 minutes, for easier handling.

Preheat oven to 400°F. Shape meat mixture into 1-inch balls (see Note). Place on a lightly sprayed or oiled baking sheet. Bake until lightly browned, 12 to 15 minutes. Serve with Dijon Mayonnaise as a dipping sauce.

Note: These also make a good hors d'oeuvre (make ½-inch balls). If making ahead, warm in the oven or microwave before serving.

DIJON MAYONNAISE

Makes ½ cup

¼ cup mayonnaise

¼ cup plain nonfat yogurt or sour cream

1 tablespoon Dijon mustard

1 teaspoon lemon juice

In a small bowl, stir together all ingredients until well blended. Cover and refrigerate.

MAKES ABOUT 20 SLICES

SAUSAGE SCRAPPLE

This sausage loaf is based on a Pennsylvania Dutch dish made of finely chopped pork scraps mixed with cornmeal mush that is sliced and fried. In this version, sausage is mixed with polenta and then sliced and fried in butter. Serve plain or with syrup.

8 ounces bulk pork sausage

1 teaspoon vegetable oil, if needed

Basic Polenta (recipe follows)

2 to 3 tablespoons butter or margarine

In a medium skillet over medium heat, fry sausage, breaking into small pieces with a spoon, until pink is no longer showing, about 5 minutes. Add oil, if needed. Add to hot polenta and mix well. Turn mixture into a lightly sprayed or oiled 4-by-8-by-2½-inch loaf pan. Cover and chill overnight.

When scrapple is firm, remove from pan. Cut into ⅜-inch slices. In a large nonstick skillet over medium-high heat, melt 1 tablespoon butter. When butter starts to foam, add 6 to 8 slices of scrapple. Fry until golden brown, about 8 minutes. Turn and fry for about 6 minutes longer. Repeat with remaining slices, adding more butter as necessary.

BASIC POLENTA

Makes 1 loaf

1 cup yellow cornmeal

3½ cups cold water, divided

½ teaspoon salt

In a small bowl, mix cornmeal with 1 cup water. In a medium saucepan over high heat, combine remaining 2½ cups water and salt and bring to a boil. Slowly stir cornmeal mixture into boiling water. Reduce heat to low and simmer, uncovered, stirring constantly, until cornmeal mixture is thick and smooth, about 3 minutes. Proceed with scrapple recipe.

If making polenta for another purpose, turn into a 4½-by-8-by-2½-inch loaf pan lightly coated with cooking spray or oil. Cover and chill for several hours.

FRESH PORK SAUSAGE LINKS

Sausage links vary in size, shape, and ingredients used. Fresh sausage needs to be thoroughly cooked until pink is no longer showing. Fully cooked smoked sausage needs only to be warmed by frying, grilling, or steaming.

BAKED FRESH PORK SAUSAGE LINKS

This is an easy way to cook links, especially for a number of people.

Serves 12

- 2 pounds fresh pork sausage links

Preheat oven to 400°F. Arrange sausage links in a single layer on a baking sheet with a rim. Bake, turning once, until sausage is lightly browned, about 20 minutes.

STEAMED FRESH PORK SAUSAGE LINKS

Serves 4

- 1 pound fresh pork sausage links
- ½ cup cold water

Place sausages in a cold medium skillet over medium-high heat. Add water and bring to a boil. Reduce heat to medium-low, cover, and simmer for about 8 minutes. Uncover, increase heat to medium, and cook, turning several times, until water evaporates and sausage is browned, 8 to 10 minutes longer.

GRILLED FRESH PORK SAUSAGE LINKS

Serves 4

- 1 pound fresh pork sausage links
- ½ cup cold water

Follow directions for steaming sausages. Finish on the grill for about 8 minutes, turning several times.

SERVES 4

BREAKFAST KABOBS

For a big, bold summer breakfast, serve this complete meal on a skewer. Sip a Delux Bloody Mary (page 28) while the kabobs are grilling.

3 new (2-inch) potatoes, unpeeled, halved

4 smoked sausages, cut into 1-inch pieces (about ¾ pound)

½ red bell pepper, seeded and cut into 1-inch pieces

½ green bell pepper, seeded and cut into 1-inch pieces

½ small yellow onion, cut into 1-inch pieces

4 large mushrooms

8 cherry tomatoes

1 Granny Smith apple, unpeeled, cored and cut into thick slices

Honey-Mustard Barbecue Sauce (recipe follows)

In a medium saucepan over medium heat, cook potatoes in water until almost tender, about 10 minutes. Drain and set aside to cool.

Preheat grill. Alternate kabob ingredients on 4 or more skewers. Brush with Honey-Mustard Barbecue Sauce. Place skewers on grill and grill until heated through, about 15 minutes, turning and brushing with sauce several times.

HONEY-MUSTARD BARBECUE SAUCE

This sauce is good on chicken too.

Makes about ½ cup

¼ cup ketchup

2 tablespoons dry red wine

1 tablespoon soy sauce

1 tablespoon prepared mustard

1 tablespoon honey

1 teaspoon Worcestershire sauce

2 drops Tabasco sauce

In a small bowl, mix together all ingredients.

SERVES 4

ORIGINAL JOE

This famous dish is said to have originated at the Original Joe's restaurant in San Francisco. It is a longtime favorite for breakfast, brunch, or supper. In this version, mushrooms have been added. Serve with Broiled Tomato Slices (page 79).

¾ pound ground beef

4 ounces medium mushrooms, sliced (optional)

6 green onions, including some tender green tops, sliced

2 teaspoons vegetable oil, if needed

6 large eggs, beaten

2 tablespoons water

½ teaspoon salt

Freshly ground pepper

Dash of ground nutmeg

½ package (5 ounces) frozen chopped spinach, thawed and squeezed dry

Grated Parmesan cheese for topping

Chopped parsley for topping

In a large skillet over medium heat, combine beef, mushrooms (if desired), and green onions and cook until pink is no longer showing in meat and vegetables are tender, 6 to 7 minutes. Add oil, if needed. In a medium bowl, whisk together eggs, water, salt, pepper to taste, and nutmeg. Pour over meat and vegetable mixture in skillet. Let set for 20 seconds. Cook, stirring, for 2 minutes. Fold in spinach and stir until eggs are cooked, about 5 minutes longer. Sprinkle with grated Parmesan and parsley and serve immediately.

Potatoes appear on almost every restaurant breakfast menu, and they are just as good served for breakfast at home. They are filling and satisfying and add substance to the meal. Here you will find all of your favorite potato dishes to serve for breakfast or brunch.

POTATOES

SERVES 4 TO 6

COUNTRY POTATOES

These potatoes are cooked with red and green onions and sprinkled with lots of salt and pepper. The heartiness of this combination makes this skillet entrée great for a brunch. Add a poached egg (see page 40) on top, if desired.

1 tablespoon butter or margarine

1 to 2 tablespoons vegetable oil

4 medium russet potatoes (about 2 pounds), unpeeled, cut into ⅜-inch slices

1 cup chopped red onion

6 green onions, including some tender green tops, sliced

Coarse salt

Freshly ground pepper

Paprika

In a large heavy skillet over medium-high heat, melt butter with 1 tablespoon oil. Add potatoes and cook, stirring occasionally, until lightly browned, about 10 minutes. Reduce heat to medium. Add red and green onions and salt, pepper, and paprika to taste, and cook until potatoes are tender, about 10 minutes longer. Add more oil, if needed.

SERVES 4

HOME FRIES

These homey potatoes are baked first and then fried until crisp and brown. Serve with Fried Eggs (page 44) and Oven-Baked Bacon (page 240)

4 medium russet potatoes (about 2 pounds), unpeeled

2 tablespoons vegetable oil

Coarse salt

Freshly ground pepper

Preheat oven to 350°F. Prick each potato with a sharp fork in several places. Bake until tender, about 1 hour. When cool enough to handle, cut unpeeled potatoes into ½-inch-thick slices.

In a large nonstick skillet over medium-high heat, warm oil. Add potatoes and cook until browned on one side, about 5 minutes. Turn and cook until brown and crisp, about 5 minutes longer. Season with salt and pepper to taste.

SERVES 4

TRUCK STOP HASH BROWNS

This classic breakfast side dish is served at almost every restaurant throughout the country. Serve with "two eggs, any style" (see page 44) and Basic Baking Powder Biscuits (page 280).

3 large russet potatoes (about 2 pounds), peeled

3 to 4 tablespoons vegetable oil, bacon drippings, or shortening

Coarse salt

Freshly ground pepper

In a food processor, using the grating attachment, grate potatoes, or use a hand grater. In a medium non-stick skillet over medium heat, warm 3 tablespoons oil. Spread potatoes in a layer in the skillet and press down with a spatula. Sprinkle generously with salt and pepper. Cook until bottom is browned, about 5 minutes. Do not stir. For easier handling, cut potatoes in half and turn over with a spatula. Add more oil, if needed. Cook until crisp on the other side, about 5 minutes longer.

SERVES 4

CHEESY POTATOES

Try these potatoes and onions smothered with cheese for a popular side dish to serve with Honey-Baked Ham with Pineapple (page 242).

- 8 small new potatoes (about 1 pound), unpeeled, quartered
- 2 tablespoons vegetable oil, divided
- 1 cup sliced green onions, including some tender green tops
- Salt and freshly ground pepper
- 1 cup grated Cheddar cheese

Place potatoes in a medium saucepan over high heat, and add salted water to cover. Bring to a boil. Reduce heat to medium-low and simmer until almost tender, 8 to 10 minutes.

In a large skillet over medium-high heat, warm 1 tablespoon oil. Add potatoes and sauté for about 5 minutes. Add remaining 1 tablespoon oil. Add green onions and cook, stirring occasionally, until potatoes are browned and onions are tender, about 5 minutes longer. Season with salt and pepper to taste. Place mixture in a flat, ovenproof dish and sprinkle with cheese.

Preheat broiler. Broil until cheese melts, about 1 minute.

MAKES 6 PANCAKES

POTATO PANCAKES

Serve these crispy cakes with Chunky Spiced Applesauce (page 319) and sour cream as a side dish for a breakfast or a brunch.

5 medium russet potatoes (about 2 pounds), peeled and grated (use a food processor)

½ yellow onion, finely chopped

1 large egg, beaten

2 tablespoons all-purpose flour

½ teaspoon salt

Freshly ground pepper

2 tablespoons chopped parsley

2 tablespoons vegetable oil

Place grated potatoes in a bowl of salted water to prevent discoloring. When ready to use, drain and pat with a clean towel to remove excess moisture. In a large bowl, combine potatoes with onion, egg, flour, salt, pepper to taste, and parsley. On a plate, divide mixture into 6 mounds (about ⅓ cup each).

In a large nonstick skillet over medium-high heat, warm oil. Place mounds of potato mixture in skillet with hot oil and flatten with a spatula. Cook until golden brown and crisp, 5 to 6 minutes on each side. Remove with a spatula. Serve immediately, or keep warm in a 300°F oven for up to 15 minutes.

MAKES 6 CAKES

MASHED-POTATO CAKES

Use leftover mashed potatoes to make these tasty patties. They go well with Ham Loaf (page 244).

2½ cups mashed potatoes

1 to 2 tablespoons sour cream

¼ teaspoon dried marjoram

¼ teaspoon dried dill weed

¼ teaspoon salt

Freshly ground pepper

1 to 2 tablespoons vegetable oil

In a medium bowl, mix mashed potatoes, sour cream, herbs, salt, and pepper to taste. Shape into 6 patties.

In a large nonstick skillet over medium-high heat, warm 1 tablespoon oil. Add potato cakes. Cook until golden brown, about 3 minutes on each side. Add more oil, if needed.

SERVES 6

ONE BIG POTATO CAKE

In this attractive dish, potatoes are layered in a circular pattern in a skillet and baked until browned and crispy. Use a food processor for quick and even slicing. Ketchup and sour cream make good accompaniments.

4 tablespoons melted butter or margarine, divided

4 large russet potatoes (about 2 pounds), peeled and cut into ⅛-inch slices (see Note)

Coarse salt

Freshly ground pepper

Preheat oven to 425°F. Spread 2 tablespoons melted butter in bottom of a large, heavy skillet (a cast-iron skillet works well). Arrange a single layer of potato slices, slightly overlapping, in circles covering the bottom of the skillet. Season lightly with salt and pepper to taste. Drizzle a little butter over potatoes. Repeat with 3 more layers, ending with butter. Press down on potatoes with the back of a spoon. Cover and bake for 20 minutes. Remove cover and bake until potatoes are golden brown, about 25 minutes longer. Run a knife around the edge to loosen potatoes. Place a large plate over skillet. Turn upside down and invert cake onto plate. Cut into wedges and serve.

Note: Once potatoes are sliced, cover them with cold water until ready to use. Drain and pat dry before using. Do not assemble until ready to bake, as potatoes will discolor.

SERVES 6

HASH BROWN POTATO PIE

Here's a diner-style breakfast dish for big appetites. Serve it with Basic Muffins (page 274). The recipe calls for frozen hash browns for convenience, but you can also make your own (page 256).

4 large eggs

¼ cup milk

½ teaspoon salt

Freshly ground pepper

6 green onions, including some tender green tops, sliced

3 cups frozen hash brown potatoes, thawed

½ cup grated Cheddar cheese

4 thick slices bacon, cooked and crumbled

½ cup grated Monterey Jack cheese

Preheat oven to 350°F. In a large bowl, whisk together eggs, milk, salt, and pepper to taste. Add green onions, hash browns, grated Cheddar, and bacon and mix well. Pour into a lightly sprayed or oiled 9-inch pie plate. Bake until set, about 25 minutes. Sprinkle with grated Monterey Jack and bake until cheese is melted, 2 minutes longer. Cut into wedges and serve.

SERVES 4 TO 6

POTATO AND COTTAGE CHEESE PIE

This is a nice way to use leftover cooked potatoes. Make it ahead and then bake it when needed.

3 cups cold cooked russet potatoes, peeled and grated (about 3 medium; see Note)

½ cup cottage cheese

½ cup sliced green onions, including some tender green tops

¼ cup sour cream

½ teaspoon salt

Freshly ground pepper

2 or 3 drops Tabasco sauce

1 cup grated Cheddar cheese

Preheat oven to 350°F. In a large bowl, mix potatoes, cottage cheese, green onions, sour cream, salt, pepper to taste, and Tabasco sauce. Spread evenly in a buttered 9-inch pie plate. Bake until lightly browned on top, about 45 minutes. Sprinkle with cheese and bake until cheese is melted and pie is crispy around the edges, about 10 minutes longer. Let set for 5 minutes. Cut into wedges and serve.

Note: Potatoes should still be slightly firm.

SERVES 4

SKILLET NEW POTATOES, BELL PEPPER, AND BACON

Cook the potatoes ahead so they can be chilled before frying. Serve with fried or poached eggs.

10 small (1½-inch) red-skinned potatoes, unpeeled

6 slices bacon, diced

½ cup chopped red bell pepper

6 green onions, including some tender green tops, sliced

¼ teaspoon salt

Freshly ground pepper

Place potatoes in a medium saucepan over high heat, and add water to cover. Bring to a boil. Reduce heat to medium-low and cook until tender, about 20 minutes. Drain and refrigerate until cold. Cut potatoes into quarters.

In a large skillet over medium-high heat, cook bacon until crisp, 6 to 7 minutes. Drain on a paper towel, leaving 2 tablespoons bacon drippings in skillet. Reduce heat to medium. Add potatoes, bell pepper, green onions, salt, and pepper to taste and cook until vegetables are tender and potatoes are browned, 5 to 6 minutes, stirring occasionally. Add bacon and cook for 1 to 2 minutes longer.

SERVES 8

BRUNCH POTATOES

This makes a wonderful casserole to serve for a brunch along with Baked Ham and Eggs Gratin (page 161), Honey-Baked Ham with Pineapple (page 242), and Fresh Fruit Compote (page 308).

- 3 large russet potatoes (about 2 pounds), peeled and grated (use a food processor)
- 2 cups grated Cheddar cheese, divided
- 1½ cups grated Swiss cheese
- 3 large eggs
- ¼ cup melted butter
- 2 cups sour cream
- 1 cup milk
- ¼ cup chopped parsley
- ½ teaspoon salt
- Freshly ground pepper

Preheat oven to 350°F. In a large bowl, mix potatoes with half of the grated Cheddar and all of the Swiss. In another large bowl, whisk eggs. Add melted butter, sour cream, milk, parsley, salt, and pepper to taste and whisk until blended. Add to potato-cheese mixture and gently mix. Turn into a lightly sprayed or oiled 9-by-13-inch baking dish. Smooth the top with a spatula. Sprinkle with remaining grated Cheddar.

Bake, uncovered, until bubbly and potatoes are tender, 50 to 55 minutes. Let stand for 5 to 10 minutes before serving.

GRAINS AND CEREALS

Cereals and grains as a breakfast choice have many health benefits. They are satisfying and filling and will provide nourishment throughout the day.

SERVES 4

MIXED-GRAIN CEREAL

This healthy combination of grains has a lot of texture and body and is very filling. The dates and brown sugar add a sweet flavor, and extra sugar is not needed. Serve with milk or nonfat yogurt.

6 cups water

½ cup brown rice

½ cup pearl barley, rinsed thoroughly

½ cup quick oats

½ cup bulgur (cracked wheat)

½ cup chopped pitted dates

¼ cup raisins

2 tablespoons packed brown sugar

1 tablespoon butter or margarine

½ cup chopped walnuts (optional)

In a large saucepan over medium-high heat, bring water to a boil. Stir in all ingredients, except walnuts. Reduce temperature to low and simmer, covered, until grains are tender and water is absorbed, about 40 minutes, stirring occasionally. Sprinkle with walnuts, if desired.

SERVES 4

CREAM OF WHEAT WITH DRIED APRICOTS AND DRIED CRANBERRIES

One of the pleasures of breakfast on a cold winter morning is a hot bowl of homemade cereal. This creamy cereal with sweet dried fruit will add variety to your morning routine. It does not need additional sugar.

4 cups milk, plus more as an accompaniment

½ teaspoon salt

¾ cup quick cream of wheat

½ cup chopped dried apricots

¼ cup dried cranberries

¼ cup chopped almonds (optional)

In a medium saucepan over medium-high heat, bring 4 cups milk and salt to a boil. Slowly whisk in cream of wheat. Add apricots and cranberries. Reduce heat to medium-low and whisk constantly until mixture thickens, 3 to 4 minutes. Serve in bowls, sprinkled with almonds, if desired. Pass additional milk at the table.

SERVES 4

OATMEAL BRÛLÉE

This deluxe oatmeal is made in individual ramekin dishes with a brown sugar topping. Broiling them briefly produces a caramelized finish.

2 cups water

Dash of salt

1 cup quick oats

2 tablespoons half-and-half, plus more as an accompaniment

4 tablespoons brown sugar

Preheat broiler. In a medium saucepan over high heat, bring water to a boil. Stir in salt and oats. Reduce heat to medium-low and cook, uncovered, until mixture is thick, stirring occasionally, 3 to 4 minutes. Add half-and-half. Spoon into 4 buttered ramekin dishes. Sprinkle 1 tablespoon brown sugar over each serving. Broil until sugar is bubbly and melted, 2 to 3 minutes. Pass additional half-and-half at the table.

SERVES 4

BROWN RICE BREAKFAST BOWL

For a nutritious flavor boost, enjoy this healthful starter of nutty brown rice, raisins, and walnuts. Top with fat-free milk.

In a medium saucepan over medium-high heat, bring water to a boil. Add rice and salt. Reduce heat to medium-low and cook, covered, until tender, about 40 minutes. Stir in raisins and walnuts. Cook, uncovered, 5 minutes longer. Serve in bowls with milk and brown sugar, if desired, or serve as a side dish.

2½ cups water

1 cup brown rice

¼ teaspoon salt

¼ cup raisins

¼ cup chopped walnuts

Fat-free milk as an accompaniment (optional)

Brown sugar for sprinkling on top (optional)

MAKES ABOUT 12 CUPS

HOMEMADE GRANOLA

This granola is my grandchildren's favorite. It makes a lot, so store it in large covered plastic containers or covered jars.

2 pounds old-fashioned rolled oats (not quick or instant), about 10 cups

1 cup raisins

½ cup chopped walnuts

½ cup chopped almonds

¼ cup honey

1 teaspoon salt

1 teaspoon ground cinnamon

2 cups sugar

1 cup water

¼ cup butter

Milk or half-and-half as an accompaniment

Preheat oven to 250°F. In a large mixing bowl, combine oats, raisins, walnuts, almonds, honey, salt, and cinnamon and mix well. In a small saucepan over medium-high heat, bring sugar and water to a boil and boil for 1 minute. Add butter to saucepan in small pieces and whisk until smooth. Pour mixture over oats and stir until mixed. Transfer to 2 lightly sprayed or oiled 9-by-13-inch baking dishes. Bake for 25 minutes. Stir around the edges. Turn off oven and leave granola in oven for 1½ hours. It should be dry and chunky. Serve with milk or half-and-half.

VARIATION

Serve the granola with yogurt and a little Fresh Blueberry Sauce (page 233) swirled through it.

SERVES 2 TO 3

INSTANT GRANOLA

This granola goes together quickly and does not have to be baked. Serve it topped with fresh fruit or yogurt. This recipe can easily be doubled.

2 tablespoons butter or margarine

2 tablespoons honey

2 tablespoons sesame seeds

1 or 2 tablespoons unsalted sunflower seeds

1 cup quick oats

3 tablespoons chopped walnuts

In a large nonstick skillet over medium heat, melt butter. Add honey, sesame seeds, and sunflower seeds and cook, stirring, for 2 minutes. Add oats and nuts and toss and turn with 2 wooden spoons until golden, about 5 minutes. Spread on a piece of aluminum foil to cool. Serve warm or cold. Store in a covered container.

SERVES 4

CREAMY GRITS

This term "grits" can mean any coarsely ground grain, such as corn, oats, or rice, but it most commonly refers to hominy grits made from corn. It is similar to cream of wheat but has a coarser texture. In the South, grits are served with almost every breakfast as a side dish.

3 cups water

½ teaspoon salt

¾ cup quick grits

2 tablespoons half-and-half or milk, plus more as an accompaniment

1 tablespoon butter or margarine

In a large saucepan over high heat, bring water and salt to a boil. Stir in grits. Reduce heat to low and cook, covered, stirring occasionally, until thick and fluffy, about 5 minutes. Stir in half-and-half and butter. Spoon into bowls. Pass additional half-and-half at the table.

VARIATIONS

Add 1 cup grated Cheddar and stir until melted, about 1 minute.

Add 1 cup raisins or chopped dates.

Who can resist homemade breakfast breads and the inviting aroma that fills the air as they bake in the oven? They make any meal special. Here you will find basic quick breads and coffee cakes with new and creative variations, plus popular yeast breads.

BREAKFAST BREADS AND CAKES

MAKES 16 MUFFINS

BASIC MUFFINS

Muffins are like cupcakes but not as sweet. They can be served with any meal but are especially good with breakfast and brunches. Muffins are easy to make and are always a success. You can vary this basic recipe by using different flours and by adding chopped nuts, berries, fruits, raisins, or spices.

2 cups all-purpose flour

⅔ cup sugar

2 teaspoons baking powder

½ teaspoon salt

2 large eggs

1 cup milk

6 tablespoons melted butter or vegetable oil

1 teaspoon vanilla extract

Preheat oven to 400°F. In a large bowl, stir together flour, sugar, baking powder, and salt. In a medium bowl, whisk eggs. Add milk, melted butter, and vanilla and whisk until blended. Add egg mixture all at once to dry ingredients and whisk until moistened.

Spoon batter into paper-lined muffin tins, filling them about three-fourths full. Bake until a toothpick inserted in the center comes out clean, about 20 minutes. Remove from pan and cool on a rack for 5 minutes. Serve warm.

VARIATIONS

Use whole-wheat flour.

Add ½ cup grated Cheddar cheese to dry ingredients.

MAKES 18 MUFFINS

BLUEBERRY MUFFINS

These are a favorite among muffins. Blueberries add extra tang and color to these muffins that will melt in your mouth. Use paper muffin tin liners for easy removal from the pan.

- 2 cups all-purpose flour
- 2 teaspoons baking powder
- ½ teaspoon salt
- ½ cup butter or margarine
- ¾ cup sugar, plus 1½ tablespoons for sprinkling on top
- 2 large eggs
- ½ cup milk
- 1 teaspoon vanilla extract
- 2 cups fresh or frozen blueberries (thawed if frozen), rinsed and dried (see Note)

Preheat oven to 375°F. In a medium bowl, combine flour, baking powder, and salt. In a large bowl, using an electric mixer, beat butter and ¾ cup sugar until light and fluffy. Add eggs, one at a time, beating well after each addition. Add dry ingredients alternately with milk and vanilla and mix until batter is smooth. Gently fold in berries with a spatula.

Spoon batter into paper-lined muffin tins, filling them about three-fourths full. Sprinkle with remaining 1½ tablespoons sugar.

Bake until a toothpick inserted in the center comes out clean, 25 to 30 minutes. Remove from pan and cool on a rack for 5 minutes. Serve warm.

Note: To keep blueberries from sinking to the bottom of the muffins, dust them lightly with flour.

MAKES ABOUT 20 MUFFINS

PUMPKIN-APPLE SPICE MUFFINS WITH STREUSEL TOPPING

The kitchen will fill with a sweet, spicy aroma as these muffins bake. They suggest fall, but they can go on the breakfast table any time of the year. They are moist and light, with a streusel topping.

2½ cups all-purpose flour
2 cups sugar
1 teaspoon baking powder
¼ teaspoon salt
½ teaspoon ground cinnamon
¼ teaspoon ground cloves
Dash of ground nutmeg
2 large eggs
1 cup canned pumpkin
½ cup vegetable oil
1 teaspoon vanilla extract
2 cups peeled, chopped apples
¼ cup chopped walnuts (optional)
Streusel Topping (recipe follows)

Preheat oven to 350°F. In a large bowl, combine flour, sugar, baking powder, salt, and spices. In a medium bowl, whisk together eggs, pumpkin, oil, and vanilla. Add to dry ingredients and mix well. Stir in apples and nuts, if desired. Spoon batter into paper-lined muffin tins, filling them about three-fourths full. Sprinkle with topping. Bake until a toothpick inserted in the center comes out clean, about 25 minutes. Remove from pan and cool on a rack.

STREUSEL TOPPING

2 tablespoons all-purpose flour
¼ cup packed brown sugar
½ teaspoon ground cinnamon
1 tablespoon butter, cut up

In a small bowl, combine flour, brown sugar, and cinnamon. Using a pastry cutter, cut in butter until crumbly. Sprinkle lightly over muffins.

MAKES 12 MUFFINS

CALIFORNIA ORANGE-DATE MUFFINS

The whole orange, rind and all, is included in these muffins for a real orange flavor. Mixed in the food processor, the muffins go together fast. Their taste and texture are outstanding.

1 large whole orange, washed and unpeeled

½ cup orange juice

½ cup chopped dates (use kitchen scissors)

1 large egg

½ cup butter or margarine, cut up

1½ cups all-purpose flour

1 teaspoon baking soda

1 teaspoon baking powder

¾ cup sugar

½ teaspoon salt

Preheat oven to 400°F. Cut orange into chunks and remove seeds. Place chunks in a food processor and process until finely ground. Add juice, dates, egg, and butter and process until blended.

In a medium bowl, combine flour, baking soda, baking powder, sugar, and salt. Pour orange mixture over dry ingredients and stir until blended. Spoon batter into paper-lined muffin tins, filling them about three-fourths full. Bake until a toothpick inserted in the center comes out clean, 15 to 18 minutes. Remove from pan and cool on a rack for 5 minutes. Serve warm.

MAKES 12 MUFFINS

WHOLE WHEAT–WALNUT MUFFINS

Simple and satisfying, these prize-winning muffins with nuts will add variety to breakfast.

¼ cup butter or margarine, cut up

1 cup packed brown sugar

1 large egg

1¼ cups milk

1 teaspoon vanilla extract

2 cups whole-wheat flour

1 teaspoon baking powder

¼ teaspoon salt

¾ cup chopped walnuts or other nuts

1 tablespoon granulated sugar

Preheat oven to 425°F. In a large bowl, using an electric mixer, beat butter and sugar until well mixed. Add egg, milk, and vanilla and blend. Add flour, baking powder, salt, and nuts and mix until moistened.

Spoon batter into paper-lined muffin tins, filling them about three-fourths full. Sprinkle with sugar. Bake until a toothpick inserted in the center comes out clean, about 15 minutes. Remove from pan and cool on a rack for 5 minutes. Serve warm.

VARIATION

Add ¾ cup peeled, chopped apple.

MAKES 18 TO 20 MUFFINS

REAL BRAN MUFFINS

Bran is the outer layer of grains (wheat or oats) that is removed during milling. It is a good source of carbohydrates, calcium, phosphorous, and fiber. You can make the batter for the muffins ahead and store it, covered, in the refrigerator for up to 1 week, and bake it when needed. These muffins stay moist for several days. Rewarm them in the microwave for 20 seconds.

1¾ cups wheat bran

1 cup boiling water

1¼ cups whole-wheat flour

1 cup all-purpose flour

2½ teaspoons baking soda

½ teaspoon salt

¾ cup honey

⅓ cup light molasses

6 tablespoons vegetable oil

¼ cup packed brown sugar

2 teaspoons grated orange zest

2 large eggs

1 cup chopped walnuts

1 cup raisins (optional)

Preheat oven to 400°F. In a large bowl, stir together bran and boiling water and let stand for 15 minutes. In a medium bowl, combine flours, baking soda, and salt. Add honey, molasses, oil, brown sugar, and orange zest to bran mixture. Whisk in eggs. Stir in nuts and raisins, if desired. Add flour mixture and stir until dry ingredients are moistened (batter will be thick.)

Spoon batter into paper-lined muffin tins, filling them three-fourths full. Bake until a toothpick comes out clean, 15 to 18 minutes. Let cool in muffin tins for 2 to 3 minutes before serving.

MAKES 10 TO 12 BISCUITS

BASIC BAKING POWDER BISCUITS

Biscuits are a quick, popular breakfast bread. If sweetened, they can be topped with fruit to make shortcake. The texture should be tender and light, and the biscuits golden brown on top.

- 2 cups all-purpose flour
- 1 tablespoon baking powder
- 1 teaspoon sugar
- ½ teaspoon salt
- 5 tablespoons cold butter or shortening, cut into pieces
- ¾ cup milk

Preheat oven to 450°F. In a large bowl, combine flour, baking powder, sugar, and salt. Using a pastry blender or 2 knives, cut in butter until mixture resembles coarse crumbs. Add milk all at once and stir with a fork or wooden spoon until mixture holds together. Gather dough into a ball. Turn dough out onto a lightly floured surface and knead for about 30 seconds. Pat or roll dough with a floured rolling pin into a circle ½ inch thick. Cut biscuits with a 2½-inch biscuit cutter or a drinking glass. Place on an ungreased baking sheet, 1 inch apart for crusty biscuits, closer together for biscuits with soft sides. Reroll scraps and cut additional biscuits. Bake until golden brown, about 12 minutes. Serve immediately.

VARIATION

Sprinkle biscuits with sugar, grated Parmesan cheese, or paprika before baking.

SQUARE BISCUITS

To avoid scraps and rerolling, follow the basic biscuit recipe. Roll dough into a square or rectangle ½ inch thick. Place on an ungreased baking sheet. Trim edges, then cut into 2-inch squares.

DROP BISCUITS

Follow the basic biscuit recipe, increasing milk to 1 cup. Don't knead or roll dough; instead drop it by heaping tablespoons onto baking sheet.

DESSERT BISCUITS

Follow basic biscuit recipe, increasing sugar to 1 tablespoon.

MAKES ABOUT 12 BISCUITS

OLD-FASHIONED BUTTERMILK BISCUITS WITH HONEY BUTTER

Buttermilk makes a tender biscuit with a slightly tangy flavor. Serve these topped with a "melt in your mouth" Honey Butter.

2 cups all-purpose flour

1 tablespoon baking powder

½ teaspoon baking soda

2 teaspoons sugar

½ teaspoon salt

5 tablespoons cold shortening

¾ cup buttermilk

Honey Butter (recipe follows) or jam for topping

Preheat oven to 450°F.

Bowl method: In a large bowl, combine flour, baking powder, baking soda, sugar, and salt. Using a pastry blender or 2 knives, cut in shortening until mixture resembles coarse crumbs. Add buttermilk all at once and stir with a fork until mixture holds together.

Food processor method: Place flour, baking powder, baking soda, sugar, salt, and shortening in a food processor and process until mixture resembles coarse crumbs. Add buttermilk and pulse with off/on pulses until dough holds together.

Gather dough into a ball and turn onto a lightly floured surface and knead for about 30 seconds. Pat or roll dough with a floured rolling pin into a circle ½ inch thick. Cut biscuits with a floured 2 ½-inch biscuit cutter. Place biscuits on an ungreased baking sheet, 1 inch apart for crusty biscuits, closer together for biscuits with soft sides. Reroll scraps and cut additional biscuits. Bake until golden brown, about 12 minutes. Serve immediately with Honey Butter or jam.

HONEY BUTTER

Makes ¾ cup

½ cup butter, at room temperature

¼ cup honey

In a small bowl, blend butter and honey until smooth.

MAKES 12 BISCUITS

LEMON-SCENTED BISCUITS

These rich biscuits with a subtle hint of lemon are the base for Strawberry-Rhubarb Shortcake (page 325), but they are also good served on their own, with jam or Honey Butter (page 281).

2 cups all-purpose flour

1 tablespoon baking powder

½ teaspoon salt

1 tablespoon sugar

1 teaspoon grated lemon zest

5 tablespoons cold butter or shortening, cut up

¾ cup half-and-half

Preheat oven to 450°F. In a large bowl, combine flour, baking powder, salt, sugar, and lemon zest. Using a pastry blender or 2 knives, cut in butter until mixture resembles coarse crumbs. Add half-and-half all at once and stir with a fork until mixture holds together.

Gather dough into a ball and turn onto a lightly floured surface. Knead for about 30 seconds. Pat or roll dough with a floured rolling pin into a circle ½ inch thick. Cut biscuits with a floured 2½-inch biscuit cutter. Place on an ungreased baking sheet. Reroll scraps and cut additional biscuits. Bake until golden brown, about 12 minutes. Serve immediately.

MAKES 18 BISCUITS

BACON-CHEESE DROP BISCUITS

Drop biscuits are the easiest to make because they require no kneading or cutting and there is less cleanup. These savory biscuits are mixed in the food processor.

2 cups all-purpose flour

1 tablespoon baking powder

1 teaspoon baking soda

1 tablespoon sugar

½ teaspoon salt

5 tablespoons shortening, cut up

1 cup buttermilk

2 thick slices bacon, cooked, drained, and crumbled

1 cup grated Cheddar cheese

Preheat oven to 450°F. In a food processor, mix flour, baking powder, baking soda, sugar, and salt. Add shortening and pulse off and on until mixture resembles coarse crumbs. Add buttermilk and process briefly until dough holds together. Fold in bacon and cheese.

Drop heaping tablespoons of dough for each biscuit onto an ungreased baking sheet and bake until golden brown, about 12 minutes. Serve immediately.

MAKES 8 SCONES

RICH SCONES WITH LEMON CURD

Scones originated in Scotland. They are a richer, fancier version of biscuits, with eggs added for flavor. The dough is formed into a round disk, cut into wedges, and baked in the oven. Scones have always been served for tea, but now they also appear on the breakfast or brunch table. These scones, made with butter and half-and-half, are extra rich and flaky. Serve them warm, split, with Lemon Curd or jam or both.

2 cups all-purpose flour

1 tablespoon baking powder

¼ cup sugar

½ teaspoon salt

½ cup butter, cut into small pieces

1 large egg

½ cup half-and-half

Lemon Curd (recipe follows) as an accompaniment

Preheat oven to 425°F. In a medium bowl, combine flour, baking powder, sugar, and salt. Add butter and cut into flour mixture with a pastry blender or 2 knives until coarse crumbs form.

In a small bowl, whisk together egg and half-and-half. Add to flour mixture and stir with a fork until ingredients are moistened and hold together. Gather into a ball and transfer to a lightly floured surface; knead several times. Pat into an 8-inch round and with a sharp knife cut into 8 equal wedges. Place wedges slightly apart on an ungreased baking sheet.

Bake until golden brown, about 12 minutes.

LEMON CURD

This tangy-sweet mixture is used as a topping on scones or as a filling for desserts.

Makes 1⅔ cups

2 large eggs

½ cup sugar

3 tablespoons strained lemon juice

1 teaspoon grated lemon zest

¼ cup butter (no substitute), cut into small pieces

In a medium stainless-steel saucepan, whisk eggs, sugar, and lemon juice until light in color. Add lemon zest and butter. Cook over medium-low heat, whisking constantly, until mixture thickens to a pudding consistency, about 8 minutes. Transfer to a small bowl. Cover with plastic wrap and chill for 2 to 3 hours. Serve cold.

MAKES 8 SCONES

CRANBERRY SCONES

These fruity scones make a breakfast or brunch special. They are best when freshly made and served warm from the oven.

Preheat oven to 425°F. In a medium bowl, combine flour, ¼ cup sugar, salt, baking powder, and baking soda. Add butter and cut in with a pastry blender or 2 knives until crumbs form. (Or place dry ingredients in food processor and cut in butter with on/off pulses until crumbs form.) Stir in cranberries.

In a small bowl, whisk together egg and buttermilk. Add to flour mixture and stir with a fork until ingredients are moistened and hold together. Gather dough into a ball and transfer to a lightly floured surface; knead several times. Pat into an 8-inch round. Sprinkle with sugar. With a sharp knife, cut into 8 equal wedges. Place wedges slightly apart on an ungreased baking sheet. Bake until golden brown, about 12 minutes. Serve immediately.

VARIATIONS

Apricot Scones: Omit cranberries and add ¾ cup chopped dried apricots.

Date Scones: Omit cranberries and add ¾ cup chopped dried dates (use kitchen scissors for easy chopping).

2 cups all-purpose flour

¼ cup sugar, plus more for sprinkling on top

¼ teaspoon salt

2 teaspoons baking powder

½ teaspoon baking soda

½ cup cold butter, cut into small pieces

¾ cup dried cranberries

1 large egg

½ cup buttermilk

MAKES 8 SCONES

CHOCOLATE CHIP–ORANGE SCONES

Add a bit of glamour to the menu by serving these sweet, orange-flavored scones with chocolate chips for a brunch dessert.

2 cups all-purpose flour

¼ cup sugar

1 tablespoon baking powder

½ teaspoon salt

6 tablespoons cold butter, cut up

⅓ cup chocolate chips

1 large egg

½ cup half-and-half or milk

1 tablespoon grated orange zest

Preheat oven to 425°F. In a medium bowl, combine flour, sugar, baking powder, and salt. Add butter and cut in with a pastry blender or 2 knives until crumbs form. Stir in chocolate chips.

In a small bowl, whisk together egg, half-and-half, and orange zest. Add to flour mixture and stir with a fork until ingredients are moistened and hold together. Gather dough into a ball and transfer to a lightly floured surface; knead several times. Pat dough into an 8-inch round. With a sharp knife, cut into 8 equal wedges. Place wedges slightly apart on an ungreased baking sheet. Bake until golden brown, about 12 minutes. Serve immediately.

MAKES 8 SCONES

SCONES WITH SPICED SUGAR-NUT TOPPING

A sprinkling of brown sugar and pecans on these scones adds flavor and crunch.

2 cups all-purpose flour

1 tablespoon baking powder

3 tablespoons sugar

½ teaspoon salt

6 tablespoons butter or margarine, cut into small pieces

1 large egg

½ cup half-and-half or milk

Spiced Sugar-Nut Topping (recipe follows)

Preheat oven to 425°F. In a medium bowl, combine flour, baking powder, sugar, and salt. Add butter and cut into flour mixture with a pastry blender or 2 knives until crumbs form.

In a small bowl, whisk together egg and half-and-half. Add to flour mixture and stir with a fork until ingredients are moistened and hold together. Gather into a ball and transfer to a lightly floured surface; knead several times. Pat into an 8-inch round. Sprinkle with topping. Cut into 8 equal wedges with a sharp knife. Place wedges slightly apart on an ungreased baking sheet.

Bake until golden brown, about 12 minutes.

SPICED SUGAR-NUT TOPPING

Makes about ¼ cup

3 tablespoons packed brown sugar

¼ teaspoon ground cinnamon

Dash of ground nutmeg

3 tablespoons chopped pecans or other nuts

In a small bowl, combine all ingredients.

MAKES 14 SCONES

SENSATIONAL SCONES

Scones can be various shapes, including triangles, rounds, squares, or diamonds. These round scones with oats complement many egg dishes and casseroles.

SCONES

1¾ cups all-purpose flour

½ cup whole-wheat flour

½ cup quick oats

2 teaspoons baking powder

½ teaspoon baking soda

1 tablespoon sugar

1 teaspoon salt

1 cup butter

2 large eggs

½ cup buttermilk

2 tablespoons maple syrup

TOPPING

2 tablespoons sugar

1 tablespoon maple syrup

1 teaspoon water

¼ teaspoon vanilla extract

Pinch of quick oats

To make the scones: Preheat oven to 425°F. In a large bowl, combine flours, oats, baking powder, baking soda, sugar, and salt. With a pastry blender or 2 knives, cut in butter until crumbs form. In a medium bowl, whisk together eggs, buttermilk, and syrup until blended. Add flour to mixture and mix well.

Turn dough onto a lightly floured surface and pat into a circle ¾ inch thick. Cut with a floured 2½-inch biscuit cutter. Place on an ungreased baking sheet.

To make the topping: In a small bowl, stir sugar, syrup, water, and vanilla until sugar is dissolved. Spread on top of each scone and add a pinch of oats. Bake until golden brown, about 10 minutes. Serve warm.

MAKES 24 SCONES

BLUEBERRY DROP SCONES

Drop scones are quick to make because they are not shaped, but they still have the same great flavor. The blueberries impart a burst of fresh flavor with every bite.

- 2 cups all-purpose flour
- ¼ cup sugar, plus more for sprinkling on top
- 2 teaspoons baking powder
- ¼ teaspoon salt
- 6 tablespoons cold butter, cut into small pieces
- ⅔ cup fresh or frozen blueberries, thawed if frozen
- 1 large egg
- ¾ cup milk

Preheat oven to 425°F. In a medium bowl, combine flour, sugar, baking powder, and salt. Add butter and cut in with a pastry blender or 2 knives until crumbs form. Stir in blueberries.

In a small bowl, whisk together egg and milk. Add to flour mixture and stir with a fork until ingredients are moistened and hold together. On a baking sheet, drop batter by heaping tablespoons 2 inches apart. Sprinkle with sugar and bake until golden brown, about 12 minutes. Serve immediately.

MAKES 9 SERVINGS

CORNBREAD

This all-American quick bread originated with the early settlers and is still popular today, especially in the South. There are many different recipes and variations. This one is light and fluffy. Serve with Honey Butter.

1 large egg

¼ cup sugar

1 teaspoon salt

1 cup buttermilk

1 teaspoon baking soda

2 tablespoons melted butter

1 cup all-purpose flour

1 cup cornmeal

Honey Butter (page 281) for topping

Preheat oven to 400°F. In a medium bowl, using an electric mixer, beat egg and sugar. Add salt, buttermilk, baking soda, melted butter, flour, and cornmeal and beat for 30 seconds. Pour into a lightly sprayed or oiled 8-by-8-inch glass baking dish. Bake until golden and a toothpick inserted in the center comes out clean, about 25 minutes. To serve, cut into squares. Serve warm with Honey Butter.

VARIATION

Add 1 cup grated pepper Jack cheese to batter. Omit Honey Butter.

MAKES 1 LOAF

DATE BREAD

This bread is delicious when first baked and will stay moist for several days. It also freezes well. Make it ahead and freeze it for the holidays.

- 8 ounces dates, coarsely chopped (use kitchen scissors)
- 1 cup boiling water
- 1 teaspoon baking soda
- 1 cup sugar
- 2 tablespoons butter or margarine
- 1 large egg
- ½ teaspoon vanilla extract
- ½ teaspoon salt
- 1½ cups all-purpose flour
- ½ cup chopped walnuts

Place dates in a medium bowl. Mix boiling water and baking soda. Pour over dates and stir. Let stand for 1 hour.

Preheat oven to 325°F. In a large bowl, using an electric mixer, beat sugar, butter, egg, vanilla, and salt. Stir in dates and liquid. Add flour and nuts and mix well. Pour mixture into a lightly sprayed or oiled 4½-by-8-by-2½-inch loaf pan. Bake until a toothpick inserted in the center comes out clean, about 1 hour. Cool in pan on a rack for 10 minutes. Run a knife around edges and remove bread from pan. When cool, wrap in aluminum foil to store.

MAKES 1 LOAF

BANANA BREAD

Use very ripe bananas to make this moist bread. Serve as a side bread for breakfast or with afternoon coffee or tea. It is best made a day before serving. This bread also freezes well.

- ⅓ cup melted butter or margarine
- 1 cup sugar
- 2 large eggs
- 1 to 1½ cups mashed ripe bananas (3 or 4)
- ⅓ cup water
- 1⅔ cups all-purpose flour
- 1 teaspoon baking soda
- ¼ teaspoon baking powder
- ½ teaspoon salt
- ½ cup chopped walnuts or other nuts

Preheat oven to 350°F. In a large bowl, using an electric mixer, beat butter and sugar. Add eggs, bananas, and water and beat for 30 seconds. Add flour, baking soda, baking powder, and salt and mix until blended. Stir in nuts. Pour mixture into a lightly sprayed or oiled 4½-by-8½-by-2½-inch loaf pan.

Bake until a toothpick inserted in the center comes out clean, 55 to 60 minutes. Cool in pan on a rack for 10 minutes. Run a knife around edges and remove bread from pan. When cool, wrap in foil to store.

MAKES 1 LOAF

ORANGE-NUT BREAD WITH DRIED CRANBERRIES

This bread with nuts and plump dried cranberries is nice to serve for a holiday brunch. Make it at least one day before serving to give it a chance to mellow.

- 2 cups all-purpose flour
- 1 cup sugar
- 1 tablespoon baking powder
- 1/4 teaspoon ground nutmeg
- 1/4 teaspoon salt
- 2 large eggs
- 3/4 cup orange juice
- 1/4 cup vegetable oil
- 1 cup dried cranberries
- 1/2 cup coarsely chopped walnuts
- 2 teaspoons grated orange zest

Preheat oven to 350°F. In a large bowl, combine flour, sugar, baking powder, nutmeg, and salt. In a medium bowl, whisk together eggs, orange juice, and oil. Make a well in the dry ingredients and add egg–orange juice mixture all at once. Stir until just blended. Fold in cranberries, nuts, and orange zest. Do not overmix. Pour batter into a lightly sprayed or oiled 4½-by-8½-by 2½-inch loaf pan.

Bake until a toothpick inserted in the center comes out clean, about 50 minutes. Cool in pan on a rack for 10 minutes. Run a knife around edges and remove bread from pan. When cool, wrap in foil to store.

MAKES 2 LOAVES

ZUCCHINI BREAD

This is a great bread to make when you have an abundance of zucchini in the garden. The recipe makes two loaves. Freeze one to have on hand for unexpected company.

3 large eggs

2 cups sugar

1 cup vegetable oil

2 zucchini (about ¾ pound), unpeeled, grated (about 2 cups)

1 teaspoon vanilla extract

3 cups all-purpose flour

1 teaspoon salt

1 teaspoon baking soda

¼ teaspoon baking powder

1 tablespoon ground cinnamon

1 cup chopped walnuts

Preheat oven to 350°F. In a large bowl, whisk eggs. Add sugar, oil, zucchini, and vanilla and mix well. In a medium bowl, combine flour, salt, baking soda, baking powder, and cinnamon. Add to egg mixture and mix well. Fold in nuts. Pour into 2 lightly sprayed or oiled 4½-by-8½-by-2½-inch loaf pans. Bake until a toothpick inserted in the center comes out clean, about 1 hour.

Cool in pan on a rack for 10 minutes. Run a knife around edges and remove bread from pans. When cool, wrap in foil to store.

MAKES 2 LOAVES

CHOCOLATE ZUCCHINI BREAD

This chocolate zucchini bread is so good you can serve it for dessert. It's another good way to use plentiful garden zucchini.

Preheat oven to 350°F. In a large bowl, combine flour, sugar, salt, cinnamon, baking soda, baking powder, cocoa, walnuts, and chocolate chips. In a medium bowl, whisk eggs slightly. Whisk in oil and vanilla. Stir in zucchini and add mixture to dry ingredients, mixing thoroughly. Pour into 2 lightly sprayed or oiled 4½-by-8½-by-2½-inch loaf pans. Bake until a toothpick inserted in the center comes out clean, 50 to 55 minutes. Cool in pan on a rack for 10 minutes. Run a knife around edges and remove bread from pans. When cool, wrap in aluminum foil to store.

2⅓ cups all-purpose flour

2 cups sugar

1 teaspoon salt

1 teaspoon ground cinnamon

2 teaspoons baking soda

¼ teaspoon baking powder

½ cup unsweetened cocoa powder

½ cup chopped walnuts

½ cup mini chocolate chips

3 large eggs

1 cup vegetable oil

2 teaspoons vanilla extract

3 cups unpeeled, grated zucchini (about 1 pound)

MAKES 20 PIECES

COFFEE CRUMB CAKE

This tender cake is a family favorite. Serve it for a brunch or an afternoon tea or coffee, warm or at room temperature. It will stay moist for several days.

2¼ cups all-purpose flour

¼ teaspoon salt

2 teaspoons ground cinnamon, divided

1 cup packed brown sugar

¾ cup granulated sugar

¾ cup vegetable oil

1 cup chopped pecans or walnuts

1 teaspoon baking powder

1 teaspoon baking soda

1 tablespoon ground nutmeg

1 large egg

1 cup buttermilk

Preheat oven to 325°F. In a large bowl, combine flour, salt, 1 teaspoon cinnamon, brown sugar, granulated sugar, and oil. Beat with an electric mixer until blended. Transfer ¾ cup to a small bowl for use as topping. Stir in nuts and set aside.

To remaining mixture, add baking powder, baking soda, remaining 1 teaspoon cinnamon, nutmeg, egg, and buttermilk and beat until smooth. Turn batter into a 9-by-13-inch lightly sprayed or oiled baking dish. Sprinkle reserved topping over batter and lightly pat it down. Bake until a toothpick inserted in the center comes out clean, 35 to 40 minutes. Cool on a wire rack.

SERVES 12

OVERNIGHT SPICE-NUT COFFEE CAKE

Make this cake the night before and pop it in the oven for a guest breakfast.

½ cup butter or margarine
¾ cup granulated sugar
1 cup packed brown sugar, divided
2 large eggs
2 cups all-purpose flour
1 teaspoon baking powder
1 teaspoon baking soda
½ teaspoon salt
2 teaspoons ground cinnamon, divided
½ teaspoon ground nutmeg
1 cup buttermilk
1 cup chopped walnuts

In a large bowl, using an electric mixer, beat butter, granulated sugar, ½ cup brown sugar, and eggs. Add flour, baking powder, baking soda, salt, 1 teaspoon cinnamon, nutmeg, and buttermilk and beat until blended. Stir in nuts. Pour into a lightly sprayed or oiled 9-by-13-inch baking dish. In a small bowl, mix remaining ½ cup brown sugar and remaining 1 teaspoon cinnamon and sprinkle on top. Cover and refrigerate for several hours or overnight. Bring to room temperature before baking.

Preheat oven to 350°F. Bake, uncovered, until a toothpick inserted in the center comes out clean, 30 to 35 minutes.

SERVES 12

WALNUT SOUR CREAM COFFEE CAKE

This rich coffee cake has a sugar-nut mixture that serves as both filling and topping. It is a great cake to serve for a brunch or a morning coffee.

¾ cup butter (no substitute), at room temperature

1 cup sugar

2 large eggs

2 cups all-purpose flour

1 teaspoon baking powder

1 teaspoon baking soda

1 cup sour cream

1 teaspoon vanilla extract

Sugar-Nut Filling (recipe follows)

Preheat oven to 350°F. In a large bowl, using an electric mixer, beat together butter and sugar until fluffy. Add eggs, one at a time, beating well after each addition.

In a medium bowl, combine flour, baking powder, and baking soda. Add to butter-sugar mixture, alternating with sour cream, starting and ending with dry ingredients. Beat well. Stir in vanilla.

Pour half the batter into a lightly sprayed or oiled 9-by-13-inch glass baking dish. Sprinkle half the filling mixture over batter. Pour remaining batter over filling and sprinkle with remaining filling mixture.

Bake until a toothpick comes out clean when inserted in the center, 30 to 35 minutes. Cool on a rack and cut into squares to serve.

Note: This cake can also be made in a sprayed and floured Bundt pan.

SUGAR-NUT FILLING

Makes about 1½ cups

⅓ cup packed brown sugar

¼ cup granulated sugar

1 cup chopped walnuts

1 teaspoon ground cinnamon

¼ teaspoon ground nutmeg

In a small bowl, mix together all ingredients.

SERVES 12

BLUEBERRY CRUMB COFFEE CAKE

I took this coffee cake, warm from the oven, to a Bible study meeting and not a crumb was left.

CAKE

1¼ cups all-purpose flour

1½ teaspoons baking powder

¼ teaspoon baking soda

¼ teaspoon salt

½ cup butter or margarine, at room temperature

¾ cup granulated sugar

1 large egg

1 teaspoon vanilla extract

⅓ cup milk

TOPPING

¼ cup all-purpose flour

¼ cup packed brown sugar

½ teaspoon ground cinnamon

¼ teaspoon ground nutmeg

2 tablespoons cold butter or margarine

⅓ cup chopped walnuts or other nuts

1 cup fresh or frozen blueberries, thawed if frozen, rinsed and dried

To make the cake: Preheat oven to 350°F. In a medium bowl, combine flour, baking powder, baking soda, and salt. In a large bowl, using an electric mixer on medium speed, beat butter and sugar until creamy, 1 to 2 minutes. Add egg and vanilla and beat until smooth. On low speed, beat in dry ingredients alternately with milk, starting and ending with dry ingredients, until blended.

To make the topping: In a small bowl, combine flour, brown sugar, cinnamon, and nutmeg. Add butter and cut in with a pastry blender or 2 knives until mixture resembles coarse crumbs. Stir in nuts.

Spread batter into a lightly sprayed or oiled 8-by-8-inch baking dish. Sprinkle blueberries evenly over batter. Sprinkle topping over blueberries. Bake until a toothpick inserted in the center comes out clean, 45 to 50 minutes.

SERVES 6

SUMMER FRUIT CUSTARD COFFEE CAKE

This special, rich coffee cake with custard and seasonal fruit is sweet enough to serve for dessert.

CAKE

1 cup plus 3 tablespoons all-purpose flour, divided

½ cup butter or margarine

2 tablespoons water

1 pear, peeled and chopped

1 peach, peeled and chopped

1 cup blueberries, rinsed, drained, and dried

1 cup plain nonfat yogurt

¾ cup granulated sugar

1 teaspoon vanilla extract

½ teaspoon salt

TOPPING

¼ cup all-purpose flour

¼ cup packed brown sugar

2 tablespoons butter or margarine

To make the cake: Preheat oven to 350°F. In a medium bowl, using an electric mixer, beat 1 cup flour, butter, and water until crumbs form. Press dough into the bottom of a lightly sprayed or oiled 8-by-8-inch baking dish. Layer fruit on top.

In a medium bowl, beat yogurt, sugar, remaining 3 tablespoons flour, vanilla, and salt. Pour over fruit.

To make the topping: In a small bowl, mix topping ingredients with a pastry blender or 2 knives until crumbly. Sprinkle on top of the batter.

Bake until top is golden brown and a toothpick comes out clean when inserted in the center, 45 to 50 minutes. Cool on a rack for 15 minutes. Serve warm or at room temperature.

SERVES 6 TO 8

FOCACCIA

This popular bread is quickly mixed in the food processor. Serve it warm as an accompaniment to brunch dishes.

1 package (¼ ounce) active dry yeast

¾ cup warm water (105° to 115°F)

2 cups all-purpose flour

1 teaspoon salt

3 tablespoons olive oil, plus more for brushing on top

½ teaspoon coarse salt

½ teaspoon dried rosemary

In a small bowl, stir yeast with water until dissolved. Let stand for 5 minutes. In a food processor, combine flour and salt. Add olive oil and process until mixed, about 30 seconds. Add yeast mixture and process until dough forms a ball. Process 1 minute longer. Turn out onto a lightly floured surface and knead until smooth, 8 to 10 times. Place dough in an oiled bowl. Turn dough over to oil top. Cover with a clean towel and let rise in a warm place for about 1 hour. Punch dough down and let rest for 5 minutes.

Preheat oven to 425°F. Fit dough into an oiled 10-inch deep dish pie plate and press down. Dimple the dough with your fingertip in about 12 places and brush with olive oil. Sprinkle with coarse salt and dried rosemary. Bake until bread is slightly browned, 18 to 20 minutes. Remove from pie plate and cool on a wire rack.

MAKES ABOUT 12 ROLLS

FAMOUS CINNAMON ROLLS

Treat your friends and family to these delicious cinnamon rolls for Easter breakfast. These are the easiest and best ones I've found.

DOUGH

1 package (¼ ounce) active dry yeast

1 cup warm milk (105° to 115°F)

½ cup granulated sugar

⅓ cup melted butter

1 teaspoon salt

2 large eggs, lightly beaten

4 cups all-purpose flour

FILLING

1 cup packed brown sugar

2 tablespoons ground cinnamon

½ cup coarsely chopped walnuts

¼ cup butter at room temperature

GLAZE

1½ cups confectioners' sugar

3 tablespoons melted butter

3 tablespoons milk

½ teaspoon vanilla extract

To make the dough: In a large bowl, stir yeast into milk until dissolved Add sugar, melted butter, salt, eggs, and flour and mix well. Turn dough out onto a lightly floured surface and knead 10 to 15 times, then shape into a ball. Return to bowl and cover with a clean towel. Let rise in a warm place until dough has doubled in size, about 1 hour.

Preheat oven to 375°F. Place dough on a floured surface and with a lightly floured rolling pin, roll it into a rectangle about 16 by 22 inches and ¼ inch thick.

To make the filling: In a small bowl, mix brown sugar, cinnamon, and nuts. Spread butter evenly over dough, leaving a ½-inch border around the edges. Sprinkle brown sugar mixture on top.

Roll up tightly, beginning at a wide side. Seal well by pinching edges of roll together. With a sharp knife, cut into 1½-inch slices and place on a lightly sprayed or oiled baking sheet. Bake until golden brown, about 30 minutes. Place on a rack to cool.

To make the glaze: In a medium bowl, whisk together confectioners' sugar, butter, milk, and vanilla until blended. Spoon a little glaze onto each roll while hot.

PAN TOAST

Simple but good, this crispy toast is made by frying buttered bread quickly in a skillet. It has a different taste than the toaster version.

Bread (as many slices as needed)

Butter or margarine

Butter bread generously on both sides. Heat a nonstick skillet or griddle over medium-high heat. Place bread in skillet and cook until lightly browned, about 1 minute on each side. Serve immediately.

SERVES 6 TO 8

GLAZED LEMON CAKE

This lemon-flavored cake is baked in a loaf pan and is similar to a pound cake. Serve it for a brunch dessert with fresh berries and ice cream. It also freezes well.

1⅔ cups all-purpose flour

1 teaspoon baking powder

½ teaspoon salt

1½ cups sugar, divided

½ cup butter, at room temperature, cut into pieces

2 large eggs

2 teaspoons grated lemon zest

1 teaspoon vanilla extract

½ cup whole milk

¼ cup lemon juice

Fresh berries for topping (optional)

Ice cream for topping (optional)

Preheat oven to 350°F. In a medium bowl, combine flour, baking powder, and salt. In a large bowl, using an electric mixer, beat 1 cup sugar and butter until fluffy. Add eggs, one at a time, beating well after each addition. Beat in lemon zest and vanilla. Add dry ingredients to butter-sugar mixture alternately with milk, starting and ending with dry ingredients. Pour batter into a sprayed or buttered 4½-by-8½-by-2½-inch loaf pan. Bake until a toothpick inserted in the center comes out clean, about 1 hour. Remove from oven.

Meanwhile, in a small saucepan over medium-low heat, combine remaining ½ cup sugar with lemon juice and stir until sugar is dissolved, about 1 minute.

While cake is warm and still in the pan, gradually spoon lemon glaze over it, adding more as glaze is absorbed. Use all of the glaze. Cool cake completely in pan, then remove from pan. Serve warm or at room temperature with berries and/or ice cream, if desired. Wrap in foil or plastic wrap to store.

SERVES 8

SKILLET PINEAPPLE UPSIDE-DOWN CAKE

Upside-down cakes are easy and fun to make. Other fruit can be substituted for the pineapple. Use a cast-iron skillet, if you have one available.

¾ cup butter or margarine, divided

¾ cup packed brown sugar

6 pineapple rings (fresh or canned), drained

1½ cups all-purpose flour

1½ teaspoons baking powder

½ teaspoon salt

¾ cup plus 1 tablespoon sugar, divided

2 large eggs

1 teaspoon vanilla extract

½ cup whole milk

1 cup heavy cream

Preheat oven to 350°F. In a heavy 9- or 10-inch cast-iron skillet (see Note) over medium heat, combine ¼ cup of the butter and brown sugar. Cook, stirring often, until sugar melts and mixture is slightly caramelized, about 1 minute. Remove from heat. Arrange pineapple rings on top of sugar mixture.

In a large bowl, using an electric mixer, beat remaining ½ cup butter with flour, baking powder, salt, ¾ cup sugar, eggs, vanilla, and milk for 1 minute on low speed, then beat on high speed for 3 minutes, scraping bowl occasionally. Pour batter over pineapple in skillet. Bake until a toothpick inserted in the center comes out clean, about 45 minutes. Immediately invert onto an ovenproof plate. Leave skillet on top for a few minutes before removing.

In a medium bowl, using an electric mixer, beat heavy cream until peaks form. Beat in remaining 1 tablespoon sugar.

Serve cake warm, topped with whipped cream.

Note: You can also use an 8-by-8-inch glass baking dish. Melt the butter and sugar in the oven as it preheats.

VARIATION

For an updated version, use sliced fresh pears, peaches, bananas, or mango.

BREAKFAST FRUITS

Assorted fruit or fruit combinations make a good accompaniment to breakfast or brunch. They provide a contrast of flavors and textures and add variety to the meal. The recipes in this chapter feature seasonal fresh fruits.

SERVES 8

TROPICAL FRUIT PLATTER WITH STRAWBERRY PURÉE

Arrange an assortment of tropical fruits on a platter and drizzle them with a strawberry purée for an attractive presentation.

- 6 fresh pineapple rings, quartered
- 1 large papaya, peeled, seeded, and cut into strips
- 1 mango, peeled and sliced
- 3 kiwi fruit, peeled and sliced
- 2 bananas, sliced
- Strawberry Purée (recipe follows)
- Mint leaves for garnish
- 4 whole strawberries for garnish

On a large, decorative platter, arrange each kind of fruit in a row, slightly overlapping them. Drizzle purée over fruit in a zigzag pattern. (Do not try to cover all of the fruit.) Garnish with strawberries and mint leaves.

STRAWBERRY PURÉE

This simple sauce is also good on ice cream.

Makes 1 cup

- 1½ cups strawberries, hulled, rinsed, and halved
- 1 tablespoon sugar
- 1 to 2 tablespoons curaçao (orange-flavored liqueur) or Grand Marnier liqueur (optional)

In a food processor or blender, process strawberries until smooth. Add sugar and liqueur (if desired) and blend. Cover and chill until ready to use.

SERVES 6 TO 8

FRESH FRUIT COMPOTE

This colorful fruit salad is eye-catching when served in a pretty glass bowl and garnished with mint.

1 medium pineapple, peeled, cored, sliced, and cut into bite-sized pieces

2 red apples, unpeeled, cored and sliced

2 green apples, unpeeled, cored and sliced

1 cantaloupe, rind removed, cut into bite-sized pieces

1 bunch seedless green grapes, removed from stems

¼ cup confectioners' sugar

2 tablespoons brandy (optional)

2 tablespoons lemon juice

2 cups hulled whole strawberries

¼ bottle champagne or ginger ale

Mint leaves for garnish

In a large bowl, combine fruit (except strawberries), confectioners' sugar, brandy (if desired), and lemon juice. Toss lightly. Cover and chill for several hours (not overnight).

Just before serving, transfer to a large, decorative glass bowl. Top with strawberries. Pour champagne over fruit mixture. Do not stir. Garnish with mint leaves. Serve in sherbet dishes, spooning some of the champagne over the fruit.

SERVES 6

TROPICAL FRUIT BOWL

Tropical fruits are known for their fragrant flavors and vivid colors. Here, they are artfully layered in a pretty glass bowl, making a decorative centerpiece for a brunch table.

- 2 kiwi fruit, peeled and sliced
- 1 papaya, peeled, seeded, and sliced
- 1 mango, peeled and diced
- 2 to 3 bananas, sliced
- 1 cup fresh pineapple chunks
- ½ cup chopped macadamia nuts
- Mint leaves for garnish
- Yogurt-Honey-Mint Sauce (recipe follows) for topping

In a large glass bowl, layer fruit. Sprinkle with nuts and garnish with mint leaves. Top each serving with Yogurt-Honey-Mint Sauce.

YOGURT-HONEY-MINT SAUCE

Makes about 1 cup

- 1 cup plain nonfat yogurt
- 1 tablespoon honey
- 1 tablespoon chopped fresh mint
- Dash of ground nutmeg

In a small bowl, combine all ingredients.

SERVES 6

IT'S THE BERRIES IN SYRUP

Marinate a variety of fresh summer berries in a simple syrup and chill for several hours to make this breakfast or brunch side dish.

1 cup water

1 cup sugar

1 tablespoon fresh lemon juice

1 tablespoon chopped fresh thyme, or 1 teaspoon dried thyme

1 teaspoon vanilla extract

1 cup strawberries, rinsed, hulled, and halved or quartered if large

1 cup raspberries, rinsed and well drained

1 cup blackberries, rinsed and well drained

1 cup blueberries, rinsed and well drained

In a medium saucepan over high heat, combine water, sugar, lemon juice, and thyme and boil until sugar is dissolved, stirring occasionally, about 1 minute. Cool slightly and add vanilla.

In a large bowl, combine berries with syrup and mix gently. Cover and refrigerate for several hours (not overnight). Serve in glass bowls or goblets, with a little syrup spooned over each.

SERVES 4

FRESH FIG COMPOTE

Fresh figs are available from June to October. They are very perishable and should be used soon after you pick or purchase them. Buy figs that are soft, plump, and free from blemishes. They are also good for snacking.

In a large saucepan over medium heat, simmer sugar, water, orange juice, and zest for 5 minutes. Add figs and cook, turning once, until soft, about 2 minutes. Add curaçao and mix. Cool and serve in sherbet dishes.

½ cup sugar

6 tablespoons water

2 tablespoons orange juice

1 teaspoon grated orange zest

8 fresh figs, peeled and halved

3 tablespoons curaçao (orange-flavored liqueur)

SERVES 8

FRUIT PLATTER WITH PROSCIUTTO

Dried fruit combined with fresh fruit and topped with salty prosciutto creates an interesting contrast of flavors and textures.

Place figs and apricots in separate small bowls and cover with hot water to reconstitute. Let stand for 10 minutes. Drain, dry, and cut each into large pieces. Arrange fresh fruit and dried fruit on a platter. Top with prosciutto strips. Garnish with parsley sprigs.

4 ounces dried figs

4 ounces dried apricots

8 cups assorted fresh fruit slices and chunks (cantaloupe, pears, fresh figs, mangoes, kiwi fruit, bananas, etc.)

3 ounces thinly sliced prosciutto, cut into strips

Parsley sprigs for garnish

SERVES 6

MELON BALL FRUIT CUP

Serve this summer fruit combination flecked with mint in large wineglasses or goblets. Champagne or ginger ale poured over the top jazzes it up.

1 cup cantaloupe balls or bite-sized pieces

1 cup honeydew melon balls or bite-sized pieces

1 cup watermelon balls or bite-sized pieces

2 teaspoons chopped fresh mint, reserve a few leaves for garnish

½ cup champagne or ginger ale

¼ cup chopped pecans or walnuts

In a large bowl, mix fruit and chopped mint. Refrigerate for several hours. Spoon into 6 large wineglasses or goblets and divide champagne among the glasses, pouring it over the fruit. Sprinkle each serving with some nuts, and garnish with a mint leaf. Serve with spoons.

SERVES 6 TO 8

APPLE-ORANGE FRUIT COMPOTE

Apples and oranges form the basis of this fruit bowl, joined by other seasonal fruit. It makes a good introduction to a fall brunch featuring Pumpkin Pancakes (page 206).

2 cups apple juice

1 tablespoon lemon juice

1 teaspoon grated orange zest

1 tablespoon brown sugar

Dash of salt

1 cinnamon stick

1 tablespoon curaçao (orange-flavored liqueur; optional)

2 apples (1 red, 1 green), unpeeled, cored and sliced

2 oranges, peeled with a knife to remove white pith and cut into sections, removing seeds and membrane

2 bananas, sliced

2 pears, peeled and sliced

In a medium saucepan over high heat, bring apple juice, lemon juice, orange zest, brown sugar, salt, and cinnamon to a boil. Reduce heat to medium-low and simmer, uncovered, for 10 minutes. Add curaçao, if desired. Cool slightly; remove and discard cinnamon stick.

Arrange fruit in a large glass bowl. Pour syrup over fruit. Cover and chill for several hours, stirring once. Serve in individual bowls, spooning some of the syrup over each serving.

SERVES 6 TO 8

ORCHARD FRUIT PLATE

Seasonal fruit, fresh from the farmers' market and attractively arranged, is an appealing and timely addition to breakfast or brunch. Serve with Creamy Poppy Seed Dressing.

Assorted sliced fruit, such as peaches, pears, apples, plums, and berries in season

Creamy Poppy Seed Dressing (recipe follows)

½ cup chopped walnuts

Arrange sliced fruit on a large platter and pass a bowl of Creamy Poppy Seed Dressing and a bowl of chopped walnuts to sprinkle on top.

CREAMY POPPY SEED DRESSING

Makes about ½ cup

¼ cup mayonnaise

¼ cup plain nonfat yogurt

1 tablespoon honey

1 tablespoon poppy seeds

Dash of ground nutmeg

In a small bowl, mix together all ingredients.

SERVES 4 TO 6

COOKED FRUIT COMPOTE

This delightful fruit dish using dried fruit and apples can be made when other fruits are not in season. It goes well with quiches and baked ham.

In a large nonreactive saucepan, soak the dried apricots and prunes in the cold water for 30 minutes.

Add cinnamon, lemon slices, tapioca, and sugar to the pan holding the fruit and water and bring to a boil over high heat. Reduce heat to medium-low and simmer, covered, for 10 minutes, stirring occasionally. Stir in raisins and apples. Reduce heat and simmer, uncovered, until apples are tender, about 10 minutes longer. Cool slightly. Remove and discard cinnamon stick. Pour into a medium glass bowl, cover, and refrigerate. Serve at room temperature in individual sherbet dishes.

1 cup dried apricots, quartered

1 cup dried pitted prunes, quartered

4 cups cold water

1 cinnamon stick, or ¼ teaspoon ground cinnamon

2 lemon slices, quartered

2 tablespoons quick-cooking tapioca, uncooked

½ cup sugar

3 tablespoons raisins

1 Granny Smith apple, peeled, cored, and sliced

SERVES 6

BREAKFAST DRIED-FRUIT SOUP

Serve this traditional Scandinavian soup as a first course for a brunch or company breakfast. Include cranberries for color. Make the soup ahead and serve it hot or cold with a dollop of sour cream.

3 cups mixed dried fruit, cut up (apples, peaches, cranberries, pears, apricots), rinsed (see Note)

1 cinnamon stick

½ medium lemon, washed and thinly sliced

3½ cups water

2 cups orange juice

1½ cups canned pineapple chunks

½ cup pineapple juice

½ cup honey

Dash of salt

2 tablespoons quick-cooking tapioca, uncooked

Sour cream or plain nonfat yogurt for topping (optional)

In a large saucepan over medium-high heat, combine fruit, cinnamon, lemon slices, water, and orange juice and bring to a boil. Reduce heat to low and simmer, uncovered, for 10 minutes. Add pineapple, pineapple juice, honey, salt, and tapioca. Remove from heat and let stand for 5 minutes to allow tapioca to soften. Return pan to burner and cook, uncovered, until fruit is tender and slightly thickened, about 15 minutes longer, stirring occasionally. Remove and discard cinnamon stick. Serve hot or cold with a dollop of yogurt or sour cream, if desired.

Note: Mixed dried fruit can be purchased in packages.

MAKES ABOUT 4

CITRUS SALSA

If your brunch includes several sweet dishes, this tart, zippy salsa will add a contrasting flavor. It also goes well with Mexican dishes.

1 red grapefruit, peeled with a knife, white pith removed, diced and drained

1 large orange, peeled with a knife, white pith removed, diced and drained

½ green bell pepper, seeded and chopped

½ red bell pepper, seeded and chopped

1 jalapeño pepper, seeded and minced

3 tablespoons finely chopped red onion

1 tablespoon chopped fresh cilantro or parsley

1 tablespoon sugar

¼ teaspoon salt

In a medium bowl, combine all ingredients. Cover and let stand for several hours to develop flavors. Drain excess liquid before serving.

SERVES 2

BROILED GRAPEFRUIT HALVES

For a change, broil pink grapefruit halves with a sprinkling of sugar and cinnamon and serve them warm. The pink color gives it a pretty appearance.

1 pink grapefruit, halved and seeded

2 tablespoons brown sugar

½ teaspoon ground cinnamon

Preheat broiler. Cut a small slice off the bottom of each grapefruit half so it will sit flat. With a grapefruit knife, cut around the outer edge. Cut between the segments to loosen them from the membrane, but do not remove them from the grapefruit. Place grapefruit on a baking sheet. Spread 1 tablespoon brown sugar on each grapefruit half, and sprinkle with cinnamon. Broil until bubbly, about 5 minutes. Serve immediately.

SERVES 6 TO 8

BROILED PINEAPPLE RINGS

Broiled pineapple rings are simple to make and are a good accompaniment to ham and sausage dishes.

1 fresh pineapple, cored and cut into rings

Brown sugar for sprinkling on top

Preheat broiler. Place pineapple rings on a baking sheet. Sprinkle about 1 teaspoon of brown sugar on top of each slice. Broil until bubbly, about 2 minutes.

MAKES ABOUT 4 CUPS

CHUNKY SPICED APPLESAUCE

Fresh, homemade applesauce can't be beat. Some apples are sweeter than others, so you may need to adjust the sugar. This makes a nice accompaniment for Potato Pancakes (page 258).

3 pounds good cooking apples (9 or 10), peeled, cored, and sliced

½ to ⅔ cup water

¼ cup sugar, or to taste

Dash of salt

1 tablespoon lemon juice

¼ teaspoon ground cinnamon

Dash of ground nutmeg

Dash of ground cloves

In a large pot over high heat, combine apples and water and bring to a boil. Stir in remaining ingredients. Reduce heat to medium-low and simmer, uncovered, stirring occasionally and mashing with the back of a spoon, until soft but still chunky, 20 to 25 minutes.

Note: For smooth applesauce, blend it in a food processor or blender.

SERVES 4

CARAMELIZED APPLES

These apple slices, cooked slowly in butter and brown sugar, are a perfect accompaniment for ham and sausage dishes and also make a good topping for waffles and pancakes. They're almost as good as apple pie and easier to make.

2 tablespoons butter or margarine

3 large apples, peeled, cored, and thinly sliced

2 tablespoons brown sugar

1 teaspoon ground cinnamon

2 tablespoons chopped walnuts (optional)

In a large nonstick skillet over medium heat, melt butter. Add apple slices. In a small bowl, mix sugar and cinnamon. Sprinkle over apples. Reduce heat to medium-low and cook until golden and tender, stirring occasionally, 20 to 25 minutes. Sprinkle with nuts, if desired. Serve warm or at room temperature. Stir before serving.

SERVES 4

FILLED BAKED APPLES

Baked apples are simple to make, and with a special filling and topping, they make an elegant fruit to serve for a brunch.

- 4 large apples (Golden Delicious, Rome Beauty, Jonagold, McIntosh, or Granny Smith), unpeeled
- 3 tablespoons packed brown sugar
- 1 teaspoon ground cinnamon
- Dash of ground nutmeg
- Dash of ground cloves
- 2 tablespoons chopped walnuts or pecans
- 2 tablespoons chopped dried cranberries (use kitchen scissors)
- 1 tablespoon butter, cut into small pieces
- Apple juice or water, at room temperature
- 1 tablespoon maple syrup
- Crème Fraˆche (page 99), ice cream, or cream for topping

Preheat oven to 375°F. Core apples, removing the seeds (see Note). Peel upper third of apple to prevent them from splitting. Place apples in an ungreased 8-by-8-inch baking dish or pie plate. In a small bowl, mix brown sugar, spices, nuts, and dried cranberries. Fill each apple equally with filling and pack it down into the cavity. Dot with butter. Pour apple juice and syrup into baking dish around apples until dish is one-fourth full.

Bake until tender when pierced with a fork, 30 to 35 minutes. Spoon some of the syrup in the dish over the apples once during cooking time. Serve warm or cold with crème fraˆche, ice cream, or cream.

Note: Use an apple corer or melon baller, if available, or a paring knife, being careful not to go clear through the bottom of the apple.

SERVES 8

FRESH PEAR SORBET

Sorbets can be served at a brunch to clear the palate between courses or as a light, refreshing dessert. To make sorbet without an ice cream maker, see the note at the end of the recipe.

1 cup water

1 cup sugar

3 large, ripe pears, peeled, cored, and cut into chunks

1 tablespoon lemon juice

¼ teaspoon ground ginger

2 tablespoons Triple Sec liqueur or orange juice

In a small saucepan over medium-high heat, stir water and sugar together. Bring to a boil and stir until sugar is completely dissolved, about 2 minutes. Remove from heat, cover, and chill in refrigerator for 1 hour.

Place pears in a food processor or blender and purée. Stir purée into sugar syrup and add remaining ingredients. Freeze in an electric ice cream maker according to manufacturer's directions. Let stand for several hours in ice cream maker before serving, or transfer to another container and place in freezer. Remove from freezer 10 minutes before serving.

Note: To make sorbet without an electric ice cream maker, spread the mixture in a 9-by-13-inch glass baking dish, cover, and freeze until firm, about 3 hours. Remove from freezer and stir with a spoon, breaking up the mixture, or transfer to a food processor and process until blended. Return to dish and refreeze for several hours. Remove from freezer 10 minutes before serving.

SERVES 8

BLUEBERRY SORBET

Fruit sorbets retain the natural, sweet flavor of fresh fruit, providing a light, refreshing taste treat at the end of a brunch. The note at the end of the Fresh Pear Sorbet recipe (page 321) describes how to make sorbet without an ice cream maker.

1 pint (2 cups) fresh or frozen blueberries, thawed if frozen

½ cup sugar

½ cup water

2 tablespoons crème de cassis liqueur (optional)

1 tablespoon lemon juice

1 cup ginger ale

In a medium saucepan over medium-high heat, stir together blueberries, sugar, and water and bring to a boil. Reduce heat to medium-low and cook, uncovered, for about 2 minutes, stirring occasionally. Cool slightly. Transfer to a food processor or blender and purée until smooth. Return to pan.

Add crème de cassis (if desired), lemon juice, and ginger ale and mix well. Freeze in an electric ice cream maker according to manufacturer's directions. Let stand for several hours in ice cream maker before serving, or transfer to another container and place in freezer. Remove from freezer 10 minutes before serving.

SERVES 8

CRANBERRY SORBET

Serve this pretty pink sorbet for a holiday brunch in keeping with the season. The note at the end of the Fresh Pear Sorbet recipe (page 321) describes how to make sorbet without an ice cream maker.

1 package (12 ounces) fresh or frozen cranberries, washed and sorted

1½ cups sugar

1 cup water

1 tablespoon orange juice

1 cup ginger ale or water

In a medium saucepan over medium-high heat, stir together cranberries, sugar, and water and bring to a boil. Reduce heat to medium-low and cook, uncovered, until berries begin to pop, about 3 minutes, stirring occasionally. Cool slightly.

Transfer to a food processor or blender and purée until smooth. Transfer to a sieve over a deep bowl and, with the back of a spoon, press mixture through the sieve (not all of it will go through). Add orange juice and ginger ale and mix well. Freeze in an electric ice cream maker according to manufacturer's directions. Transfer to another container and place in freezer. Remove from freezer 5 to 10 minutes before serving.

SERVES 8

APRICOT AND BLUEBERRY FLAN

Make this rich, elegant dessert ahead for a brunch. Serve it plain or with whipped cream or crème fra^che, if desired.

½ cup butter, cut up

¾ cup sugar

1⅓ cups all-purpose flour

½ teaspoon salt

¼ teaspoon baking powder

1 teaspoon ground cinnamon

2 cans (16 ounces each) apricot halves, drained

1 cup fresh or frozen blueberries, thawed if frozen, rinsed and drained

1 cup half-and-half

1 large egg

Whipped Cream (facing page) or Crème Fra^che (page 99) for topping (optional)

Preheat oven to 375°F. In a food processor, mix butter, sugar, flour, salt, baking powder, and cinnamon until fine crumbs form. Reserve ⅓ cup for topping and set aside.

Using a 10-inch flan pan with removable bottom, press remaining crumb mixture into pan and up the sides. Arrange apricot halves, cut-side up, evenly over crust. Scatter blueberries on top. Sprinkle with reserved topping. Bake for 20 minutes.

In a medium pitcher or bowl, whisk half-and-half with egg. Pull out oven rack and pour mixture over flan while still in the oven. Slide rack back in and bake until set, 25 minutes longer. Cool on a wire rack. Remove rim from pan and cut flan into wedges. Top with whipped cream or crème fra^che, if desired.

SERVES 6 TO 8

STRAWBERRY-RHUBARB SHORTCAKE

Enjoy this flavorful sauce of tart rhubarb and sweet strawberries on Lemon-Scented Biscuits topped with whipped cream.

1 pound fresh rhubarb, cut into 1-inch slices

⅓ cup water

1 cup sugar

4 cups strawberries, sliced lengthwise (reserve 6 or 8 whole berries with stem intact for garnish), divided

6 to 8 Lemon-Scented Biscuits (page 282)

Whipped Cream (recipe follows)

Grated nutmeg for sprinkling on top

In a medium saucepan over medium-high heat, combine rhubarb and water. Bring to a boil, reduce heat to medium-low, and simmer, covered, until soft, about 10 minutes, stirring occasionally. Stir in sugar and 1 cup berries. Transfer to a food processor and purée. Return to pan, add remaining 3 cups berries, and simmer until flavors are blended, about 5 minutes.

To assemble: Split biscuits and place the bottom half on a plate. Spoon on some of the sauce. Add the biscuit top, spoon on more sauce, and top with whipped cream. Sprinkle with nutmeg. Garnish each serving with 1 whole strawberry.

WHIPPED CREAM

Makes 1 cup

1 cup heavy cream

1 tablespoon sugar

1 teaspoon vanilla extract

Place heavy cream in a small bowl and beat, using an electric mixer, until stiff peaks form. Beat in sugar and vanilla.

SERVES 6

BLUEBERRY PIE

Fresh, juicy blueberries capture the taste of summer in this easy pie for a special brunch dessert. Serve with vanilla ice cream or frozen yogurt.

9-inch Pie Shell (page 123), fully baked and cooled

4 cups fresh or frozen blueberries, thawed if frozen, washed, drained, and dried, divided

1 cup sugar

3 tablespoons cornstarch

¼ cup water

¼ teaspoon salt

1 tablespoon lemon juice

1 tablespoon butter, cut up

Vanilla ice cream or frozen yogurt for topping

Fill pie shell with 2 cups blueberries. In a large saucepan over medium heat, combine remaining 2 cups blueberries, sugar, cornstarch, water, salt, and lemon juice. Bring to a boil over medium-high heat and cook, stirring constantly, until mixture thickens slightly and turns clear, 4 to 5 minutes. Remove from heat and stir in butter. Cool for about 10 minutes, then pour mixture over berries in shell. Serve warm or chilled with ice cream or frozen yogurt.

SERVES 8

FRESH PEAR AND WALNUT TORTE

Fresh pears along with walnuts are paired in this delicious cakelike dessert. If pears are not in season, use canned pears. Top with ice cream or frozen yogurt.

2 large eggs

1½ cups sugar

1 teaspoon vanilla extract

½ cup all-purpose flour

¼ teaspoon salt

2 teaspoons baking powder

1 cup chopped walnuts

2 pears, peeled, cored, and chopped (about 1½ cups), or 1½ cups chopped canned pears

Vanilla ice cream or frozen yogurt for topping

Preheat oven to 350°F. In a large bowl, using an electric mixer, beat together eggs, sugar, and vanilla until light. In a medium bowl, combine flour, salt, and baking powder and stir into batter. Fold in nuts and pears. Pour into a lightly oiled or sprayed 8-by-8-inch baking dish.

Bake until a toothpick inserted in the center comes out clean, about 35 minutes. Cool thoroughly on a rack. Cut into squares and top with ice cream or frozen yogurt.

SERVES 6

BAKED PEARS IN WINE WITH CHOCOLATE SAUCE

Fresh, juicy pears are baked in wine and spices and then topped with a velvety smooth chocolate sauce for a quick-and-easy brunch dessert.

3 firm pears, peeled, halved lengthwise, and cored

½ cup dry red wine

¼ cup water

1 teaspoon sugar

1 cinnamon stick

4 whole cloves

Chocolate Sauce (recipe follows)

⅓ cup chopped walnuts

Mint leaves for garnish

Preheat oven to 350°F. Place pears, cut-side down, in an 8-by-8-inch baking dish. In a small bowl, stir together wine, water, sugar, cinnamon, and cloves. Pour evenly over pears.

Bake for 6 minutes, then baste generously with wine mixture and bake for 3 minutes longer. Pears should be soft but not mushy. Remove from oven, let cool, cover, and refrigerate for several hours.

Drain pears and place a pear half in each of 6 individual dessert dishes. Drizzle Chocolate Sauce on top. Sprinkle with nuts and garnish with mint leaves.

CHOCOLATE SAUCE

This sauce uses unsweetened cocoa powder, which has less fat than baking chocolate. It will not get hard when cold, so it can be kept, covered, in the refrigerator for days. It is delicious hot or cold.

Makes about 1 cup

¼ cup unsweetened cocoa powder

1 tablespoon cornstarch

½ cup sugar

1 cup hot water

1 tablespoon light corn syrup

1 tablespoon butter

½ teaspoon vanilla extract

In a small saucepan over high heat, stir together cocoa powder, cornstarch, and sugar. Slowly stir in hot water and then corn syrup. Bring to a boil and cook, stirring constantly, until slightly thickened, about 2 minutes. Remove from heat and stir in butter and vanilla.

SERVES 6

FRESH FRUIT TRIFLE

Originating in England but served in many countries, this dessert with layers of cake, custards, and fruit makes an attractive and impressive presentation.

1 sponge or pound cake (16 ounces), purchased or homemade, cut into ½-inch slices and halved

¼ cup cream sherry or rum

2¼ cups sliced strawberries (reserve 10 whole berries for garnish)

2 cups blueberries (reserve ¼ cup for garnish)

2 kiwi fruit, peeled and sliced

2 bananas, peeled and sliced

Vanilla Custard Sauce (recipe follows)

Whipped Cream (page 325)

Mint leaves for garnish

Brush cake slices with sherry. Arrange half the slices on the bottom of a trifle bowl or an 8-by-4-inch straight-sided glass bowl. Arrange a layer of half the fruit on top. Spoon half the custard sauce over fruit. Repeat the layers ending with custard sauce.

Cover and chill for several hours. Top with whipped cream and garnish with reserved strawberry slices, blueberries, and mint leaves just before serving. Serve at the table in dessert dishes.

VANILLA CUSTARD SAUCE

This delicious sauce takes constant stirring, but it is worth it. It is also good served plain or with chopped fruit folded in.

Makes about 2 cups

2 cups milk

2 tablespoons cornstarch

¼ cup sugar

2 egg yolks

1 teaspoon vanilla extract

In a small, heavy saucepan, whisk together milk, cornstarch, sugar, and egg yolks. Place over medium heat and cook, whisking constantly, until mixture thickens, 5 to 6 minutes. Mix in vanilla. Remove from heat, and let cool slightly.

Note: If not using immediately, cover and refrigerate. Serve at room temperature.

INDEX

D

E

F

G

H

Q

R

S

T

V

W

Y

Z

TABLE OF EQUIVALENTS

The exact equivalents in the following tables have been rounded for convenience.

LIQUID/DRY MEASURES

U.S.	METRIC
¼ teaspoon	1.25 milliliters
½ teaspoon	2.5 milliliters
1 teaspoon	5 milliliters
1 tablespoon (3 teaspoons)	15 milliliters
1 fluid ounce (2 tablespoons)	30 milliliters
¼ cup	60 milliliters
⅓ cup	80 milliliters
½ cup	120 milliliters
1 cup	240 milliliters
1 pint (2 cups)	480 milliliters
1 quart (4 cups, 32 ounces)	960 milliliters
1 gallon (4 quarts)	3.84 liters
1 ounce (by weight)	28 grams
1 pound	454 grams
2.2 pounds	1 kilogram

LENGTH

U.S.	METRIC
⅛ inch	3 millimeters
¼ inch	6 millimeters
½ inch	12 millimeters
1 inch	2.5 centimeters

OVEN TEMPERATURE

FAHRENHEIT	CELSIUS	GAS
250	120	½
275	140	1
300	150	2
325	160	3
350	180	4
375	190	5
400	200	6
425	220	7
450	230	8
475	240	9
500	260	10